LEGENDARY LOCALS

OF

CHICAGO LAWN AND WEST LAWN

ILLINOIS

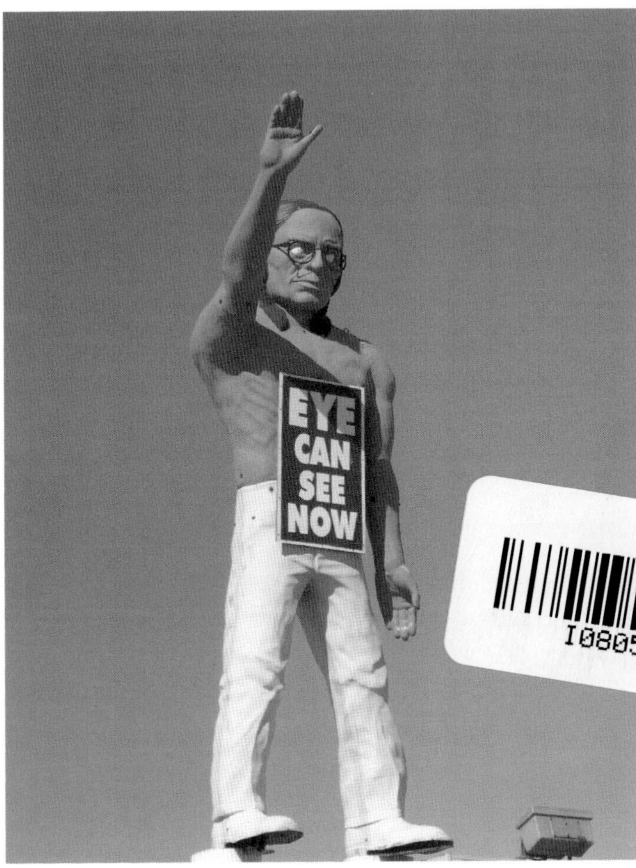

Page 1: Our Indian
The most easily recognizable member of the community is the Indian standing atop the building on the northwest corner of Sixty-Third Street and Pulaski Road. Please see page 124 for additional information. (Authors' collection.)

LEGENDARY LOCALS

OF

CHICAGO LAWN AND WEST LAWN

ILLINOIS

KATHLEEN J. HEADLEY AND TRACY J. KROL

LEGENDARY LOCALS

ISBN 978-1-4671-0215-5

Legendary Locals is an imprint of Arcadia Publishing
Charleston, South Carolina

Printed in the United States of America

Library of Congress Control Number: 2015933526

For all general information, please contact Arcadia Publishing:
Telephone 843-853-2070
Fax 843-853-0044
E-mail sales@arcadiapublishing.com
For customer service and orders:
Toll-Free 1-888-313-2665

Visit us on the Internet at www.arcadiapublishing.com

Dedication

This book is dedicated to all who have called Chicago Lawn or West Lawn home, whether putting down roots or just staying for a while, you have enriched the communities.

On the Front Cover: Clockwise from top left:
Frank Caldarone, proprietor of Palermo's of 63rd, with business partner Paul Baio (Courtesy of Frank Caldarone; see page 122), our Indian, the most easily recognizable member of the community (Authors' collection; see page 124), Clarence Edwin Eagle, the first of Chicago Lawn's sons to sacrifice his life for his country during a war (Courtesy of the Chicago Lawn Historical Society; see page 29), Capt. Steponas Darius and Lt. Stasys Girenas attempting to be the first to make a transatlantic flight from America to Lithuania (Authors' collection; see page 39), Michael Gehant, owner of J&R Variety Store (Authors' collection; see page 108), Martin McVeagh, the first mailman in the Lawn (Courtesy of the Chicago Lawn Historical Society; see page 26), Stanley Balzekas Jr., Lithuanian historian, inside Balzekas Museum of Lithuanian Culture (Authors' collection; see page 110), Jim Capraro, community developer and founding executive director of Greater Southwest Development Corporation (Courtesy of Shawn Allee; see page 106), Venerable Maria "Casimira" Kaupas, foundress of the Sisters of St. Casmir (Courtesy of the Sisters of St. Casimir; see page 24).

On the Back Cover: From left to right:
Michael Stefanos making hand-dipped Dove bars in the back room of his father's candy store where it was first created (Authors' collection; see page 92), Henry Bianco Sr. visiting with Joe DiMaggio at Club El Bianco (Courtesy of Henry Bianco Jr.; see page 73).

CONTENTS

ACKNOWLEDGMENTS

Deepest gratitude goes to Jim Vondrak for his generous help and love of neighborhood history, which has always been a source of encouragement.

For helping us come up with those hard-to-find photographs and histories, special thanks to Nancy Barrett, Alia Bilal, Joe Boyle, Gloria Contino, Bridget Ferriter, Caitlin Gath, Nneka Gunn, Tim Hadac, Patricia Hummel, Christine James, Joe Kasper, Annette Matuszewski, Rev. Thomas McCarthy, Larry O'Connell, Alan Pelt, Thomas Ramsden, Mary Russell, Imelda Salazar, Tom Schumacher, Paula Staisiunas Shultz, and Michael Headley.

Our heartfelt thanks go to those who have shared their family photographs with us. Sincere thanks to everyone that offered a thought or suggestion, for it is the suggestions that helped to make the book interesting.

And finally, thanks to our editors, Amy Perryman, Tiffany Frary, and Erin Vosgien, for their patience and assistance along the way.

Unless otherwise noted, all other images are from the collection of the authors.

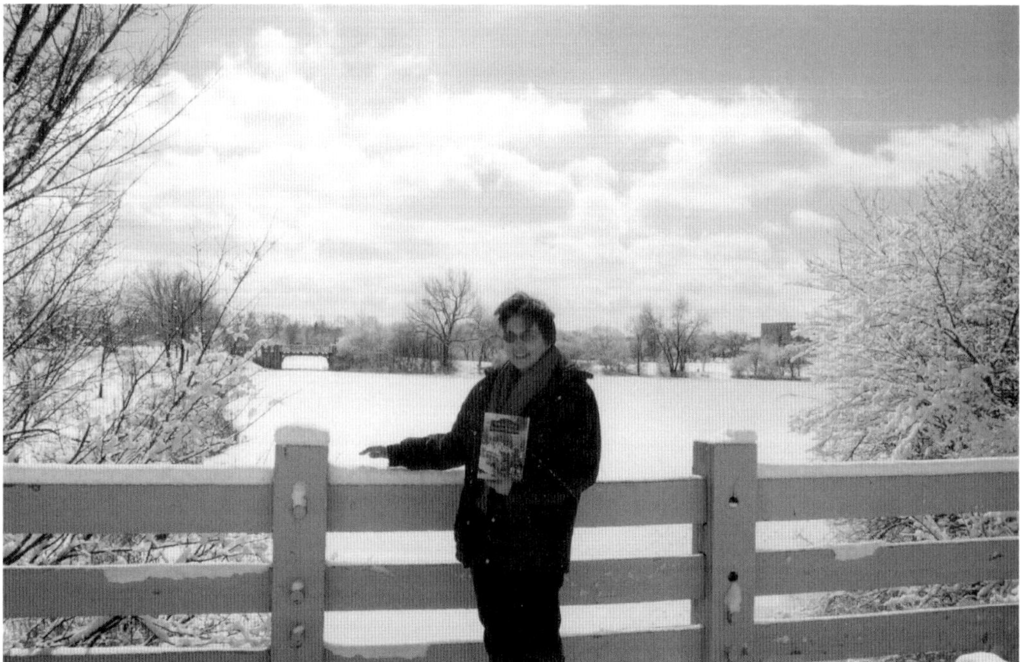

Kathleen J. Headley

The first Arcadia Book written by Kathleen J. Headley was for the Images of America series, titled *Chicago Lawn/Marquette Manor.* The author is pictured here in scenic Marquette Park.

INTRODUCTION

Chicago Lawn began as the dream of its founder, Prof. John F. Eberhart. In the beginning, it was but a vast expanse of wild strawberries, phlox, cabbages, and mushrooms. The first residents were members of the Eberhart family. Once he was able to sell officials of the Chicago, Danville and Vincennes Railway on the idea of building a trunk line running through his envisioned suburb to the city, Eberhart began to develop plots of land. Included in his agreement with the railroad was the stipulation that anyone working on the building of the line or who became a resident along the line would receive a three-year pass for the railroad. This more than anything increased the allure of his venture and caused his tiny settlement to grow quickly. The eastern section of Chicago Lawn, known as Marquette Manor, got a much later start due in part to wealthy and eccentric landowner Hetty Green, who had acquired a good portion of the land through foreclosures in 1877. While a few farms dotted the land, and one building, Pryor's General Store, sat on what is now Sixty-Third Place and Western Avenue, most of the land lay undeveloped and uninhabited until the early 1900s.

Fr. James Green, who was brought here at the invitation of Archbishop James Quigley, and Mother Maria Kaupas, who arrived just six years later and also at the archbishop's invitation, can be credited with the substantial growth and development of that eastern section of the community. The institutions they fostered appealed to specific groups, most prominently those of the Catholic faith. In Father Green's case, he established the first Catholic church and school this far southwest of the city. While Mother Maria's establishments were also Catholic in nature, they were specifically geared toward helping young Lithuanian immigrants assimilate to their new homeland.

It was not long at all before these institutions began attracting people from other areas of the city, and Marquette Manor grew by leaps and bounds. As Chicago Lawn continued to expand eastward and Marquette Manor continued to grow westward, the two communities became one. On the other side of the Chicago, Danville and Vincennes Railway, the area that would become known as West Lawn still lay undeveloped. To the folks living in Chicago Lawn, this area west of the tracks was a place they visited for swimming in the summer and ice skating in the winter, thanks to a huge pond left over from an abandoned artesian well.

It was not until the late 1920s that the marshes here were drained and the land filled in. Homes then began to sprout up west of Chicago Lawn and east of Pulaski. The growth of the Clearing Industrial District to the west and the addition of a streetcar on Sixty-Third Street that could bring workers through West Lawn all the way to Clearing aided greatly in its development. Throughout those years, the census tracts showed the population of Chicago Lawn and West Lawn as primarily German, Irish, Czech, Polish, and Italian, with the exception of the southern part of Marquette Manor, which had become a desirable location for residents of Lithuanian background.

Changing times brought a change in demographics during the latter part of the 20th century. Young people of Mexican, Arab, and Muslim heritage began to see the advantages the community could offer. While neighborhood and social groups had always been prevalent here, they had tended to bring together people with like minds and similar interests. Now, the groups center more and more on bringing people not of like minds together for the common purpose of learning about each other and strengthening community. As the process continues, new leaders develop new strategies and solutions.

Heroes do not actually leap tall buildings in a single bound, and legends are not born with infallible qualities. Heroes and legends begin as someone's neighbor. Sometimes their memorable qualities extend across the nation, sometimes throughout the city, and sometimes just in their corner of the community. For whatever reason, large or small, they have made a difference, and future generations will learn from them and be reassured that they can handle difficulties as they come and rise to the challenges of the future.

Together we have moved mountains in one way or another. And so this book is but a sampling, for everyone that has called Chicago Lawn or West Lawn home has made a difference in some way. The neighborhood would not have been quite the same without you.

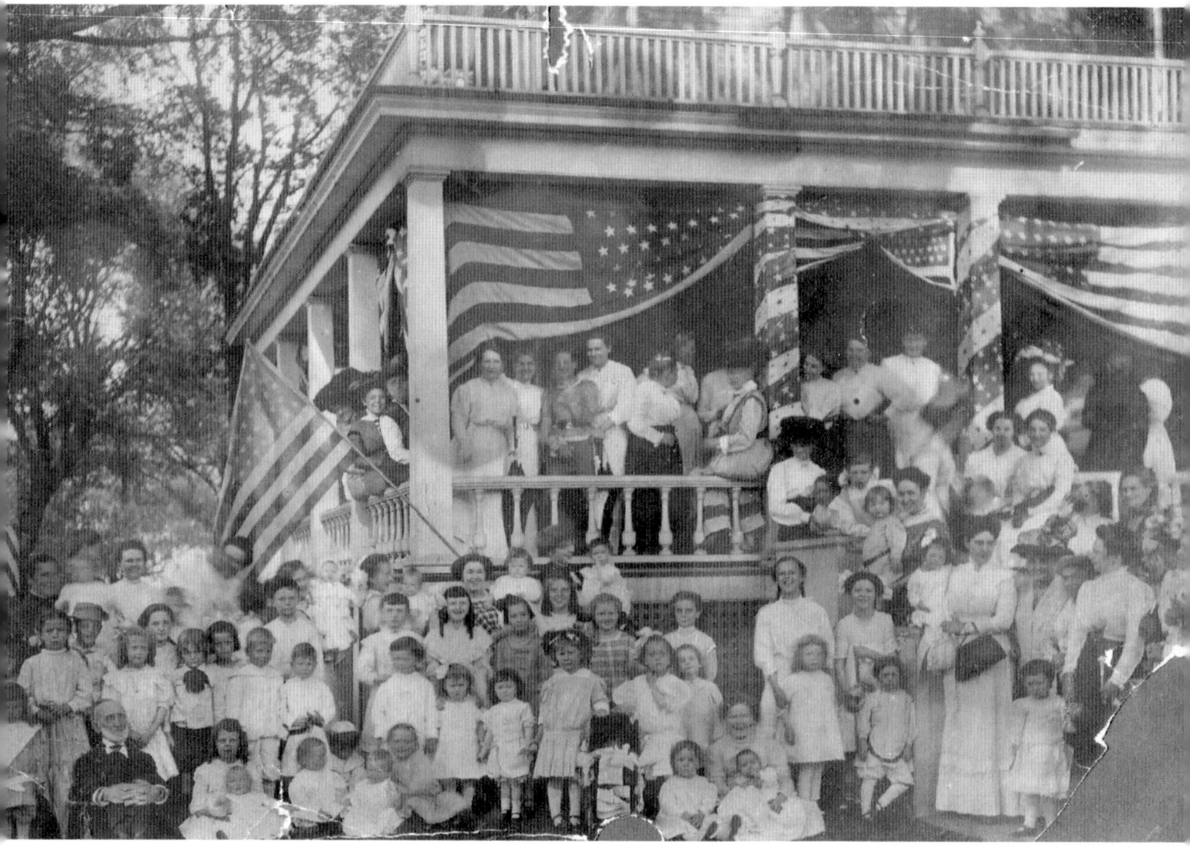

The Eberharts

Pictured here is the 1910 Fourth of July gathering at the home of John and Matilda Eberhart. (Courtesy of the Chicago Lawn Historical Society.)

CHAPTER ONE

Embarking on an Adventure

I look upon life as a reality, and that it should be made a beautiful activity. Unless one lives to better the life of someone else, his life has been a failure.

—John Eberhart

In the earliest days, this area of the city now called Chicago Lawn was home to only members of Prof. John Eberhart's immediate family. Soon, cousins joined the Eberharts. Then, word of mouth brought extended family and friends. Matilda Eberhart conducted the first school in the front parlor of their home. On Sundays, in the same front parlor, Rev. Uriah Eberhart conducted church services. Once cousin Ira Eberhart completed his studies in medicine, he also joined the family, and as the Lawn grew, he conducted his medical visits on his bicycle.

Religion and education has always been a main focus of community leaders in Chicago Lawn, West Lawn, and Marquette Manor. One generally will not have to travel more than a few blocks to find a church or school.

On the eastern end of town, it was in 1905 at the request of Archbishop James Quigley that Fr. James Green, OSA, arrived in Chicago to build a parish and school, east of Chicago Lawn proper. It was here that Father Green encountered the woman known as the "Witch of Wall Street."

A few years later, also at the invitation of the Archbishop, a new order of Lithuanian nuns headed by a young Casimira Kaupas, known as Sister Maria, arrived, settling in the Marquette Manor area of Chicago Lawn just south of Father Green's parish.

Sister Maria had grown up in a farming village in Lithuania where Catholics had been persecuted. She had founded this new order in Pennsylvania not far from her brother's parish, but when asked to come here, she made the difficult decision to start again. Arriving on a cold January day, the sisters found that the pipes had burst in their brand-new convent building, and the floors were covered in mud.

As these early pioneers were laying the foundation, their sons were engaging in another type of adventure, one which would prove fatal for Clarence Eagle, the first Chicago Lawn son to die in combat. His mother, Augusta, mourning the death of her only child, put together a scrapbook detailing his life and career that she donated to the Chicago Lawn Historical Society.

John F. Eberhart

John Frederic Eberhart, known as the "Father of Chicago Lawn" was born on a Pennsylvania farm in January 1829. Growing up, he attended school during the winter months and worked on the farm during the summer.

An educator from the beginning of his adult life, Eberhart taught his first class at the age of 16. During his early teaching career, Eberhart was a schoolmaster, served as principal of Albright Seminary in Pennsylvania, and bought and edited a newspaper in Dixon, Illinois.

While presiding over teacher-training institutes, he was one of the founders of the State Normal School and convened the first Cook County Teachers Institute in Oak Park.

In 1855, Eberhart came to Illinois from Pennsylvania at the age of 25. Within four years, he was elected the first Cook County superintendent of schools. There were 198 teachers in Cook County at the time, and Eberhart visited each one of them once a year, traveling by horse and buggy along the rough roads.

As he became familiar with the territory, he was convinced of the great opportunity for development around Chicago. The professor made up his mind that when his term was up as superintendent, he would try his hand in the real estate business.

In 1871, he and his partner bought the property that now extends from Fifty-Ninth to Sixty-Seventh streets and from Kedzie to Central Park Avenues.

He paid the Chicago, Danville and Vincennes Railway $5,000 to build a trunk line. It took three years to complete, and when the road was ready, Eberhart christened his new suburb Chicago Lawn. (Courtesy of the Chicago Lawn Historical Society.)

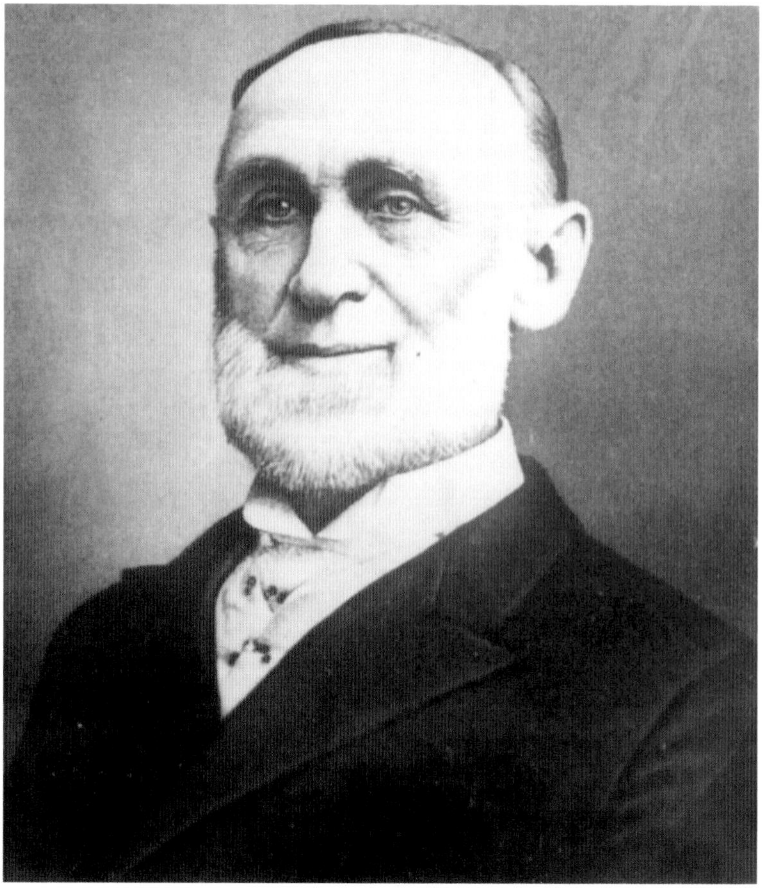

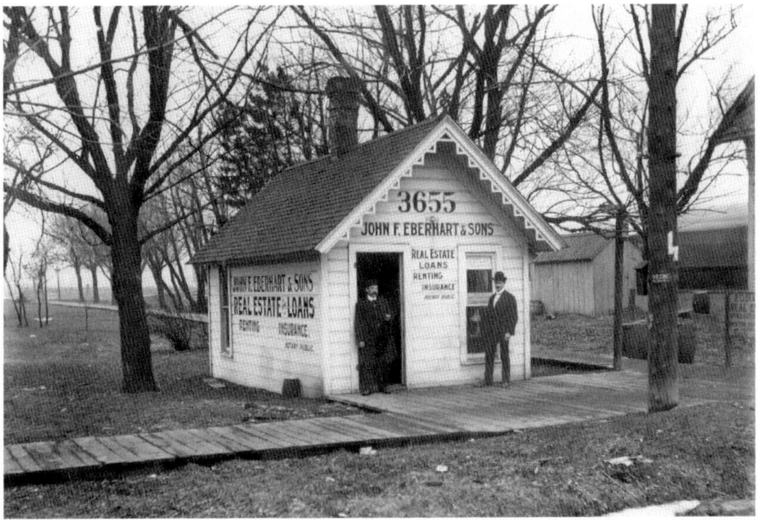

Professor Eberhart
John Eberhart knew Abraham Lincoln well. He introduced Lincoln to Stephen A. Douglas for the first time when Douglas and Lincoln were opposing candidates for the US Senate. A popular orator himself, Eberhart was quite often in demand for public speaking engagements.

Education was of utmost importance to the professor, and even though he was a real estate man, he is credited with introducing the first kindergarten into the public school system in Chicago Lawn, thus affording Cook County bragging rights as the first county to have a kindergarten in the state.

Eberhart is well remembered as a scholar, educator, writer, lecturer, and builder. In 1855, he was told by three attending doctors that his health was very poor and he would die within six months. He died at the age of 84 on January 13, 1914.

The day of his funeral was a day of mourning for the entire community. Both young and old vied with each other to pay homage to this man, who was known and respected by all. Every business in Chicago Lawn was closed for the first time in its history, from 10:00 a.m. until 12:00 p.m. during the funeral service. (Both, courtesy of the Chicago Lawn Historical Society.)

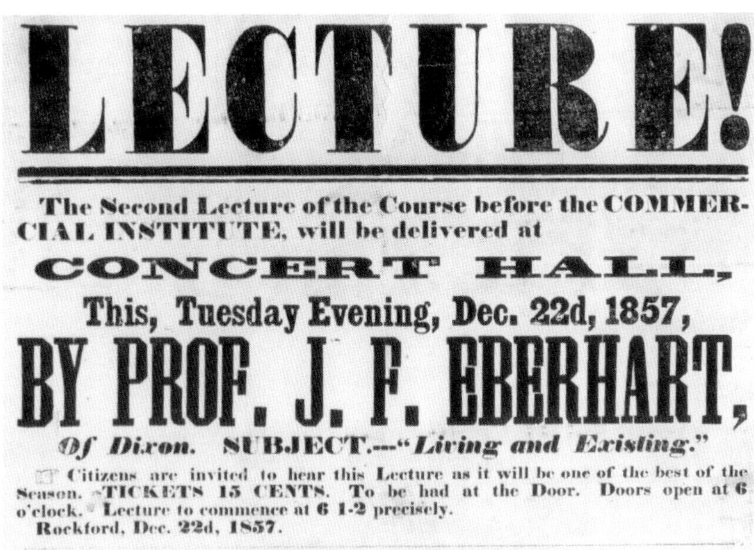

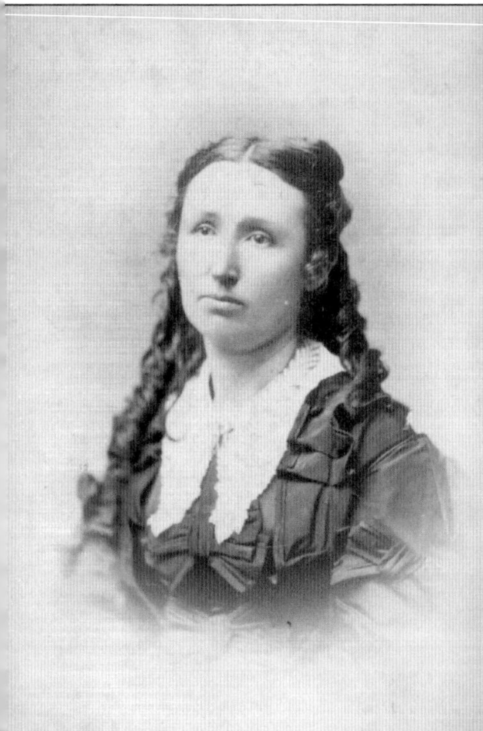

Matilda C. Eberhart

On December 25, 1864, Dr. John Frederic Eberhart was married to Matilda Charity Miller, daughter of Joseph C. and Mercie H. Miller, who were among Chicago's earliest settlers. She was educated in the schools of Aurora and Chicago and a lady of marked talent and literary ability.

When the couple started their family, the Eberharts lived in the town of Norwood Park, the first settlement the educator-turned-home builder had a hand in starting.

After her husband changed the direction of their little family's future by purchasing land here, her life became quite different from what she had been accustomed to as a young lady.

Once the yellow brick house on what is now Sixty-Fourth Street was completed, Eberhart moved Matilda and their two sons to their new home. Upon arrival, she would have found six buildings and about 30 people living here, most of them relatives of her husband.

Finding no actual school in the little settlement, Matilda became the first teacher, setting up shop and starting the first school in her parlor. Six pupils in grades ranging from kindergarten to high school attended. (Both, courtesy of the Chicago Lawn Historical Society.)

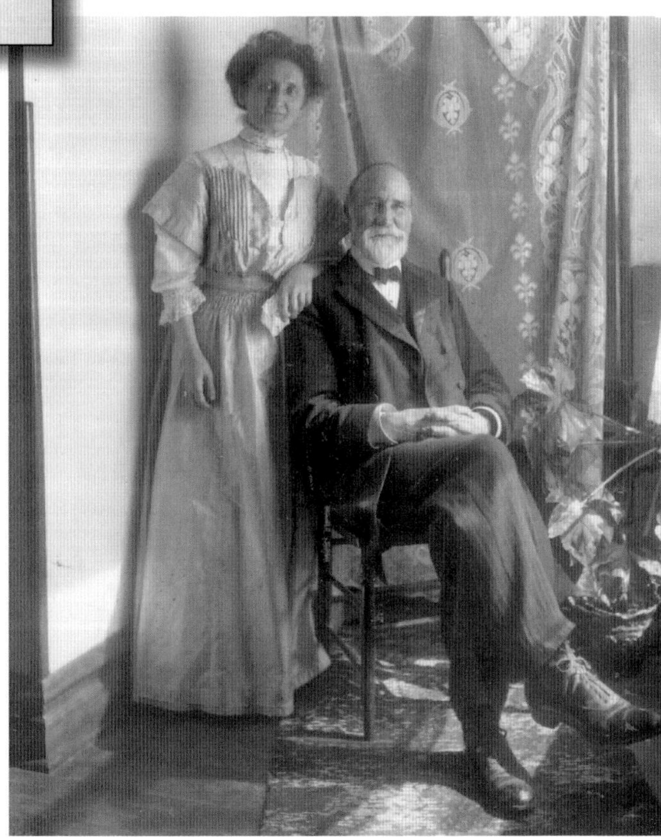

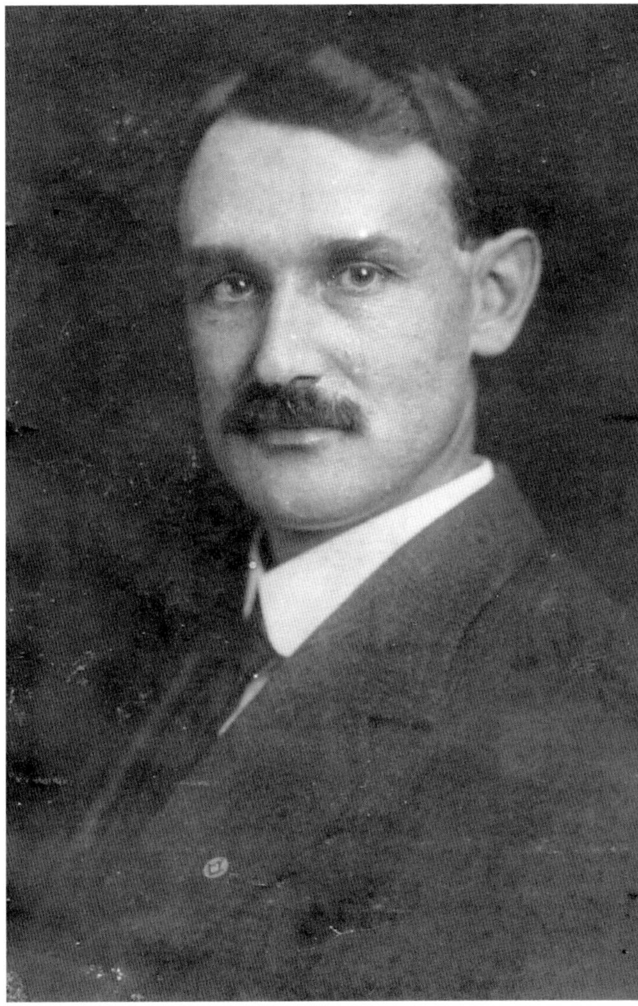

Frank N. Eberhart

Frank Eberhart, son of John and Matilda Eberhart, is today most appreciatively known in historical circles as the man with the camera; for it was his camera that took the glass slides depicting early life in the Lawn that in turn have been converted to photographs for future generations.

However, in the early 1900s, Frank was young and handsome and known to make the women swoon. He was also the manager of the Lawn Theater, and it was in this capacity that he made a bit of a name for himself as a local hero.

Locking up on a Sunday night, Frank put the evening's receipts in his pocket and grabbed the paste bucket and brush for posting new advertisements. Arriving at the billboard on the southwest corner of Sixty-Third Street and Homan Avenue, Frank found himself suddenly confronted by a revolver. Two gunshots rang out, one grazing the pocket of his jacket. The night was dark. With a split-second decision, the gunman was covered in starch and water, which combined with the midnight air, engulfed him in the sticky paste, giving Frank just enough time to bring his hands around the gunman's windpipe, pressing hard enough to subdue him. (Courtesy of the Chicago Lawn Historical Society.)

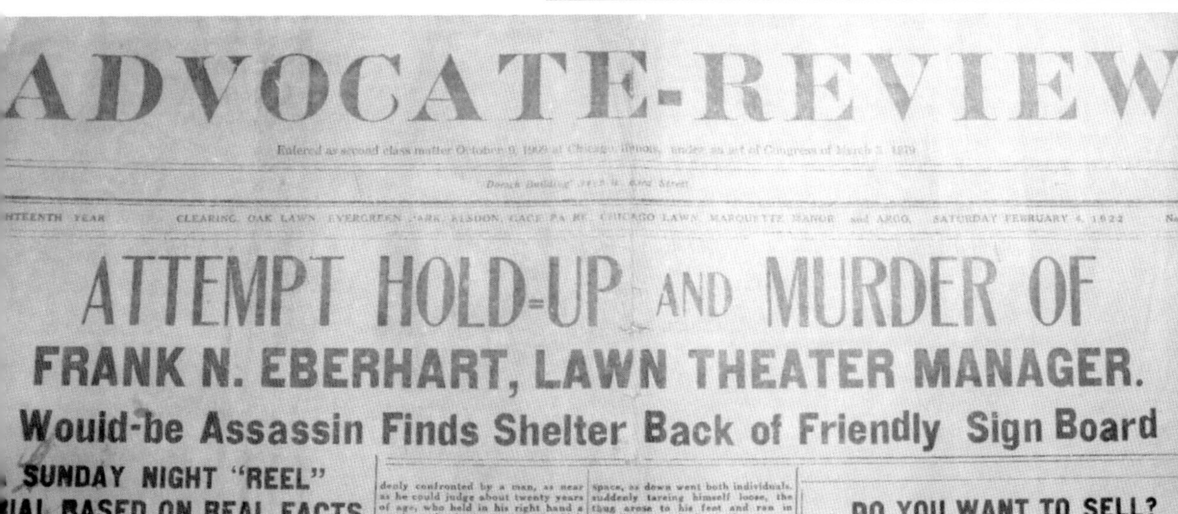

ADVOCATE-REVIEW

Entered as second class matter October 9, 1909 at Chicago, Illinois, under an act of Congress of March 3, 1879

HTEENTH YEAR CLEARING, OAK LAWN, EVERGREEN PARK, ... CHICAGO LAWN, MARQUETTE MANOR and ARGO, SATURDAY FEBRUARY 4, 1922 No.

ATTEMPT HOLD-UP AND MURDER OF

FRANK N. EBERHART, LAWN THEATER MANAGER.

Wouid-be Assassin Finds Shelter Back of Friendly Sign Board

SUNDAY NIGHT "REEL"
IAL BASED ON REAL FACTS.

denly confronted by a man, as near as he could judge about twenty years of age, who held in his right hand a revolver the business end of which

space, as down went both individuals. suddenly tareing himself loose, the thug arose to his feet and ran in the direction of the pool room on

DO YOU WANT TO SELL?

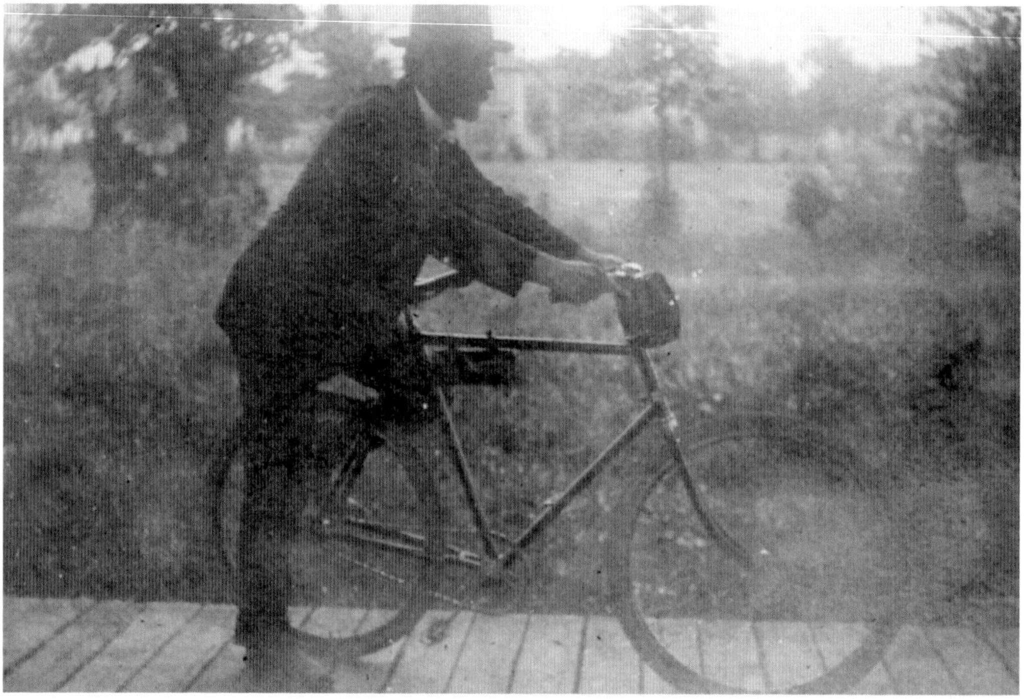

Dr. Ira Eberhart

Ira Eberhart shared an interest in photography with his cousin Frank, and he helped himself through college by taking photographs and working on farms. The doctor photographed his way through medical courses at Ames, Rush, and Jefferson College in Philadelphia, Pennsylvania, from which he graduated in the spring of 1889.

His camera and plates were forsaken when he became the first doctor in Chicago Lawn. He bought a house on Sixty-Third Place and most everyday could be seen riding his bicycle up and down the streets of the Lawn making his medical visits. He introduced three generations of babies to Chicago Lawn.

When not practicing medicine, Doctor Ira enjoyed hunting, negotiating on his bicycle with his little black cocker spaniel trotting alongside. They would go searching out into the fields for prairie chickens.

Once he retired, he also retired his bicycle, turning it in for a 1928 Ford, which he used to travel to Michigan to fish for bass and shoot some photographs of egrets and wildflowers. He continued to practice medicine a bit and lived to the age of 94. The photograph below was taken in September 1953, shortly before his death. (Both, courtesy of the Chicago Lawn Historical Society.)

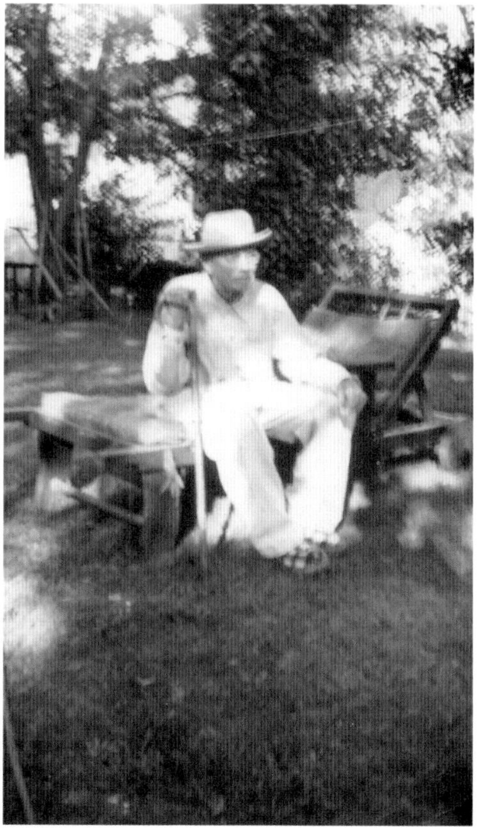

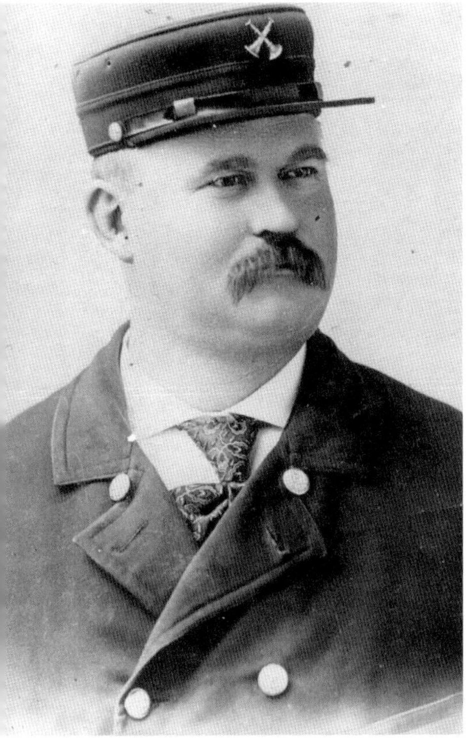

Fred Herold

In 1888, a volunteer fire department was organized, with Fred Herold as the town's first fire chief. He was a big jovial man, weighing more than 300 pounds. He is remembered in stories as the butter and egg man of the day, because when not called to fight a fire, he was the town butcher and used to make his deliveries by streetcar.

Firemen always rode free. So, every time Herold wanted to make a delivery, he just put on his fireman's uniform. Eventually, they did have to put a stop to that.

Luckily, the first fires were prairie fires, for in those days the streets were often muddy swamps or sundried ruts depending on the season. Legend says Herold's white horse, Charlie, could not be held at bay when the word fire was mentioned.

For every barn that was built, a dance was held to celebrate. Herold called the square dances and generally furnished all of the meat for the occasions.

When the first streetcar arrived on Sixty-Third Street, Herold fired a cannon to start things out, which meant a parade, music, and refreshments. (Both, courtesy of the Chicago Lawn Historical Society.)

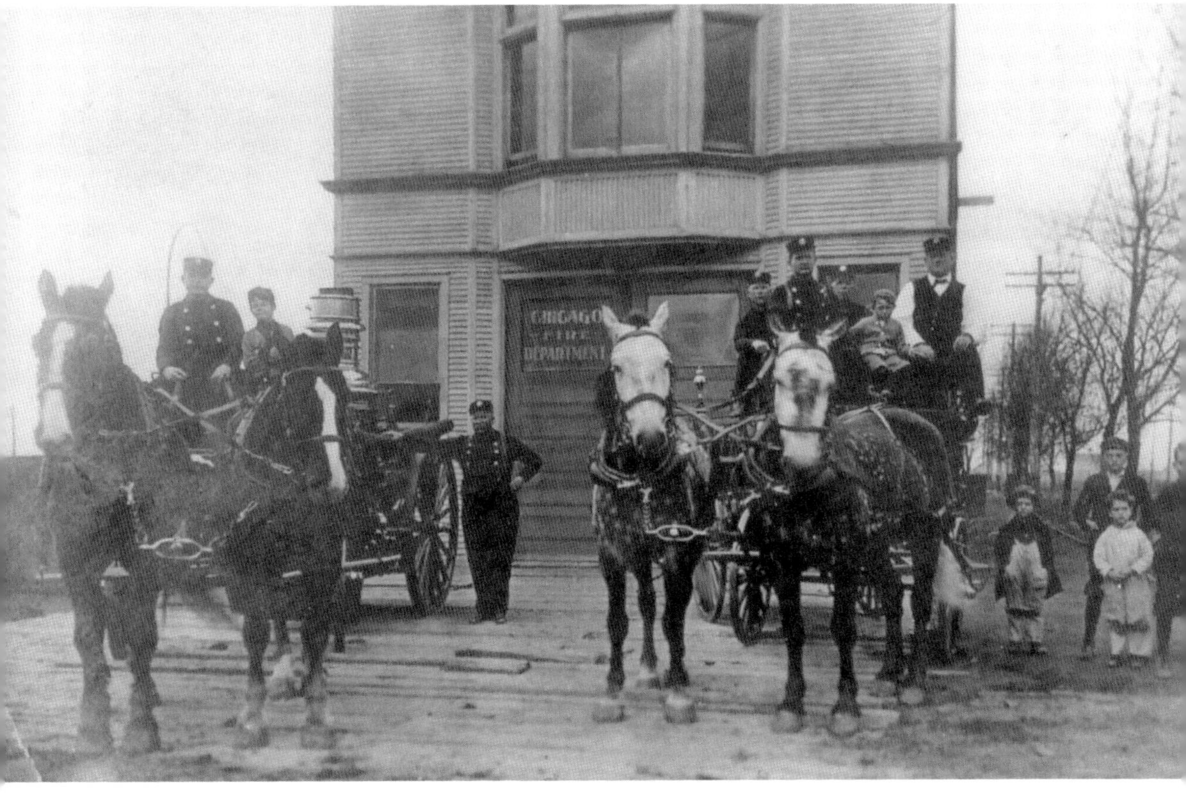

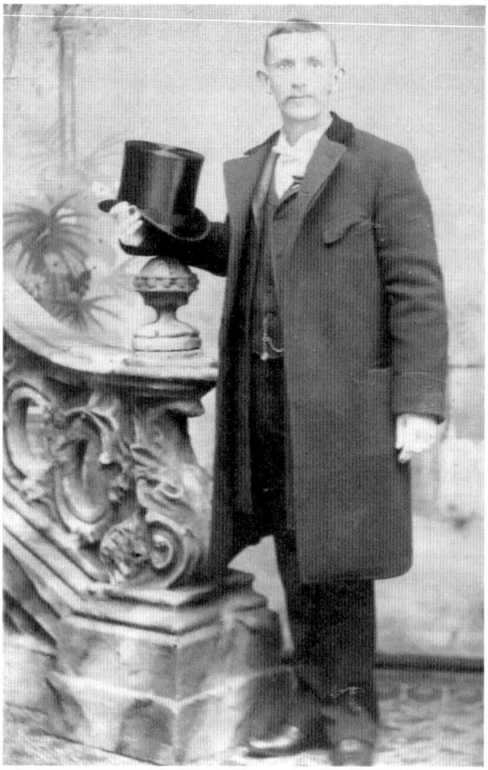

Amos W. Cravener

Amos William Cravener was a cousin of John Eberhart. Born in January 1859 in Armstrong County, Pennsylvania, he was the second son of John and Sarah Ann (Eberhart) Cravener. When he was 10 years old, the boy was placed in the Soldiers' Orphan School, remaining there six years. In February 1877, he traveled to Chicago and for several years attended school during the winter months, working in the gardening and nursery business during the summer.

His older brother Henry had studied law for three years, and when he graduated he moved to his cousin's settlement of Chicago Lawn. Henry convinced Amos to join him.

When Amos arrived, he purchased the little store Jeremiah Eberhart had built diagonally across from the train station. His was the only grocery store at the time in the Lawn. The second floor of the store was occupied by Mrs. Robb and her daughter Sarah, who in time became Mrs. Amos Cravener. They married in 1888. The following year, their union was blessed with a son, Donald Henry. (Both, courtesy of the Chicago Lawn Historical Society.)

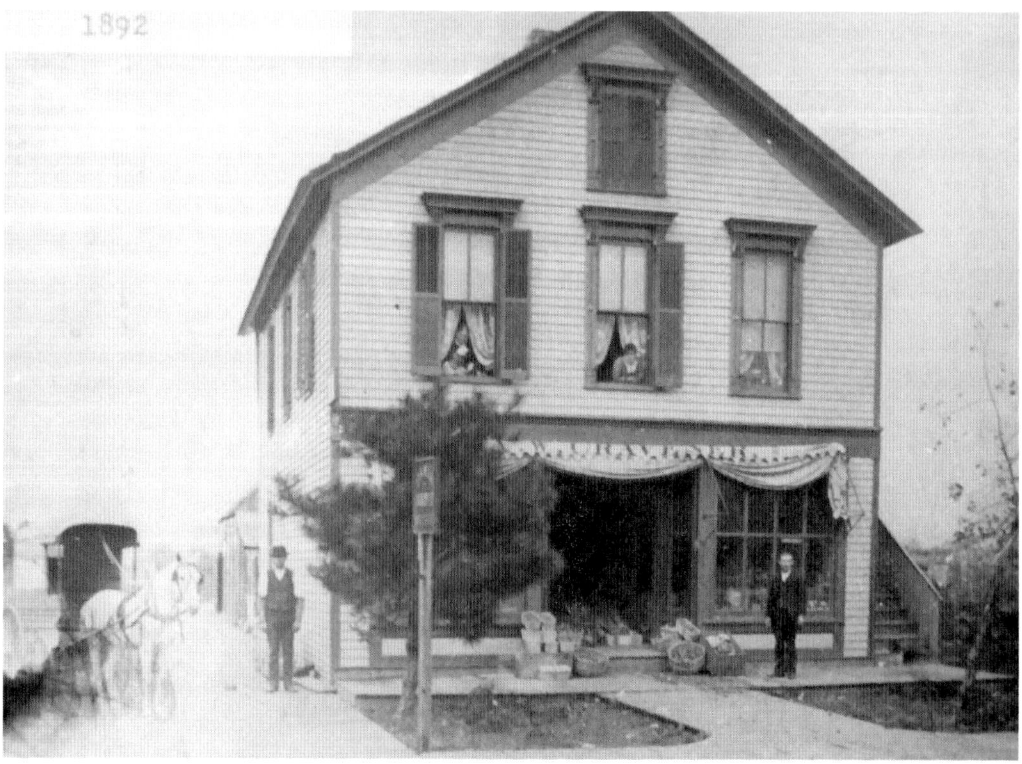

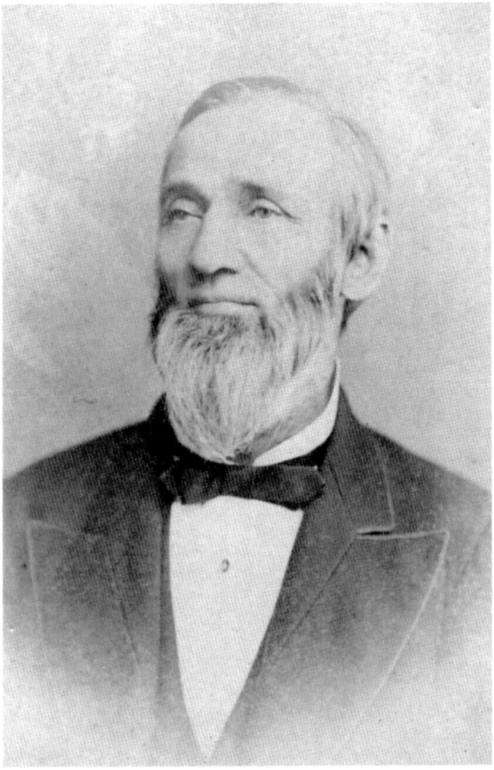

Rev. Uriah Eberhart
Rev. Uriah Eberhart founded the First Methodist Church, the first religious organization in the Lawn. He was its initial and regular pastor. In the beginning, church services were held in the parlor of John Eberhart's home. As the population began to grow, Sunday services were moved to the train depot. Reverend Eberhart also conducted the first Sunday school. (Courtesy of the Chicago Lawn Historical Society.)

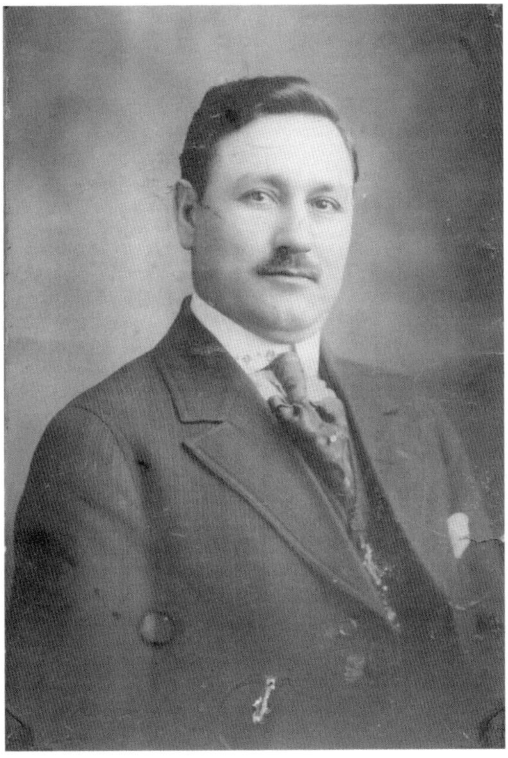

James Koovallis
James Koovallis began in business with a fruit and vegetable wagon, delivering his goods door to door in the early days of the Lawn.

After several years on the road, Koovallis opened a candy shop at the corner of Sixty-Third Street and Kedzie Avenue, of all places. Folks chided him; for at that time, Kedzie Avenue was considered the outskirts of town.

But time proved that Koovallis showed foresight. As the neighborhood grew up around the shop, his business did so well that he opened a new larger store, where he served up treats for many years to come. (Courtesy of the Chicago Lawn Historical Society.)

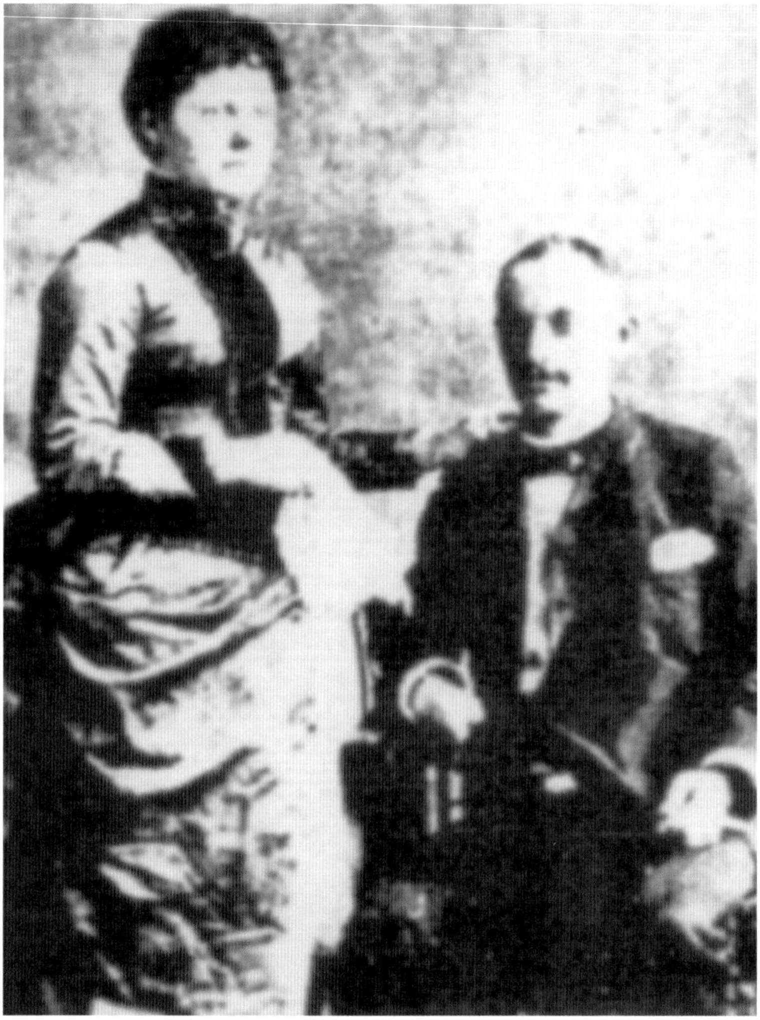

Louis and Rose G. O'Connell

Louis and Rose G. O'Connell were proprietors of a lone outpost on a dirt road that was then considered to be the longest road in the nation.

In the late 1800s, Western Avenue was only a long cleared path made of dirt and sand, but even as such it was the main artery from Chicago to Blue Island. Farmers from Blue Island traveled along the road to bring their crops to market.

The official name of the little station was Pryor's General Store, but travelers referred to it as the Half-Way House, since the corner that is now Sixty-Third Street and Western Avenue was considered to be the halfway point from Blue Island to city hall.

Rose O'Connell was a young girl when she moved to this area with her parents, John and Emma Pryor, in 1873. John built a two-story frame structure using the first floor for his general store and the upper level as a dwelling for his little family.

When Rose married Louis O'Connell, they took over as managers of the store. Farmers stopped to weigh their hay on the big scale in front, watered their horses, stayed for a cool drink, and visited before the last leg of their trip.

Both the Pryors and O'Connells were founding members of St. Rita Parish. (Courtesy of the Chicago Lawn Historical Society.)

William M. Butterworth

William Butterworth lived in Chicago Lawn for many years before it was annexed to the city of Chicago. He was very active in civic affairs and prominent in real estate and legal businesses. He was the first alderman of the original 31st Ward, which encompassed both Chicago Lawn and West Lawn. Its boundaries were State Street on the east, Fifty-Fifth Street on the north, Seventy-First Street on the south, and Central Avenue on the west.

Butterworth served in the city council under Mayor Carter H. Harrison as chairman of the health commission. He sponsored city ordinances imposing a penalty for spitting on the sidewalks and streetcar platforms as well as one enforcing a law that all dogs running at large be muzzled.

Butterworth affected the passing of regulations to have all ashes and cinders brought to the streets of Chicago Lawn as filling for base foundation of future pavements on all streets.

And, he led the first effort to rid Chicago Lawn of the rampant growth of weeds and wild clover by establishing sickle and scythe groups of citizens who made great strides in clearing the home areas during the hot summers of the early days. He is pictured here in a sketch that appeared in a Chicago newspaper in July 1901 under the title "Alderman Butterworth and his Chicago Lawn Weed Cutting Squad."

The alderman himself was the leader, working every night with his neighbors to keep the rank growth from the west side of Chicago Lawn. For a long time, the alderman was accorded the distinction of living in the last house in his ward, and at this time in history the ward was still one of the farthest west.

Pictured here are Ald. Butterworth, W.J. Diamond, policeman John Douglas, P.D. Diamond, and G.K. Glen. (Courtesy of the Chicago Lawn Historical Society.)

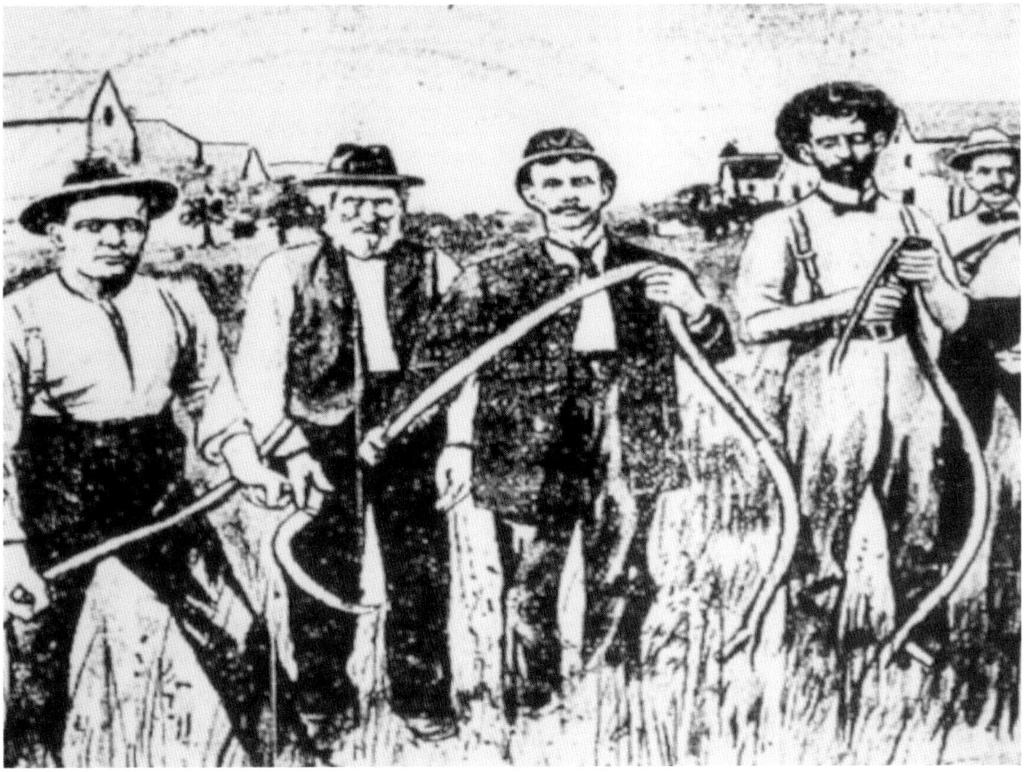

Rev. James F. Green, OSA

Reverend James Green was the founding pastor of St. Rita of Cascia, the first Catholic parish in the area. During his time here, he established a monastery, grammar school, and high school, founded three mission churches, one of them being St. Nicholas of Tolentine, and played a huge role in opening up a 450-acre tract of land formerly uninhabitable.

In 1905, Archbishop James Quigley extended an invitation to the Augustinian friars to service the Catholic population in the prairies southwest of downtown. A five-acre tract of land on Sixty-Third Street, just east of wealthy landowner Hetty Green's holdings, sitting between Oakley and Claremont Avenues, was purchased.

Father Green arrived in Chicago on June 24 of that year and immediately set about the task of building a parish. He lived at St. Ann's rectory on Garfield Boulevard as he worked on the plans.

Losing no time in inspecting the property, he found vast expanses of wilderness, marshy land with prairies of wild mushrooms, strawberries, and sunflowers, separating acres of small cabbage farms. It was no doubt hard for him to believe this was a part of the city.

In the surrounding farms, he found but seven families to form the nucleus of his new parish.

Perhaps the largest obstacle facing Father Green was one that stifled the growth of this vast expanse of land, which would become known as the section of Chicago Lawn named Marquette Manor. The problem was Hetty Green, an eccentric woman from New York who was the principal landowner of much of the property north and west of Saint Rita's original tract of land. Refusing to take responsibility and improve it with a proper sewage system or sell the land to another who could improve it caused the area to become useless during the heavy spring rains. She fought every suggestion for a drainage system.

Father Green's concern for the health of his fledgling congregation and the future of the area drove him into bitter controversy and an eventual court battle, which ended in triumph over the wealthy landowner. (Courtesy of St. Rita High School.)

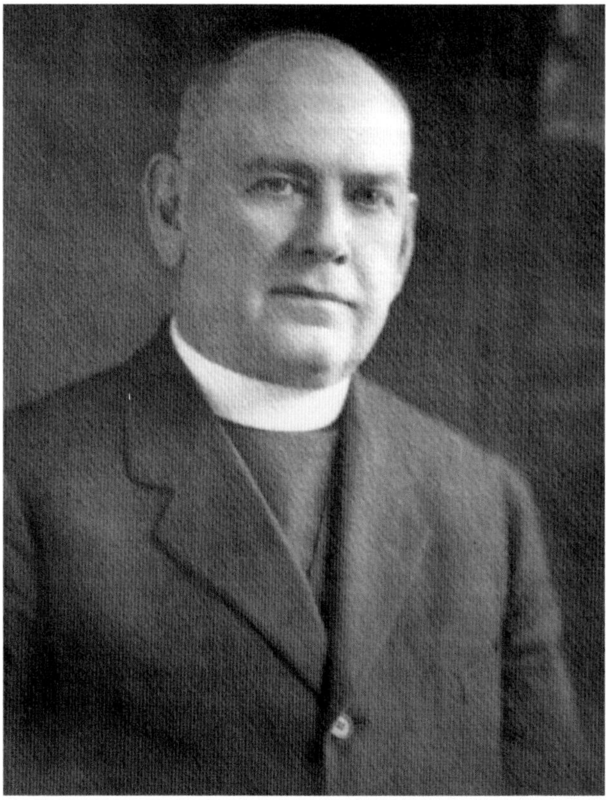

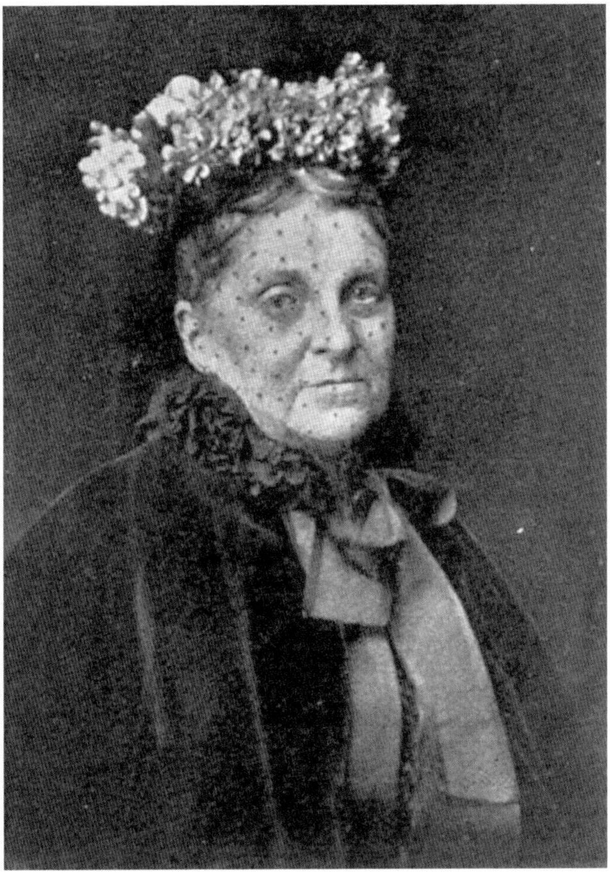

Hetty Green

Hetty Green died in 1916, but she could not take her wealth or her power with her and would forever be known in annals as the "Witch of Wall Street." Her estate was valued at over $100 million, yet she lived in poverty all of her adult life.

She ate cold oatmeal because it cost money to heat it. Legend has it that when her son fell and hurt his leg and it became infected, Green would not get it treated until she could find a clinic that would not charge her. By then, her son's leg had to be amputated.

Green came from a family of accumulated wealth. She learned at her father's knee how to be a shrewd businesswoman. When her father and aunt passed away, they left her a fortune totaling $6 million. Since she was a young woman and thought incapable of handling money, $5 million of that was kept in trust and $1 million left at her disposal. During her lifetime, Green increased that $1 million to $100 million.

Green accumulated much of her wealth at the misfortune of others. Her holdings on the Southwest Side of Chicago were obtained through foreclosure on a $100,000 loan made to Henry Gage. When Gage passed away before the loan was paid off, his heirs failed to pay the annual interest of 10 percent. This made Green the principal landowner of all the acreage from Kedzie to Western Avenues and Fifty-Sixth to Sixty-Second Streets.

At the age of 75, Hetty became seriously ill, depressed as a result of the death of her dog Dewey, whom she loved dearly. The next year, she turned the management of her holdings here to her son Ned.

Ned improved the land and was able to sell it at a profit of 10 times his mother's initial outlay. It is said that if it had been sold during those 15 years under her ownership, she most likely would have realized 20 times as much, an extra $10 million, had she agreed to improve it as originally requested in Father Green's lawsuit. (Courtesy of the Chicago Lawn Historical Society.)

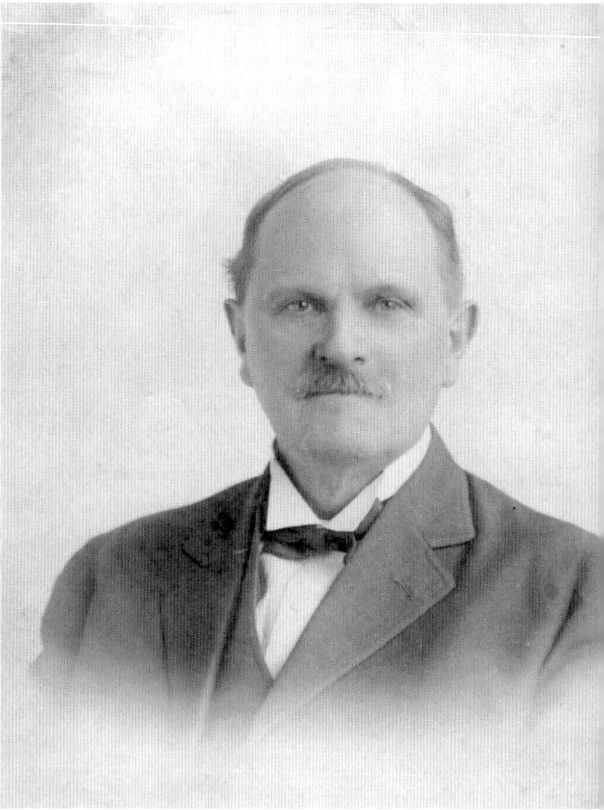

James A. Beach

When the Chicago Lawn Band was organized in 1906, its members were all Chicago Lawn residents and heads of families, which may be part of the reason the band held together for a very long time. Civil War veteran Prof. James Beach, a serious and talented music scholar, was elected director of the band at its first meeting.

The band was not organized for profit, but for the practice and benefit of the Chicago Lawn people.

Beach set up annual concerts to defray expenses and hall rent; however, they had several short vacations for lack of funds and a suitable room in which to rehearse in the winter. In the summer, he led the amateur musicians in practice on the cupola of the Lawn Club Hall.

Members of the Lawn Club Band pictured below are C.G. Carleton, Edward Westenfelder, Willis Roberts, J.M. Chubb, James Beach, Floyd Peck, John Westenfelder, Ross Topping, Frank Eberhart, and William Sherman. (Both, courtesy of the Chicago Lawn Historical Society.)

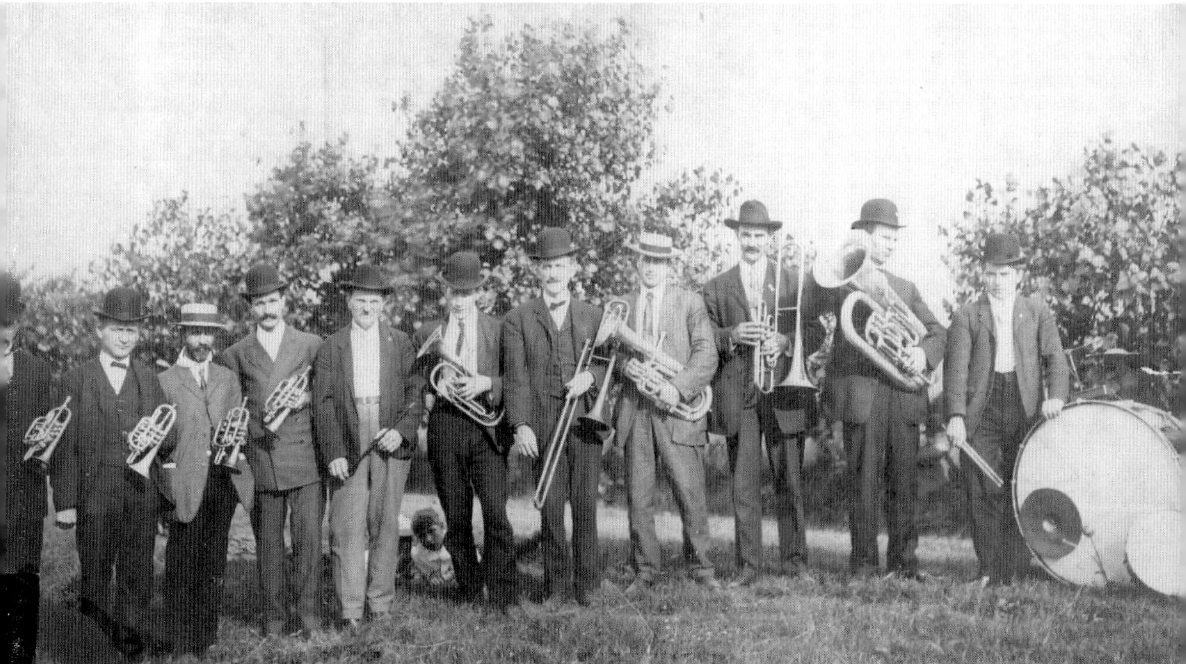

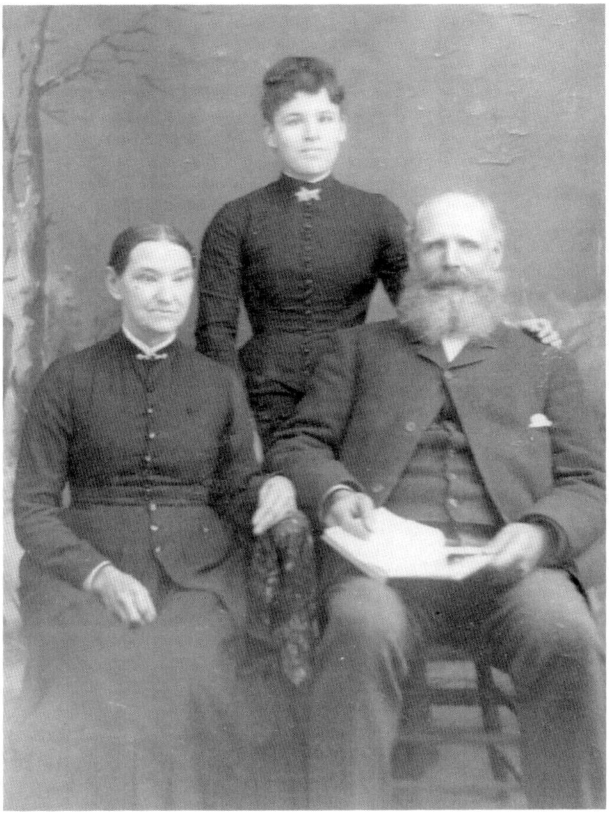

May C. Blair

May Blair (pictured here with her parents, Mr. and Mrs. Robert J. Blair) was voted the most popular girl in the community in the late 1800s. Moving to the then-village of Chicago Lawn with her parents in 1888, she quickly acclimated herself to the social goings-on in the fledgling town. Parties, dances, picnics, any kind of get together, May was there, many times responsible for orchestrating the event.

In 1902, she became the Lawn's first telephone operator when the Chicago Lawn telephone exchange was installed in her home. Because the area had no electricity at the time, it was necessary to use the imperfect shutter-board system. The 19 original subscribers were given any number of local calls at the regular monthly rate of $1.50, and a 10¢ charge was made for Chicago calls. In those early days, the operator was not only responsible for connecting the calls, he or she also had to keep an accurate record of the amount of calls placed, send out the bills at the end of the month, and collect payment from customers.

During the 1903 Iroquois Theater fire, May worked diligently throughout the night trying to get answers and relaying any new information to the locals, who were waiting anxiously for any news of their loved ones.

Any sickness or accident requiring medical attention was relayed through May. It was then her responsibility to locate the doctor and relay the message. As the exchange grew to 127 subscribers, the position became increasingly arduous.

The telephone was a luxury most often only used for important business. Known as a pal to teenagers, May helped to arrange dates for many young people who were not allowed to use the home telephone for such frivolousness.

May was a charter member of the popular Chicago Lawn Women's Club, and the Blairs were one of the founding families of St. Nicholas of Tolentine Parish. (Courtesy of the Chicago Lawn Historical Society.)

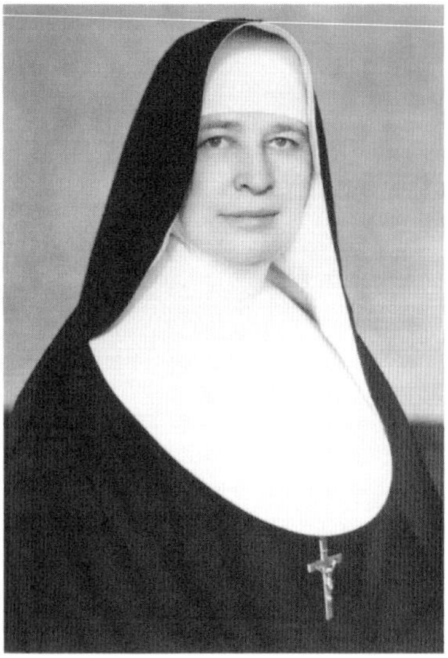

Venerable Maria "Casimira" Kaupas

The Sisters of St. Casimir hold a special place in the annals of local history, for it is to the SSCs and their foundress, Venerable Maria Kaupas, that residents owe an unending debt of gratitude for both the founding and the extensive growth of the southern portion of Marquette Manor, resulting in a motherhouse, high school, and hospital.

It was in 1907, in Scranton, Pennsylvania, that a young woman of Lithuanian heritage, Casimira Kaupas, founded a small religious community with the purpose of nourishing the faith of early Lithuanian immigrants.

The Sisters chose Chicago as their home because of the large influx of Lithuanians making their way in the young city. Within two years, the small community of nuns opened a school within the motherhouse confines and, in the next 10 years, staffed the nine Lithuanian parish schools that opened in Chicago.

Sister Maria, even as general superior, faithfully visited the schools, seeing to it that classes were of the highest standards. As long as she was able, she herself acted as school superior.

She is pictured below with Srs. Concepta Unguraitis and Immaculata Dvaranauskas on Profession Day 1907. (Both, courtesy of the Sisters of St. Casimir.)

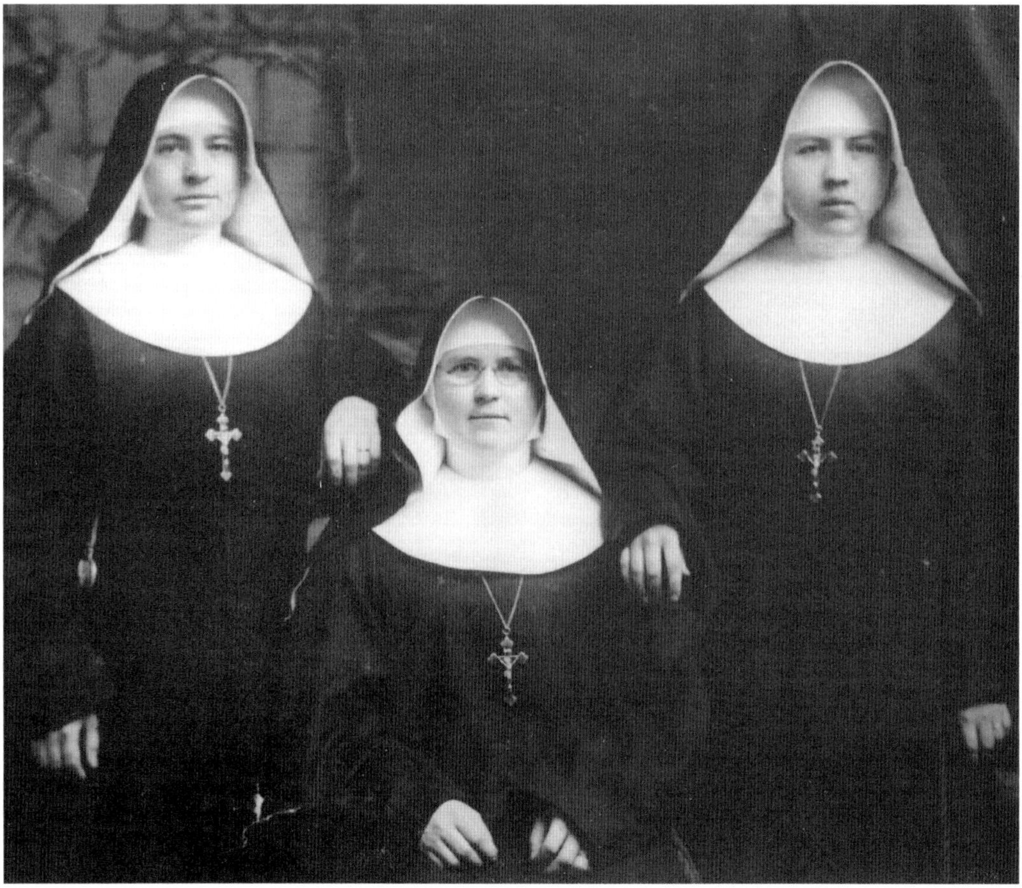

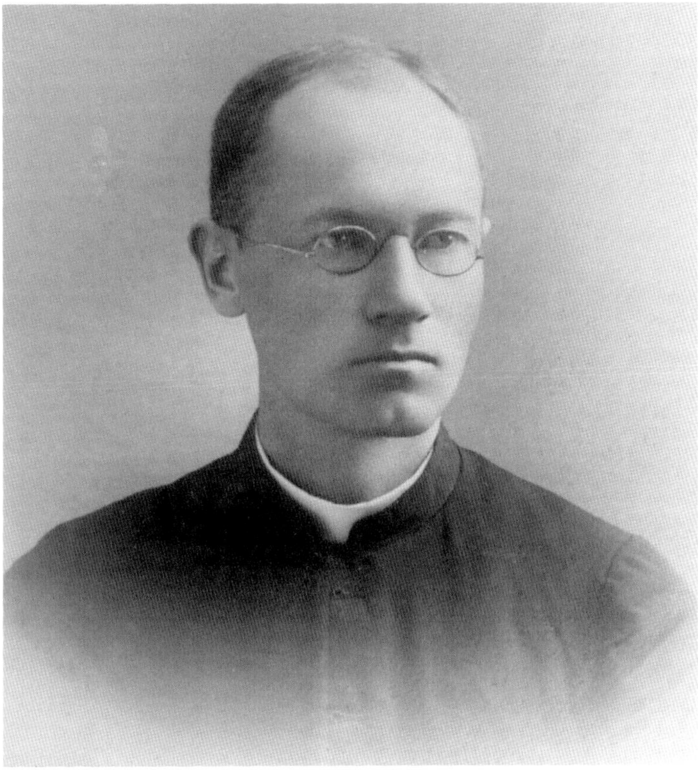

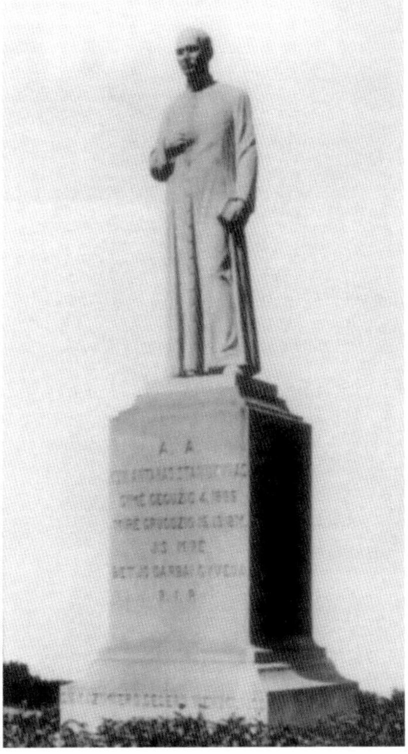

Rev. Anthony Staniukynas

Rev. Anthony Staniukynas dedicated himself to the wellbeing of young Casimira Kaupas and her dream of a Lithuanian order of nuns. Through his help and guidance, the Sisters of St. Casimir became a reality, and with his encouragement and foresight, this resulted in the growth of the southeastern section of Marquette Manor.

At the invitation of Archbishop James Quigley, he assisted the young community of nuns in purchasing land between 1907 and 1909 in an area southwest of the city limits.

Reverend Staniukynas served as chaplain to the SSCs. While collecting donations for the congregation, he also requested donations for orphans, as that cause was also close to his heart. Looking out the window of the newly built motherhouse, he longed to see an orphanage built on the adjacent 10 acres. Cardinal Mundelein preferred land outside the city limits for the orphanage and the present land be used for a hospital instead. The plan was implemented, and on February 28, 1928, Holy Cross Hospital opened its doors under the direction of the SSCs. (Above, courtesy of the Sisters of St. Casimir; below, courtesy of the Chicago Lawn Historical Society.)

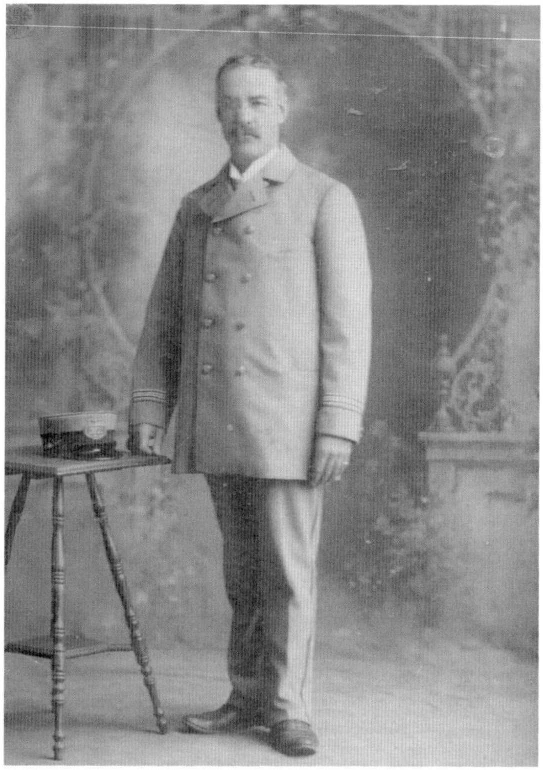

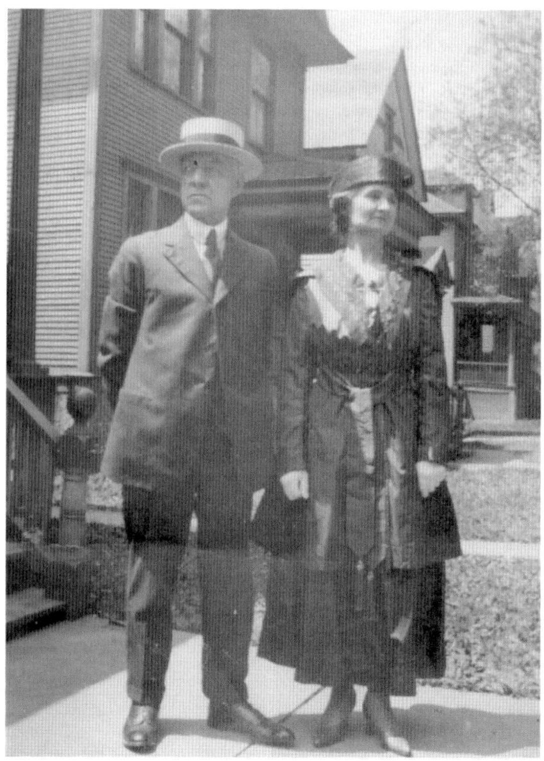

Martin McVeagh
In June 1898, Martin McVeagh received official notice that his application for transfer to the new Chicago Lawn headquarters of the city-delivery division of the US Post Office had been received and granted. He would be the first actual mailman in the Lawn and would go on to become postmaster. Prior to his appointment, the mail was brought in on the train, and any residents expecting correspondence needed to go to the train station at Sixty-Third Street and Central Park Avenue to pick it up.

An amiable and well-liked fellow, McVeagh was a welcome addition to the community. He worked for a few hours on Sundays in addition to his regular six-day work schedule.

As the area grew, he was assigned a substitute, a temporary helper, but it was not until the 1920s that six new permanent postmen were put on the job.

McVeagh is pictured here in the early days in his postman's uniform and then later on with his wife. (Courtesy of the Chicago Lawn Historical Society.)

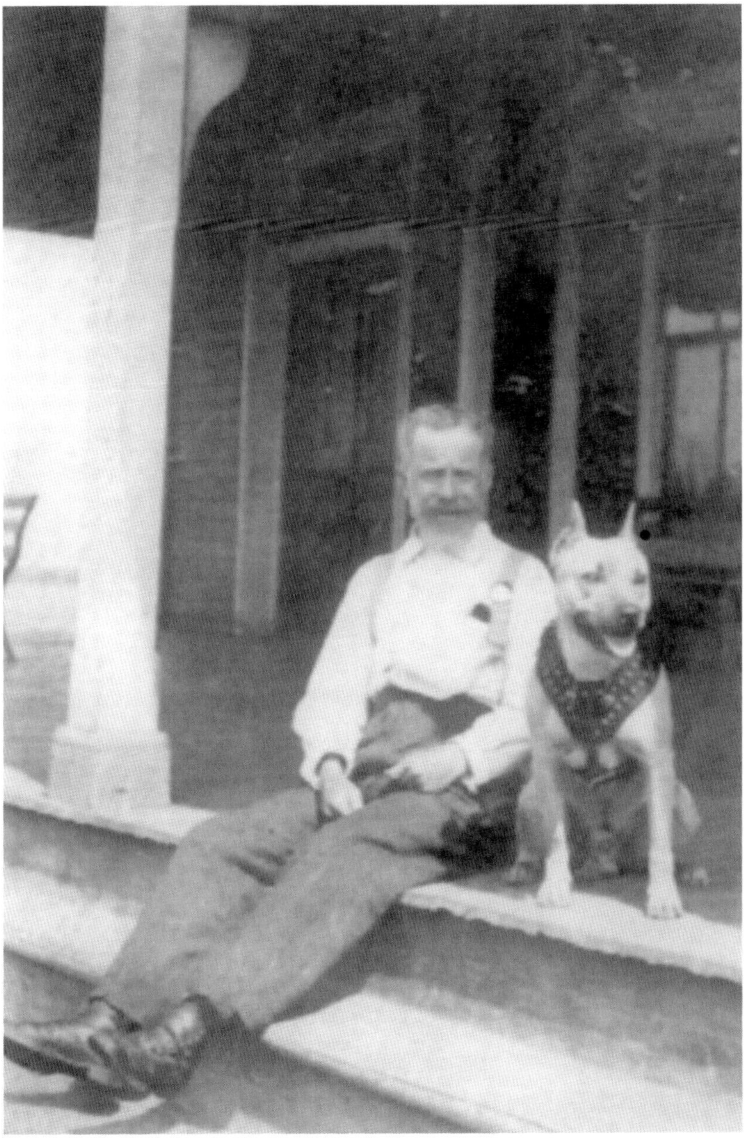

Edwin Eagle

Edwin Eagle, pictured here on the steps of the original field house, was the first foreman of Marquette Park and held that position for 23 years. It has been said that rarely a movement was made by anyone in the park that did not fall on the watchful eye of Eagle and his field glasses.

When the park first opened, the Mossler farmhouse, which sat at roughly what would now be Sixty-Eighth Street and St. Louis Avenue, was kept to serve as a field house. The first floor was for park business, and the top floor was remodeled into a five-room apartment for Eagle, his wife, Augusta, and their son Clarence.

In those early days, the park commissioners had very little money to hire extra help, so Eagle had to become a master of all trades. And he was on duty day and night, much to the sorrow of some of the young folks, as he would not allow any loafing after closing hours. Marquette Park was referred to as "the farm," and the foreman was known as "the eagle over the farm." (Courtesy of the Chicago Lawn Historical Society.)

Clarence Edwin Eagle

Born in 1896, the only child of Edwin and Augusta Eagle, Clarence became the first of Chicago Lawn's sons to sacrifice his life for his country during a war.

When Clarence was eight years old, his father accepted a position with the South Park Board, becoming the first superintendent of Marquette Park.

Clarence attended the Lawn School (now Eberhart) and later Tilden High School. He was a member of St. Elizabeth's Church on Sixty-Second Street and St. Louis Avenue.

At the age of 19, Clarence enlisted in the famous Illinois "Dandy First" division of the National Guard, serving on the border patrol. The second call on his regiment brought them to French soil, where they became part of the only division to fight under the American, British, and French flags.

His courage overseas quickly earned him the rank of corporal. Gassed and wounded time and again, he nevertheless returned to his ranks, going "over the top" on two occasions. (Both, courtesy of the Chicago Lawn Historical Society.)

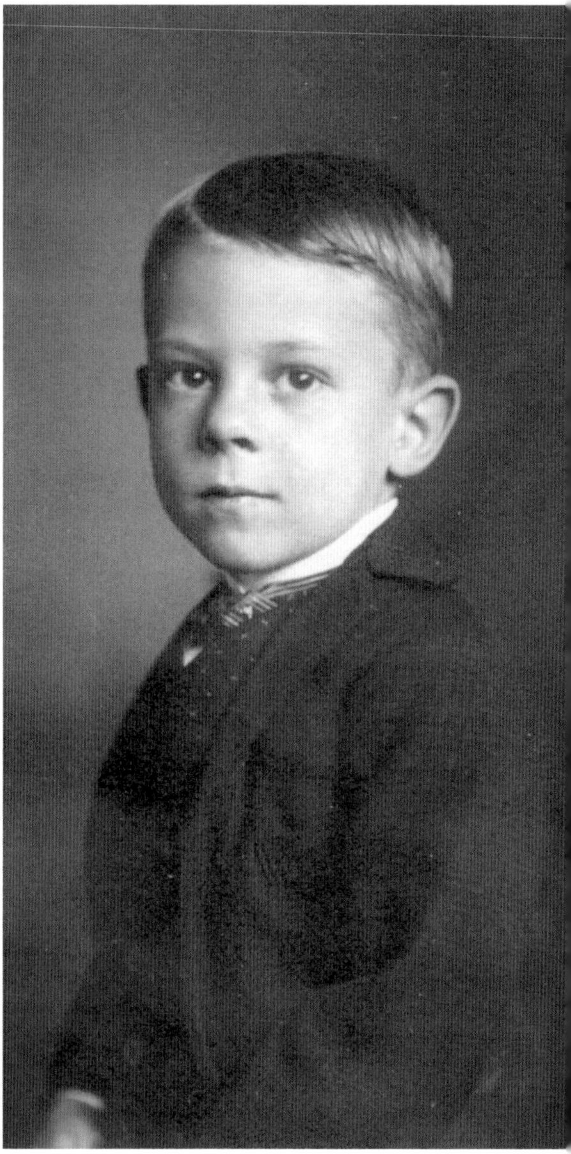

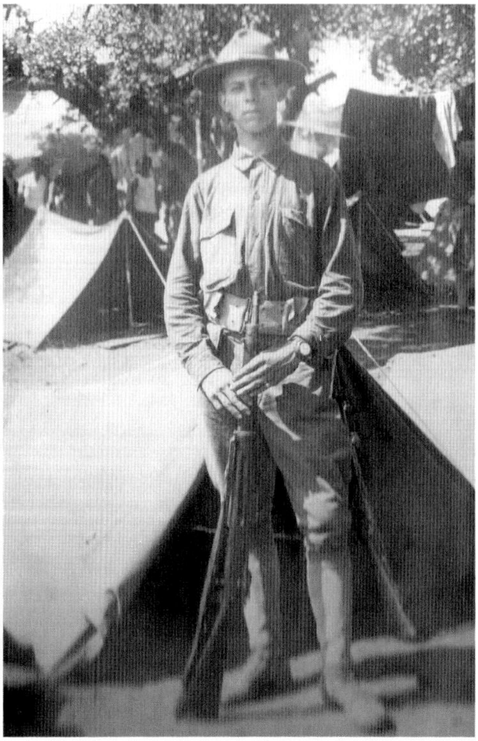

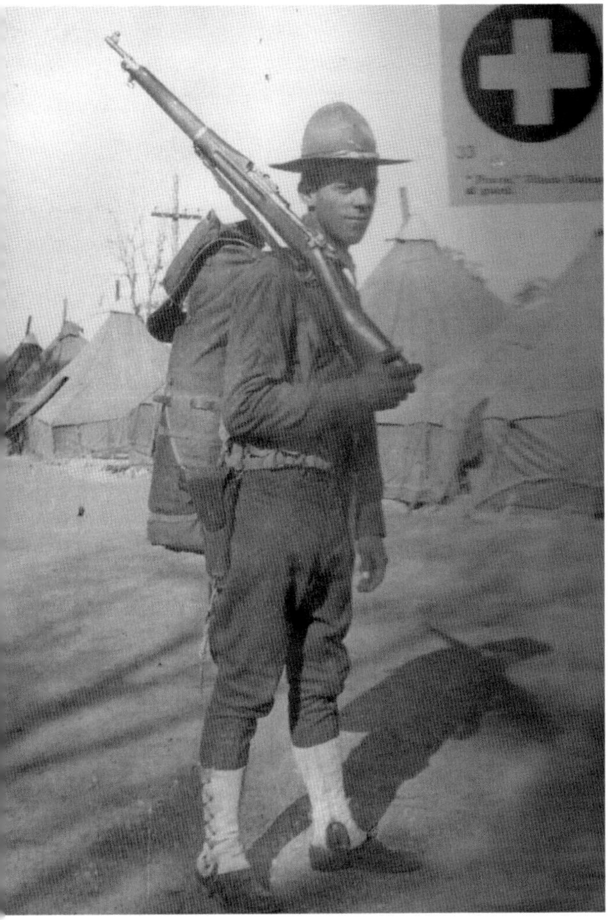

Corporal Eagle

Twice, Eagle went out alone into no man's land and brought back four and then five German prisoners. For this, he earned two medals for bravery.

Gen. John Pershing and King George of England visited the French fields and personally decorated Eagle and 12 of his fellow soldiers for their gallantry.

On August 11, 1918, Eagle's 22nd birthday, he went "over the top" at Chipilly Ridge. Out there in the open fields, in the midst of heavy showers of rifle and machine-gun fire, Cpl. Clarence E. Eagle gave his life for his country.

In a letter to Eagle's parents, a fellow soldier wrote, "During these months Clarence has often referred to you both and to his sweetheart and on several occasions he has expressed his willingness to sacrifice his own life in order that those left at home might be saved from the bloodstained and brutal hand of our common enemy."

Clarence Eagle is buried in France. The community mourned his passing, and on Easter Sunday 1925, his church unveiled a stained-glass window honoring his memory. (Both, courtesy of the Chicago Lawn Historical Society.)

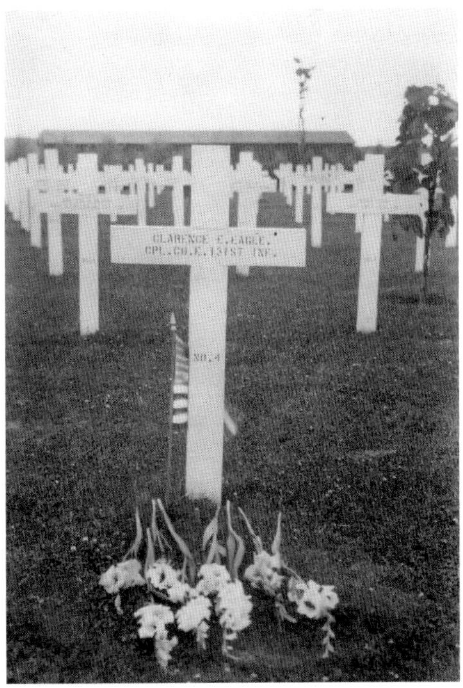

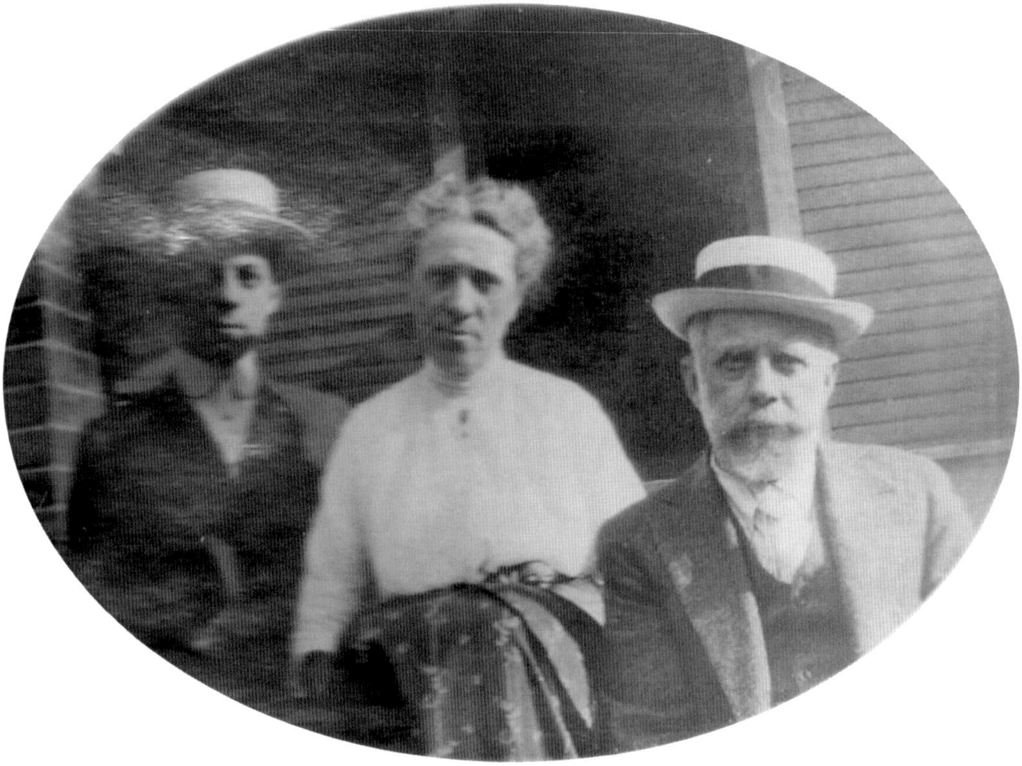

Augusta Eagle

Augusta Eagle came to Chicago Lawn with her husband, Edwin, and young son, Clarence, when Edwin won the job of foreman at Marquette Park. Moving all the way out to the Lawn from Forty-Fourth Street and Calumet Avenue was a big change, but she quickly acclimated.

The Eagles attended services at St. Elizabeth Episcopal Church, and while Augusta took part in auxiliary activities there and also served as hostess for any park activities, she gained notoriety for the saddest event in her life.

When her only child, Clarence, was killed in World War I, she became a grieving "Gold Star Mother." The US Army invited her to travel with others who had lost sons and husbands on a pilgrimage to France where they would see the graves of their beloved soldiers. She was in honored attendance the day St. Elizabeth's dedicated a stained-glass window to her son.

But her most endearing effort is what has kept both her and her son in the public eye even today. Augusta kept a scrapbook for Clarence, which she hoped to present to him upon his return. Having no descendants, she left the scrapbook to the Chicago Lawn Historical Society, and that scrapbook has been featured on Chicago's WTTW Channel 11 and NBC Channel 5 television.

The book opens to childhood photographs, even one with Clarence sporting his first pair of pants, continues on with lots of photographs of her son as a soldier interspersed with newspaper clippings and poems, and sadly ends with a photograph of his white cross forever perched in the quiet peace of Flanders Fields. (Courtesy of the Chicago Lawn Historical Society.)

CHAPTER TWO

Building the Community

Every human activity can be put at the service of the divine and of love.
We should all exercise our gift to build community.

— Jean Vanier, Community and Growth

Once the foundation was laid and word started to spread, the area attracted more and more citizens to its boundaries. Sometimes these folks were not the friendliest. As gangland turf wars began during the Prohibition era, this was a much-desired district, and it has been affirmed that the first shots fired from a Thompson machine gun in Chicago were fired here by gang leader Frank McErlane.

Politicians from the area began to make a name for themselves as William Cunnea threw his hat in the ring for mayor and John Egan, who would eventually spend a good portion of his career fighting for the airport, began a term as alderman.

The first Chicago Lawn daughter whose name would be emblazoned in bright lights throughout the country, Hazel Wood, left for vaudeville. Not long after, the bright lights beckoned to Parnell St. Aubin and Mary Ellen Bacon, who would later return here and marry.

Scotty O'Carroll brought his dream of flying an airplane to Chicago and opened up Monarch Air Service, headquartered at Municipal Airport. And down the street from the airport, Capt. Steponas Darius and Lt. Stasys Girenas were building a plane to make the first transatlantic flight from Chicago to Lithuania.

Tony Piet, who would become known as the "Father of Little League Baseball," was playing infield in the majors. Edward Landmichl was taking photographs that would become the talk of the town for years to come.

Dennis Larkin was building his coal company, which was the first official business in West Lawn, into a large lumberyard that spanned almost the whole block.

Greek immigrant Paul Stefanos was developing his famous Cupid Candies line. B.J. Glidewell had opened his pharmacy. Heim Pomerance was in business as a tailor. And John F. McCarthy was taking over the shuttered Marquette Park State Bank.

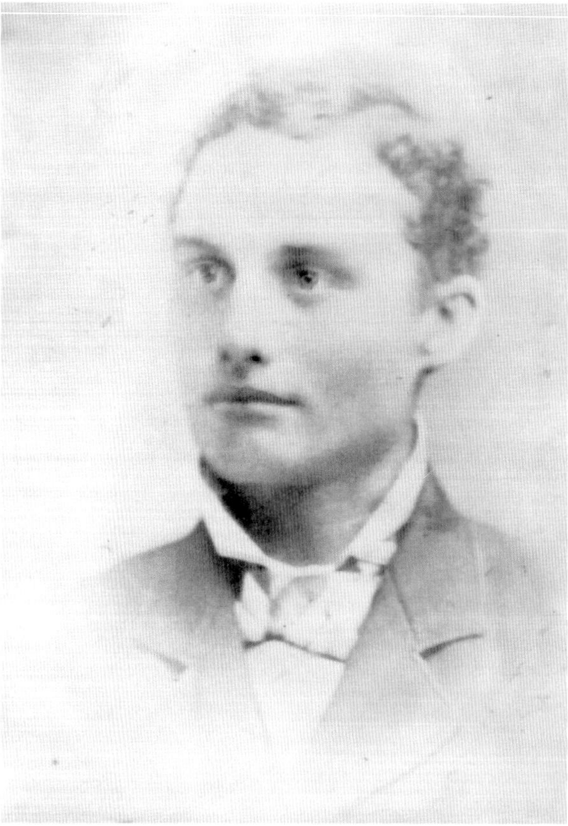

Dennis. F. Larkin

Dennis F. Larkin came to the small settlement of Chicago Lawn in the late 1880s and sunk a deep artesian well at what was then the southwest end of town, near the railroad tracks. The water furnished by this well was thought to be valuable for its medicinal qualities, and many lots were sold on the strength of that one fact.

As the population began to grow, Larkin opened the D.F. Larkin Coal and Lumber yard. Through this business, he supplied the people with much-needed building and heating materials that previously had to be purchased in Chicago.

When he erected his coal and lumber company just west of the Chicago Lawn train depot, it became the first official business in West Lawn.

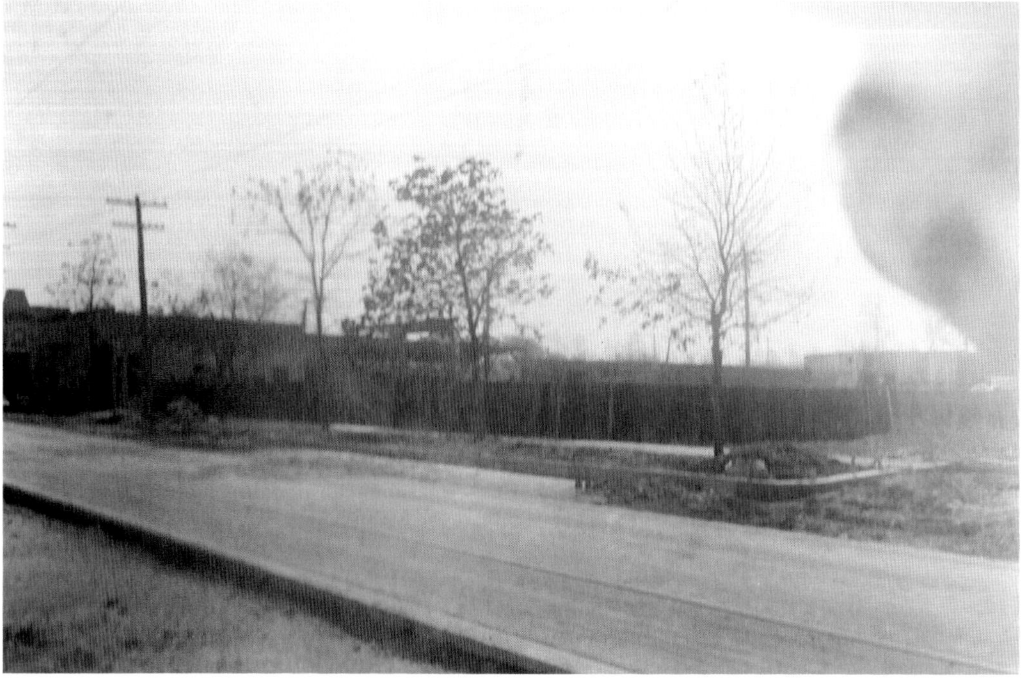

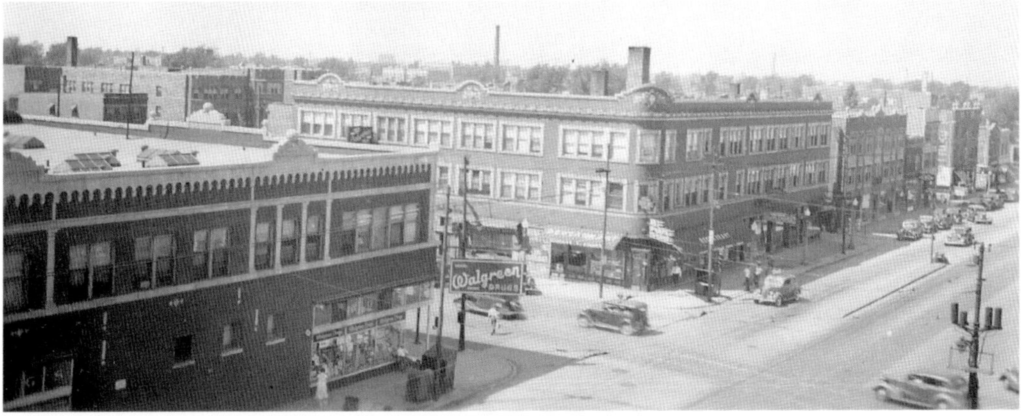

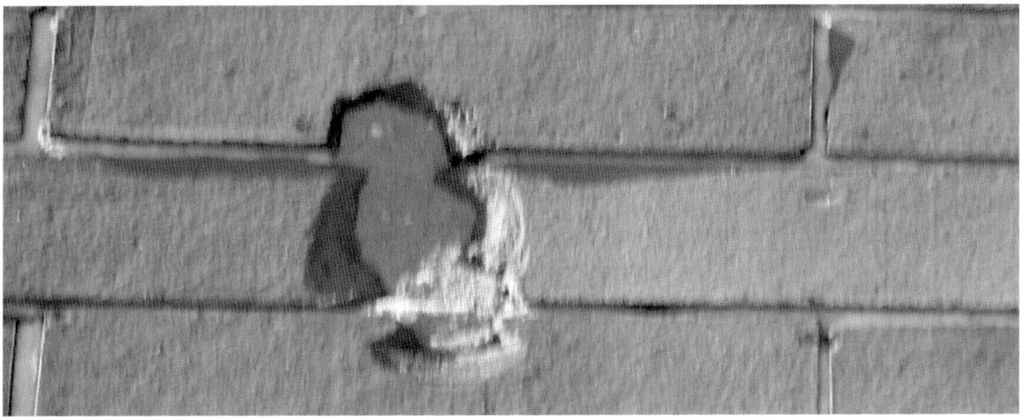

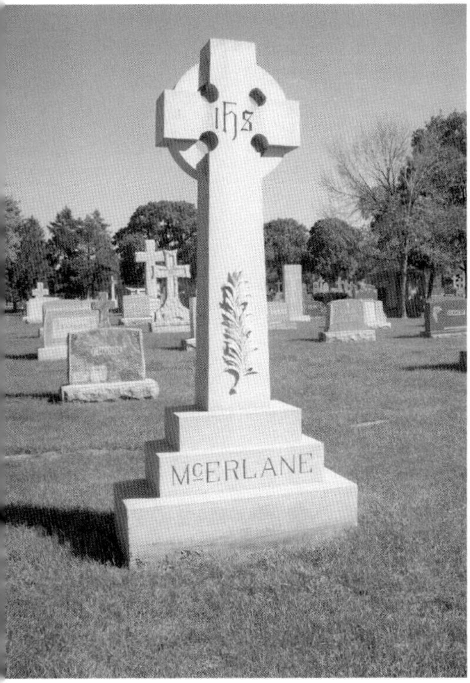

Frank McErlane

It was a sunny September morning in 1925 when Frank McErlane, an ally of Al Capone, made gangland history by firing the first known shots from a Thompson submachine gun in Chicago. The five-foot, eight-inch 190-pound leader of the Prohibition-era Soltes-McErlane gang had blue eyes, wore a perpetual scowl, and kept a rosary next to the pistol in his jacket pocket.

Rival gang member Spike O'Donnell stood in front of the Weiss Drug Store on the northwest corner of Sixty-Third Street and Western Avenue as an open touring car veered around the corner. McErlane shouted "He-e-l-l-o-o Spike," stuck his Tommy gun out the window, and pelted the corner with bullets. Though he missed his target, no one knows if that was his intention.

Most of the façade has been replaced, but if one walks north to the first doorway and looks up, chips that remain in the terra-cotta and brick can be seen. Members of the Chicago Landmarks Commission affirm in all probability these chips are from McErlane's machine gun.

In all, the murders of at least nine men and two dogs were attributed to McErlane. His remains rest in the family plot in Holy Sepulchre Cemetery in Worth.

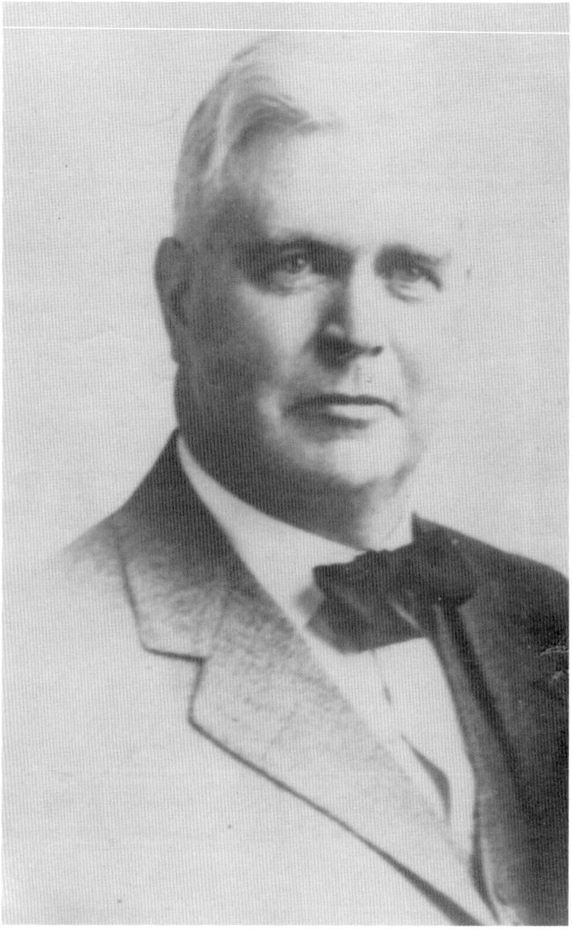

William A. Cunnea

William Alexander Cunnea was known as a fiery Chicago Socialist leader. Born in Northern Ireland in 1868, he was the youngest of 11 children and the son of a captain in the Merchant Marines. Educated at St. Mary's College in Belfast, he came to Chicago with his mother and siblings in 1884 and continued his education at Northwestern University.

The first political allegiance of this lawyer was to the Democratic Party, and he ran on that ticket for alderman in 1899. Switching to the Socialist Party, he ran for state's attorney in 1912 and 1918 and then for mayor 1923. It was during the state's attorney races that he gained notoriety and attention in national news.

In the early 1900s, it was said to be practically impossible for anyone to win an election to the office of state's attorney in Cook County without the support of either the Democratic or Republican Party. When most of the votes were in, it appeared Cunnea was the victor, but as returns came in from the last precincts, the tables turned, and his Democratic opponent ended the race with a surprising majority. While it looked suspicious, it was never proven that fraud was involved.

During the elections, Cunnea advocated for 5¢ surface-line fares and lower utility rates, but history credits the extraordinary vote he received to his promise of "forcing publishers who employ gunmen and shield murderers to answer to the law."

Even with the loss of the election, records indicate the impressive vote was a triumph for Cunnea, who became known as a brilliant orator and was much in demand as a speaker as well as a lawyer. (Courtesy of Mary Russell.)

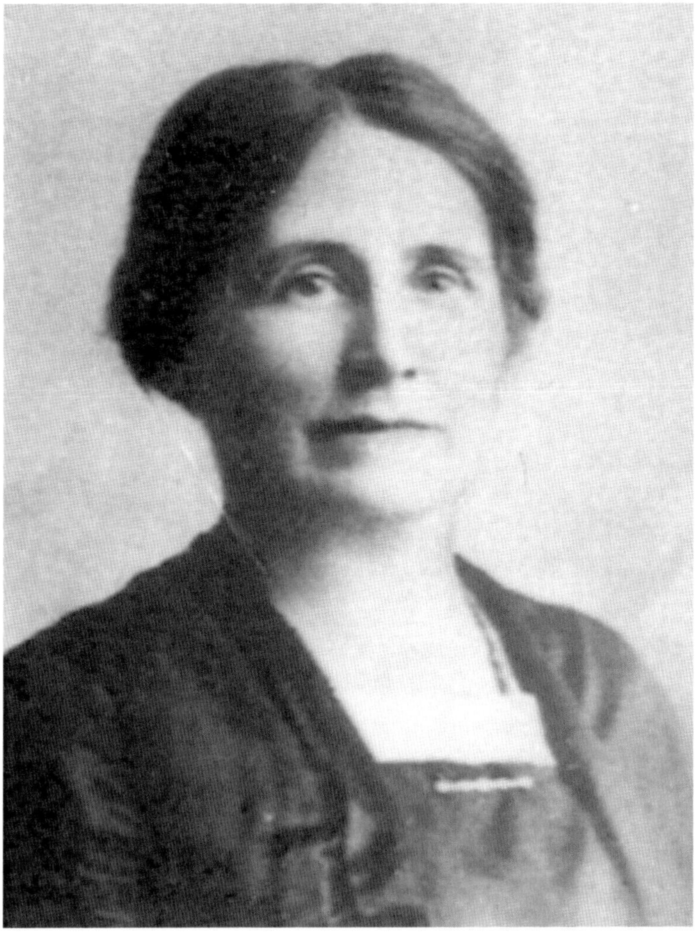

Mary A. Cunnea

On Christmas Day 1895, William Alexander Cunnea married Mary Anna Elizabeth McElherne. In 1923, she was described in a *Daily News* article by June Provines as "a woman who has the wisdom of the ages, and is not aware of it; a woman who has a charm of personality that she does not even suspect; a woman whose silences are more eloquent than most women's speeches."

Mary Cunnea was a quiet, soft-voiced slender woman with deep-blue eyes and long lashes who shared the busy life of her husband and raised eight children at the same time, six boys and two girls.

The couple lived most of their married life at 3708 West Sixty-Second Place and were early parishioners of St. Nicholas of Tolentine Church. During the period when her husband was running in the mayoral campaign, Mary was asked if she had given any thought to where they might move if he won the election.

"That is our home and we would stay there, I am sure," she answered. "We have six lots around our house and the children can play to their hearts' content. I don't think an apartment is the place for children. They either ruin their nervous system or your own."

Mary was prominently active in numerous charity organizations, the Altar and Rosary Society at her church, and the Chicago Lawn Women's Club, the latter of which elected her president shortly before her death.

When Mary passed away in 1933 after a lingering illness, her six sons carried her casket around the corner from their home to St. Nicholas of Tolentine Church. Several years after, the house was sold to her parish and then later torn down. It is now the parking lot for St. Nicholas Church. (Courtesy of Mary Russell.)

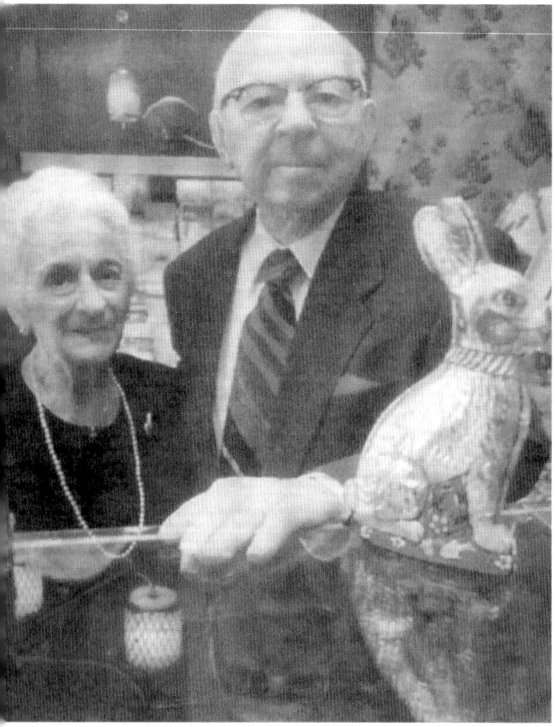

Polyhronis C. Stefanos

Polyhronis "Paul" Stefanos was the son of sheep farmers in the southern Greek town of Pedemeno. When he arrived in Chicago he had his green card, a $2 bill, and the recipes for fudge and the caramel candies he made popular and called Turks. He went to work for his brother Peter, who had started Joy Candies in Chicago a few years earlier. With only a second-grade education, Paul taught himself English by decoding the newspaper.

By 1936, Paul and his wife, Pauline, saved up enough money to rent a storefront next to the Highland Theatre, where they sold popcorn for a nickel and made toffee and fudge in the backroom.

In 1946, the Stefanos opened the Cupid Candies location at 3143 West Sixty-Third Street that would grow into the candy and soda shop best remembered by a generation of Southwest Siders.

Described as having a big heart, he often treated children at his church to his hand-dipped chocolates and hand-packed ice cream.

Stefanos lived to be 100, and it is said he attributed his longevity to eating a quarter of a pound of candy a day. (Above, courtesy of John Stefanos.)

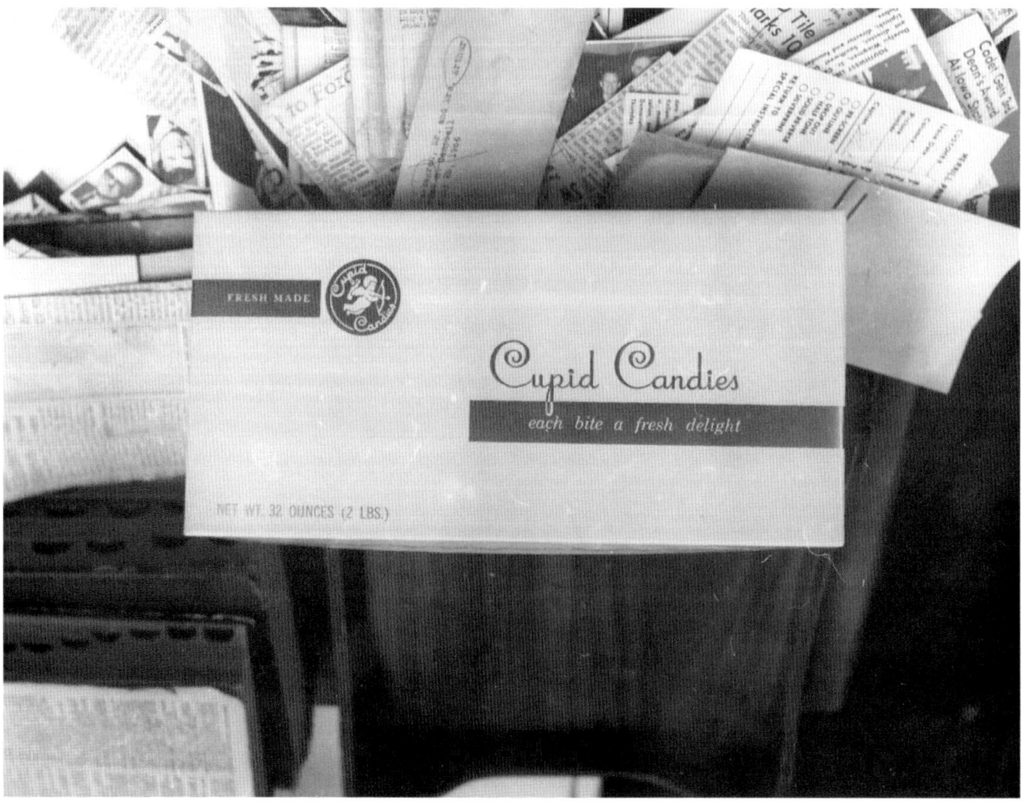

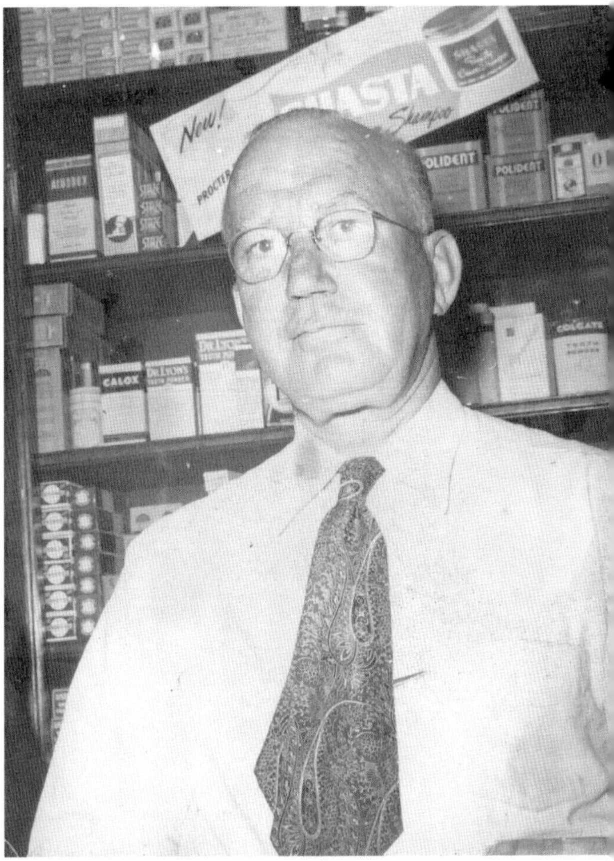

Benjamin Jackson Glidewell

B.J., as he was affectionately known, owned and operated the oldest drugstore on the Southwest Side. Born in Florida in 1888, he earned his pharmaceutical degree from Vanderbilt University. He met Constance Wallin, daughter of a Chicago Lawn pioneering family, while she was vacationing in Florida with the Eberharts. They married, moved to Chicago shortly after, purchased the pharmacy from H.E. Cain in 1919, and operated it continuously for 47 years.

Glidewell was an active well-liked member of the business community and served as the first president of the Chicago Lawn Businessmen's Association. He also had a reputation as an ardent fisherman and cook.

Father and son could be seen working together when his son Warren, also a pharmacist, joined his father at Glidewell's after a stint in the US Navy.

The family still has the clock and some of the old mortars, pestles, and bottles from the store. The clock was a pendulum about four feet in diameter. They also have a sign that reads "Glide to Glidewell's Your Druggist." (Both, courtesy of Keith Glidewell.)

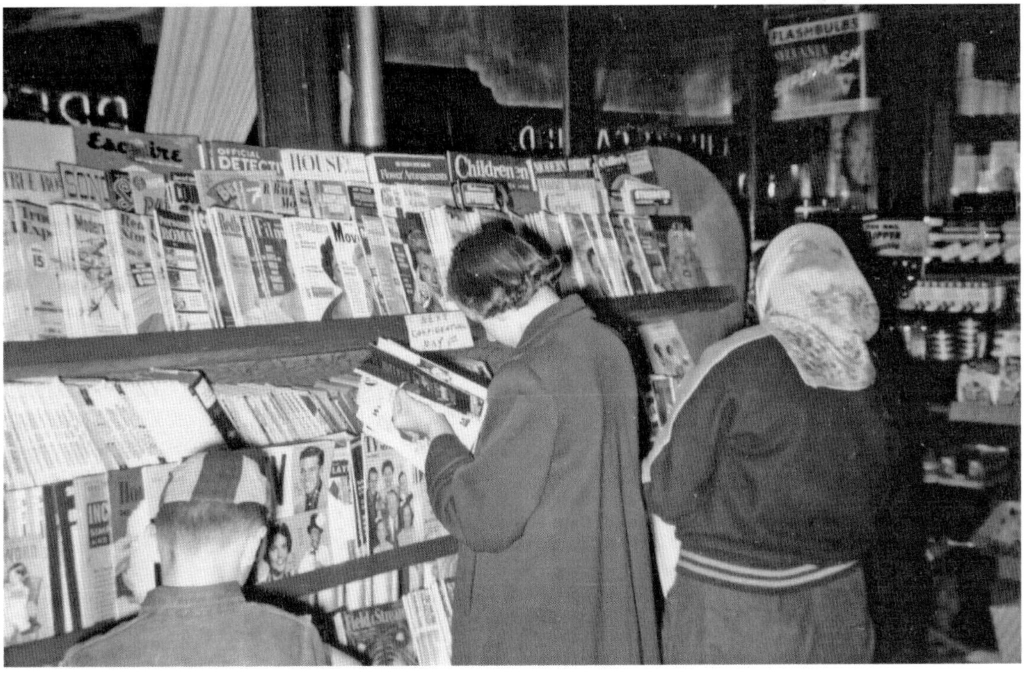

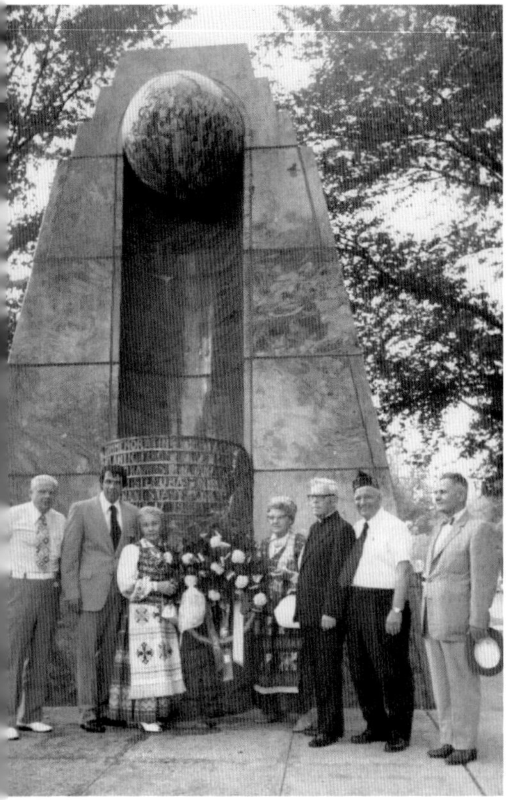

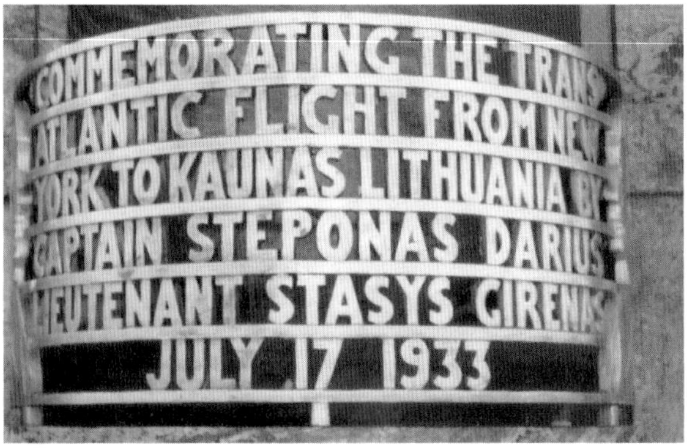

Darius and Girenas Monument
Standing on the southwest corner of Marquette and California Avenues is the Darius-Girenas monument. It honors the memory and contains the epitaphs of two men who attempted to be the first to make a transatlantic flight from America to Lithuania, crashing just 650 kilometers short of their goal.

Throughout Lithuania there are many monuments dedicated to these two pilots, for they are true heroes to the people of Lithuania. Their flight is considered to be a most noble endeavor and still stirs the patriotism of the next Lithuanian generation. In the United States there are two monuments, one in New York City and one here in Marquette Park.

Capt. Steponas Darius and Lt. Stasys Girenas (OPPOSITE)
Both Steponas Darius and Stasys Girenas were born in Lithuania, immigrated to the United States at a young age, and were educated in Chicago. Both also joined the US Army in 1917 and fought during World War I. Darius was awarded the Purple Heart for his valiant service in France. Girenas served as an aviation mechanic in the 136th Airborne Squadron.

The pilots teamed up in 1932, determined to fly over the Atlantic Ocean to Kaunas, Lithuania, then the temporary capital.

Before the flight, they wrote in their will, "We must do our share in the general work of the exploration of the North Atlantic air streams which are still poorly investigated. We hold it to be our duty to do this, being used for the benefit of mankind. We hold it to be our duty to do this job with honor."

The aviators purchased a used Bellanca CH 300 Pacemaker plane from the *Chicago Daily News*, soliciting donations to enable them to enhance the aircraft for the flight. They named it *Lituanica* and christened the plane at the Standard Oil Anchor at Municipal Airport.

Darius and Girenas had no navigational equipment and used only a compass to guide the plane, yet they were able to keep on an accurate course.

On the evening of July 16, 1933, they flew over Scotland. Darius and Girenas had successfully crossed the Atlantic but were stopped just 650 kilometers short of their goal when their plane crashed in a forest in southern Germany.

Their flight became the second-longest nonstop flight in aviation history. Their final words upon takeoff were, "To you young Lithuanians we dedicate this flight."

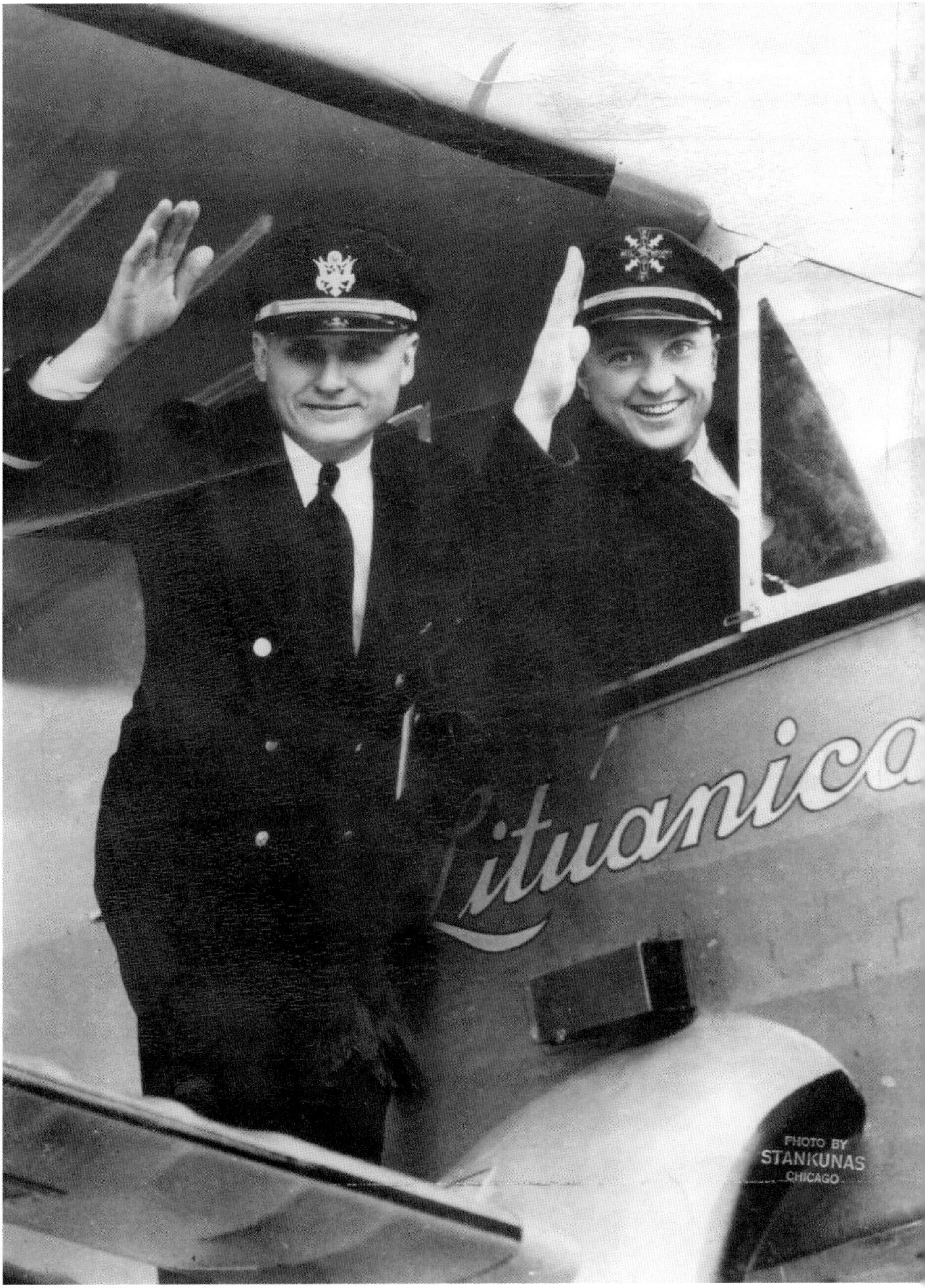
Lituanica
PHOTO BY
STANKUNAS
CHICAGO

Heim Pomerance

For many years, Heim Pomerance was known as the "Dean of Southwest Community Business Owners" due in part to his longevity as a businessman. He lived to be 102, passing away only months after retiring from the Chicago Lawn tailoring shop he ran for more than 70 years.

Immigrating to the United States from Russia in 1905, he established his first tailoring shop in Englewood. He operated the business successfully following his move to Chicago Lawn but reportedly lost the shop to creditors during the lean years of the Great Depression. Ironically, he was eventually able to buy back the business for less money than he owed on it before the Depression.

Pomerance purchased the Lawn Cleaner and Tailor at 3444 West Sixty-Third Street in 1915, keeping all of the original equipment and fixtures that came with the purchase, using them right up until he closed the shop's doors for the final time. Old-fashioned furnishings that could be seen in the shop included his sewing machine, (identical to the model he used as an apprentice in Russia), a roll-top desk, three full-length mirrors, and a cashier's cage at the counter.

For most of his life, he lived in an apartment in back of his shop. He welcomed customers and neighbors when they stopped in and was always happy to take a break and chat for a while. And Pomerance drove until he was just shy of his 99th birthday.

On his 98th birthday, he received a letter from then-president Ronald Reagan in which he wrote, "Your many years of work in your community have set a shining example for others to follow."

"We have learned that your driver's license is valid through your 100th birthday, commented Reagan. "This certainly indicates the confidence you inspire."

On his 100th birthday, Pomerance commented, "Life is just too short."

Both Heim Pomerance and neighbor Hazel Wood, who had also surpassed the magic century mark, passed away the same year and the same month. (Courtesy of Dolores Czerwinski.)

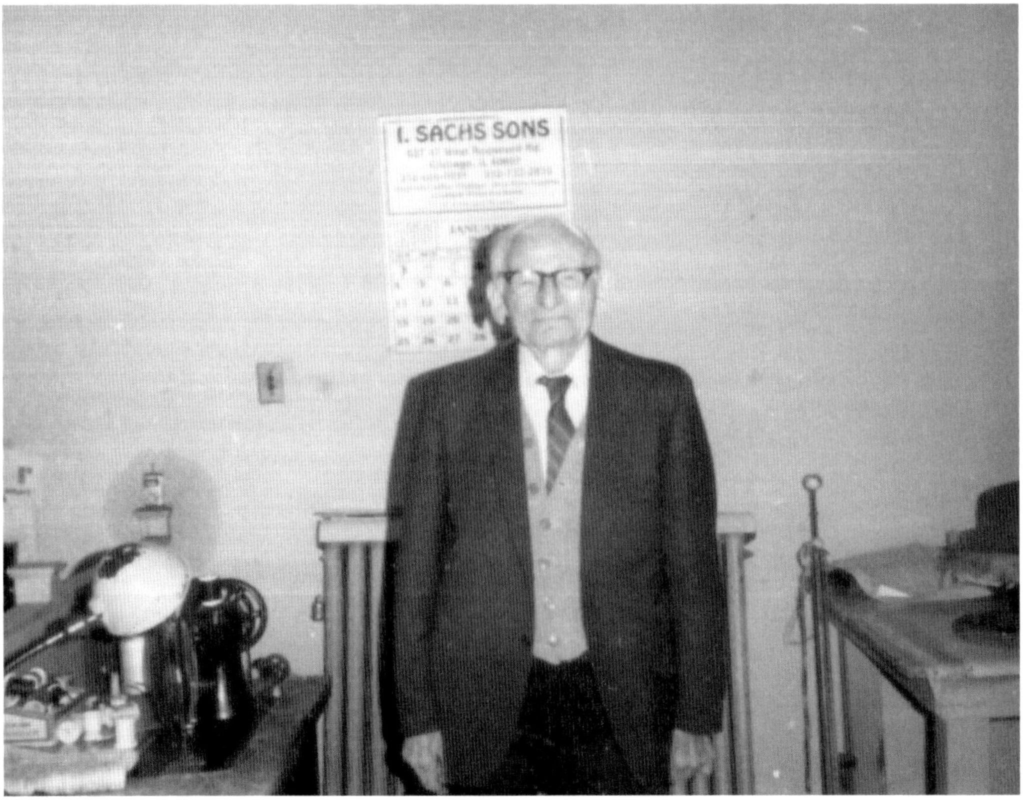

Hazel Wood

Described as "vibrant and electric with charm," Hazel Wood was the girl with the golden voice, perhaps the first Chicago Lawn daughter to be known around the country. She became an actress, excelling in light musical comedy and light opera, traveling as part of a professional road company. Her best known role was as Prima Donna with Gus Elimore's famous Cannibal Maids' Company, touring the renowned Pantages Circuit. During her career, she traveled to every state and every province in Canada except Nova Scotia.

After retiring from the road company, Wood returned to her childhood home. She taught voice and dramatic art for the Chicago Park District and volunteered as the director of the junior choir at the house of worship she attended as a girl, Thomas Memorial Congregational Church.

Stopping in to offer congratulations on her 100th birthday was a surprise visitor, Mayor Harold Washington. She told the mayor, "I lied so much over the years about my age, I never knew for sure how old I was but I do know today is my birthday. I always remember that date."

Hazel Wood died at the age of 104, in the same house in which she grew up.

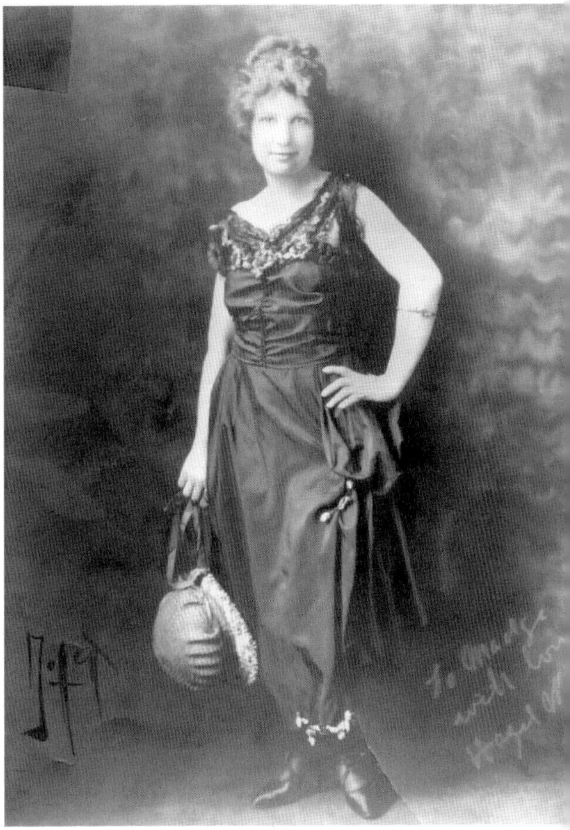

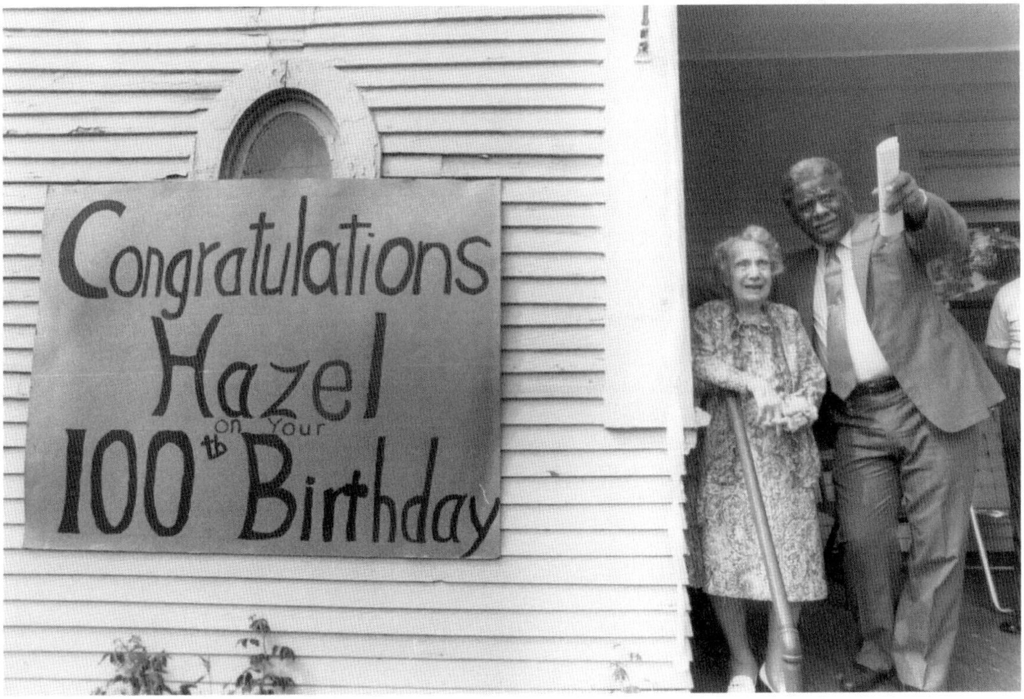

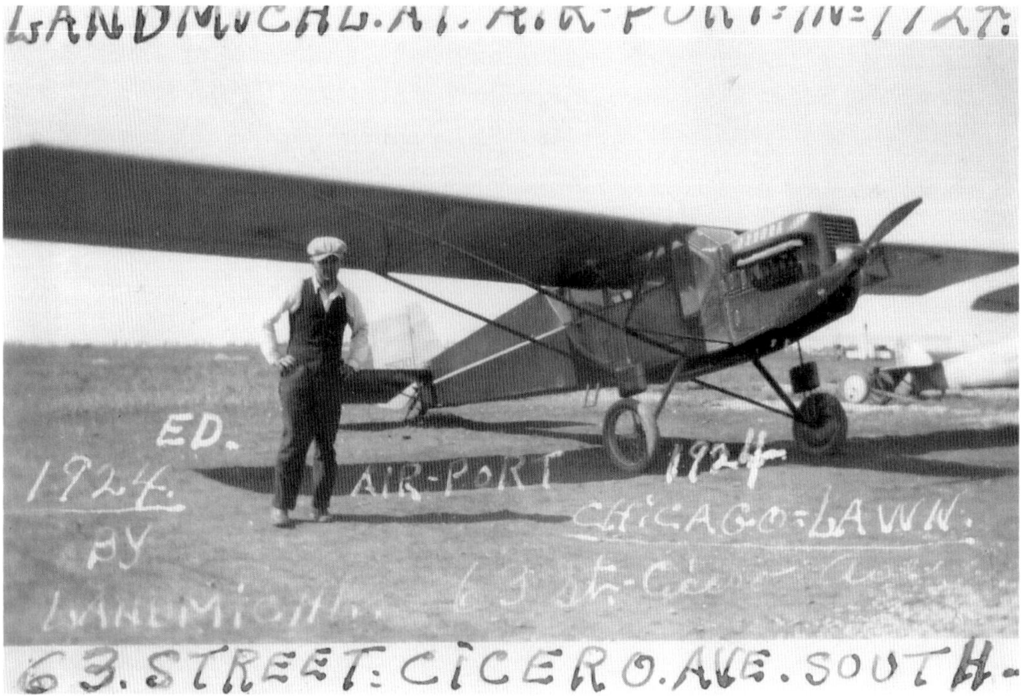

Edward Landmichl Jr.

Edward Landmichl Jr. was well known in the community as the genial proprietor of Landmichl's Place at 3824 West Sixty-Fifth Place, formerly operated under the name of the Chicago Lawn Nursery, which was started by his father on Fifty-Ninth Street in 1913.

Having come here as a young boy with his parents, he saw the communities develop from muddy prairies and often recalled his favorite boyhood sport of hunting ducks in the swamps and cattails where Ford City now stands.

Photography was his hobby, and nary a collection of historical local photographs is complete without at least a few of his images. They are easy to detect, for he wrote the descriptions right across the front. He was fond of automobiles and airplanes, as his snapshots show.

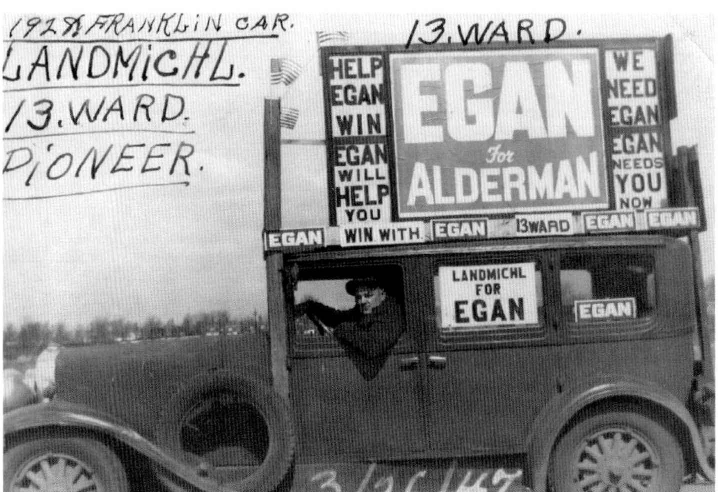

Landmichl and his wife, Lillian, raised two sons in the house they built at the above address.

He is pictured above at the Flying Field on Sixty-Third Street and Cicero Avenue in 1924, two years before it opened as Municipal Airport, and pictured at left in 1947 using his 1928 Franklin to campaign for John Egan. The almost 20-year-old air-cooled Franklin was painted red.

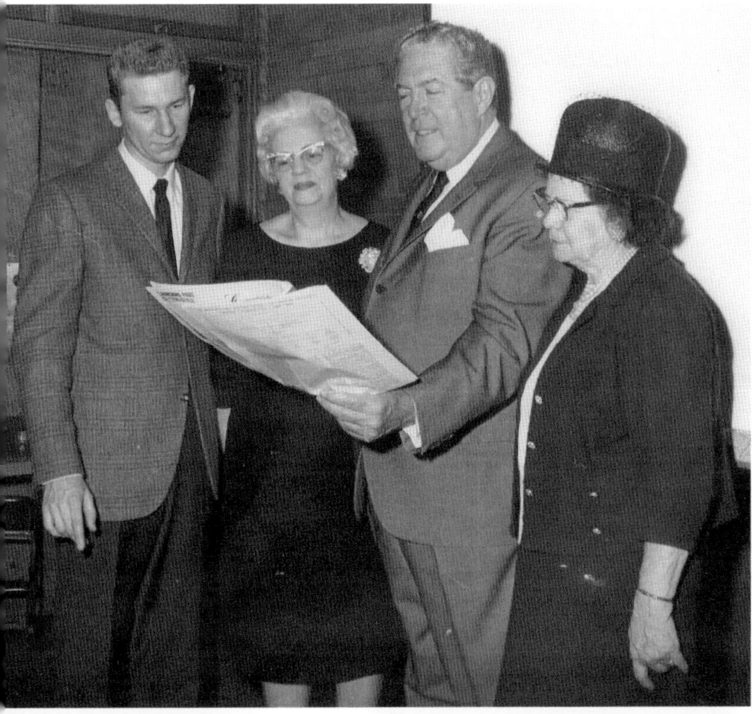

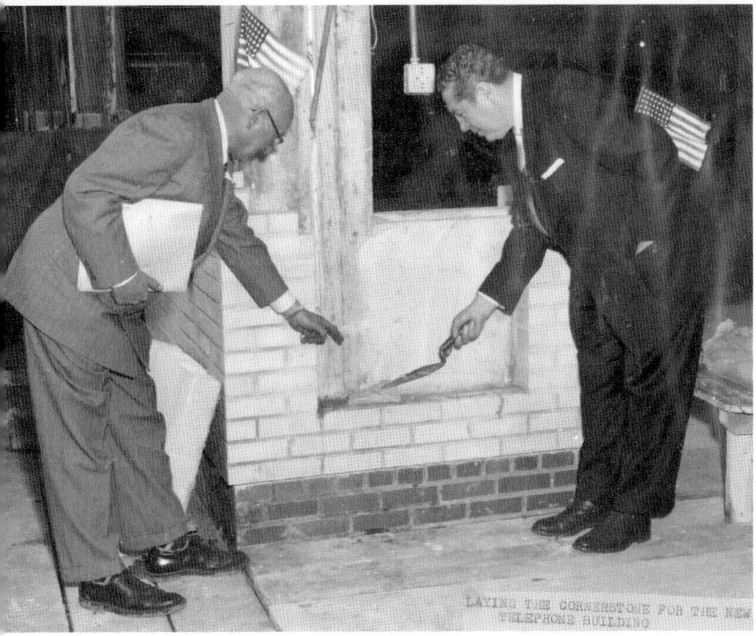

LAYING THE CORNERSTONE FOR THE NEW TELEPHONE BUILDING

John E. Egan

John E. Egan was a bouncer, boxer, blacksmith's helper, undertaker, and politician. While for many the name Egan conjures up thoughts of the huge funeral home on Sixty-Third Street, he was better known throughout the city for his career in public service. A former 13th Ward alderman, it was his old De LaSalle High School classmate Mayor Richard J. Daley who decided Egan should give up his seat as alderman in 1961 to run for trustee of the Metropolitan Sanitary District and "straighten out the mess it was in." At the sanitary district he earned a man-of-the-year award, had an innovative treatment plant named after him, and retired as president.

Egan thought of himself as an independent. Some thought of him as a rebel. His colleagues and constituents alike agreed that if John Egan said he would get something done, he did. During his 21 years as an alderman, he spent 17 on the city's aviation committee and 10 as chairman, where he worked frantically to forestall the abandonment of Midway Airport as a major air terminal. Throughout his aldermanic career he always referred to his ward as "Chicago's Great Southwest Side."

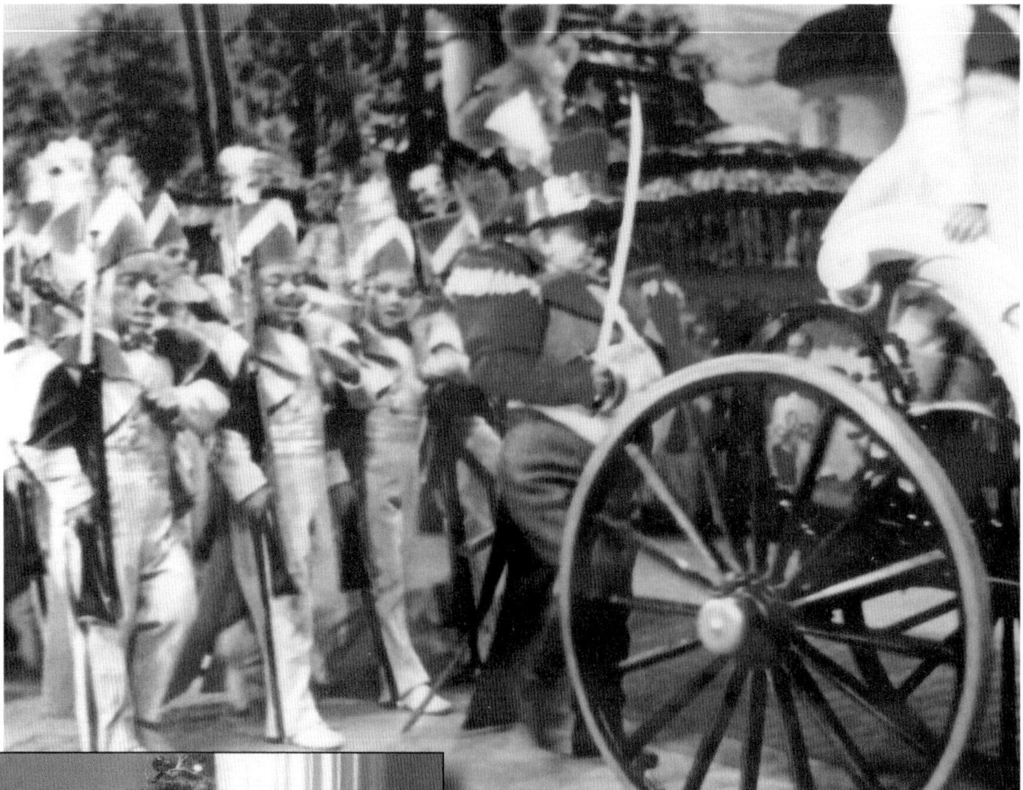

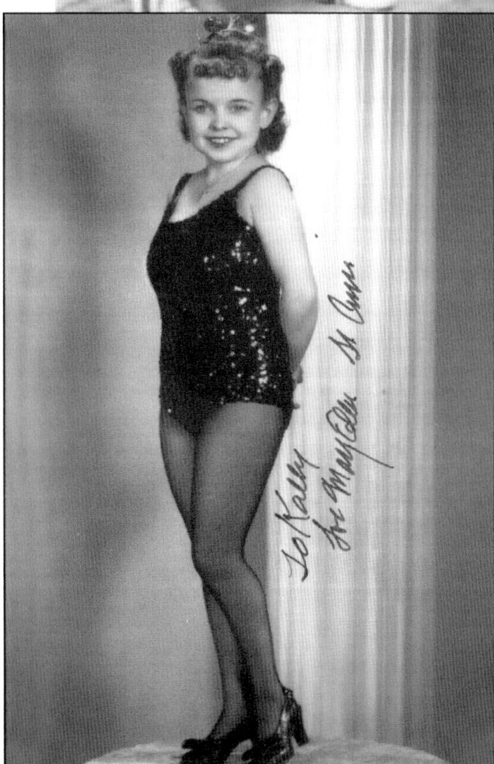

Parnell and Mary Ellen St. Aubin

Parnell St. Aubin grew up on Sixty-Fifth and Rockwell Avenue. He was just 16 when he heard of MGM's casting call for characters to populate Munchkin Land. At 43 inches tall, he was the tiniest soldier. In the *Wizard of Oz*, Parnell is the first Munchkin that comes into view when Dorothy arrives. He has a long black coat and a tall gray hat and is peeking out from under a bush. He is also distinguishable as a townsman.

Mary Ellen Bacon was also a native of Chicago Lawn, growing up on Sixty-Third and Richmond Avenue, and she attended Marquette School. A show business performer herself, she had a film role in *Three Wise Fools*. Her career spanned 15 years, beginning in vaudeville with singing and dancing roles.

While both Parnell and Mary Ellen spent childhood years in the Lawn and then went on to movie roles, they had never met. But that changed in 1946. Mary Ellen was hired as one of Santa's elves at the Goldblatt's store downtown. Parnell heard about the little elves and went to see for himself. Once he laid eyes on her, he was smitten. They dated and were married six months later. (Both, courtesy of Mary Ellen St. Aubin.)

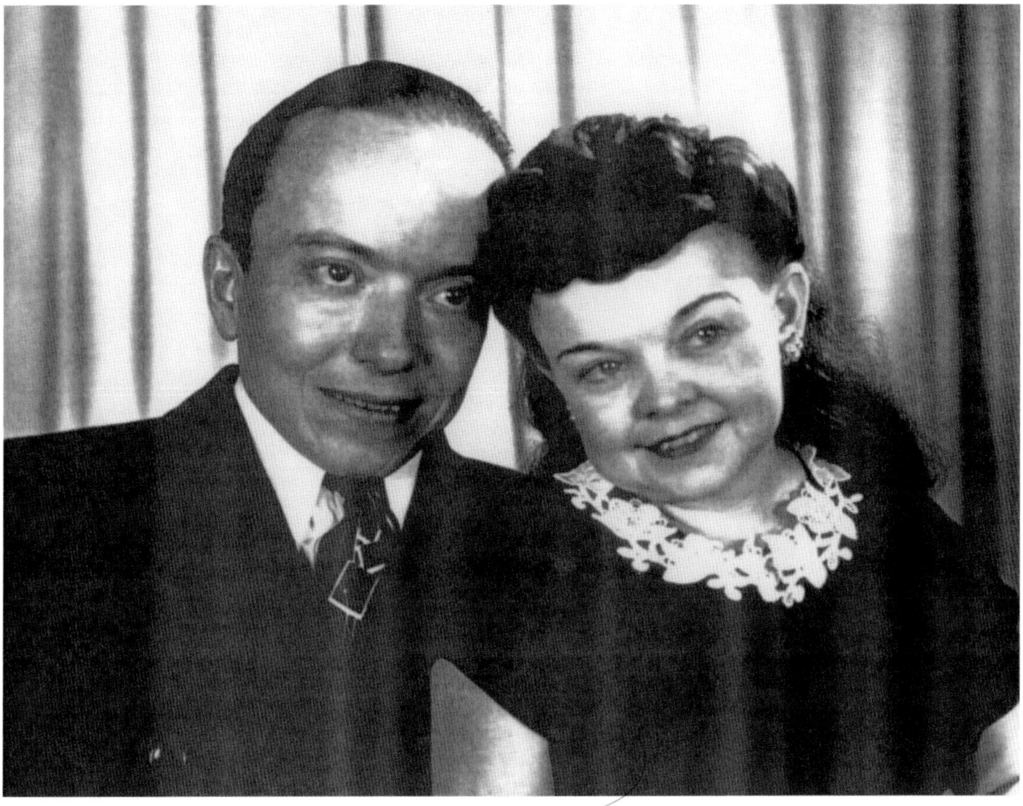

The St. Aubins

For folks living on the Southwest Side, the St. Aubins have been best known as the friendly proprietors of the Midget Club. While Parnell tried his hand in the business for a brief time on the east side, with Mary Ellen helping out as a waitress, they opened their first club in Chicago Lawn in 1953 at Sixty-Third Place and Kedzie Avenue. When the land was needed for other purposes, the St. Aubins moved their club down the street to 4016 West Sixty-Third Street in West Lawn.

Their club was a popular place even though it was small in size. The bar was only three feet tall, and Parnell had to climb up on a barstool to reach the cash register. He would lean over the bar with a big cigar in his mouth and announce, "Yeah, I got big plans for this place."

The St. Aubins had a big black Cadillac, specially fitted with extensions on the pedals for Parnell to reach, and everyone seemed to know them as they drove by. The club did a fine business at the Sixty-Third Street location until 1982, when the city needed that land for the West Lawn Branch Library. Parnell died five years later. Mary Ellen remained active in the annual Munchkin Festival in Chesterton, Indiana, where she retained the title of "Munchkin by Marriage." Years later, her blue eyes still light up at mention of Parnell. (Courtesy of Mary Ellen St. Aubin.)

John F. McCarthy

The son of immigrant parents, John McCarthy was founding chairman of Marquette Bank. He was "a gentle person of the old school" according to his son Paul, who succeeded him as chairman. "He lived during the Depression and became aware of the evils of speculation, having handled tons of foreclosed properties." In 1945, he helped found Marquette in the historic Western Avenue building, which was acquired through foreclosure. The new bank was the former home of Marquette Park State Bank, which went under during the Great Depression. (Both, courtesy of Marquette Bank.)

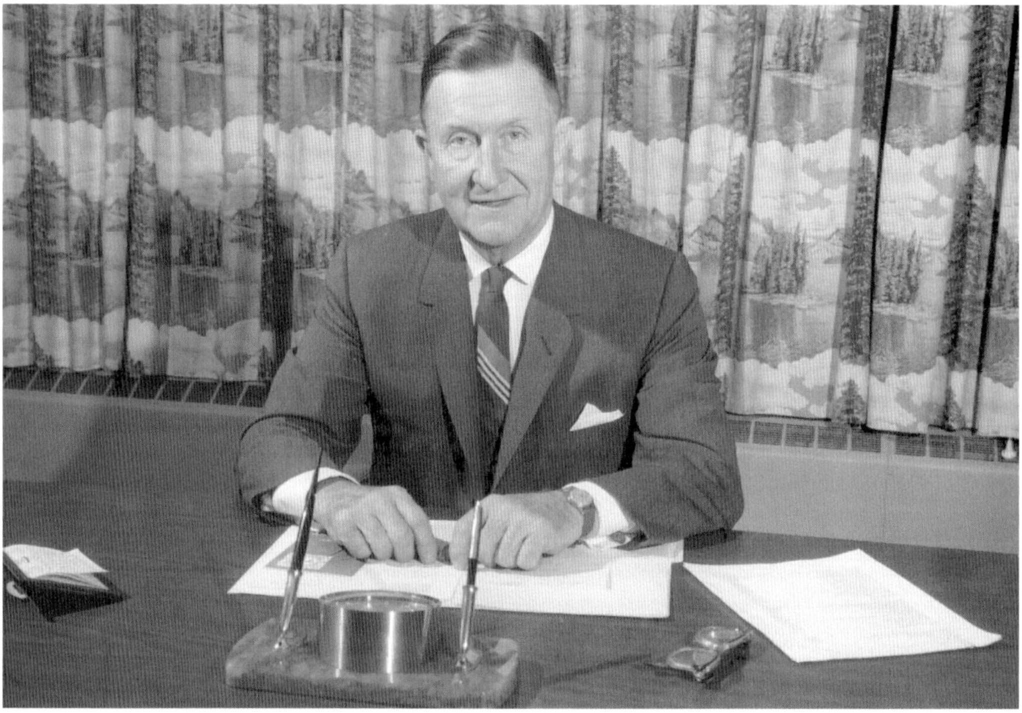

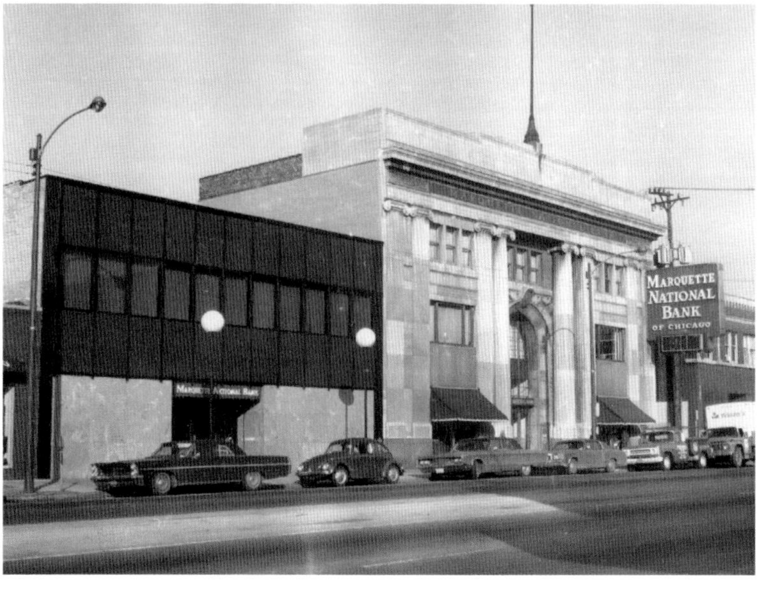

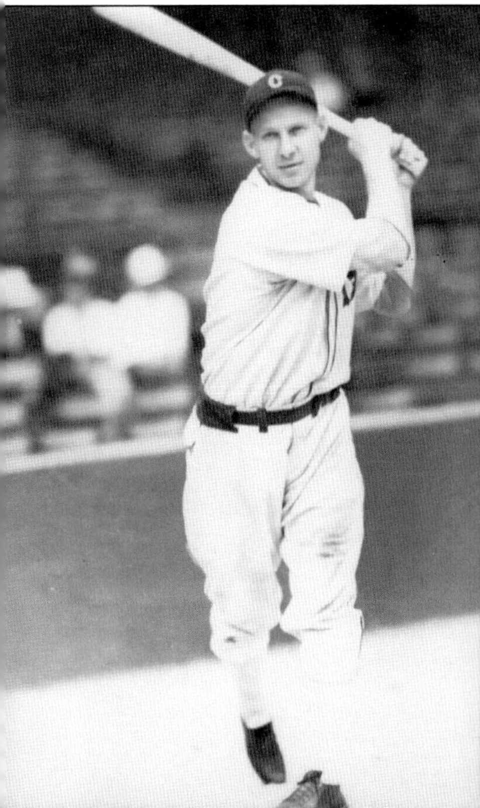

Anthony F. Piet

Former major-league baseball player Anthony Francis Piet believed that every boy should have a chance to play ball and proved it by his actions in planning and organizing the Southwest Side Little and Pony Leagues at Marquette Park. With a farm-team system in place, the Marquette organization was looked on as one of the finest at the time.

Dubbed the "Father of Little League," Piet said he just wanted kids to have an opportunity to participate in something that could build their character.

Tony Piet was an infielder in the major leagues and platyed for the Pittsburgh Pirates, Cincinnati Reds, Detroit Tigers, and the Chicago White Sox. His second year in the majors, he was second in stolen bases in the National League (NL). The following year, with a batting average of .323, he led the NL in most games played.

After retiring from baseball, he opened a car dealership and decorated the walls with huge portraits of 25 baseball legends such as Ted Williams and Rogers Hornsby, which he commissioned artist Carl Tolpo to create.

When he enlarged his dealership he renamed it Pontiac City. His slogan was "Shop for it anywhere, But buy it at Piet."

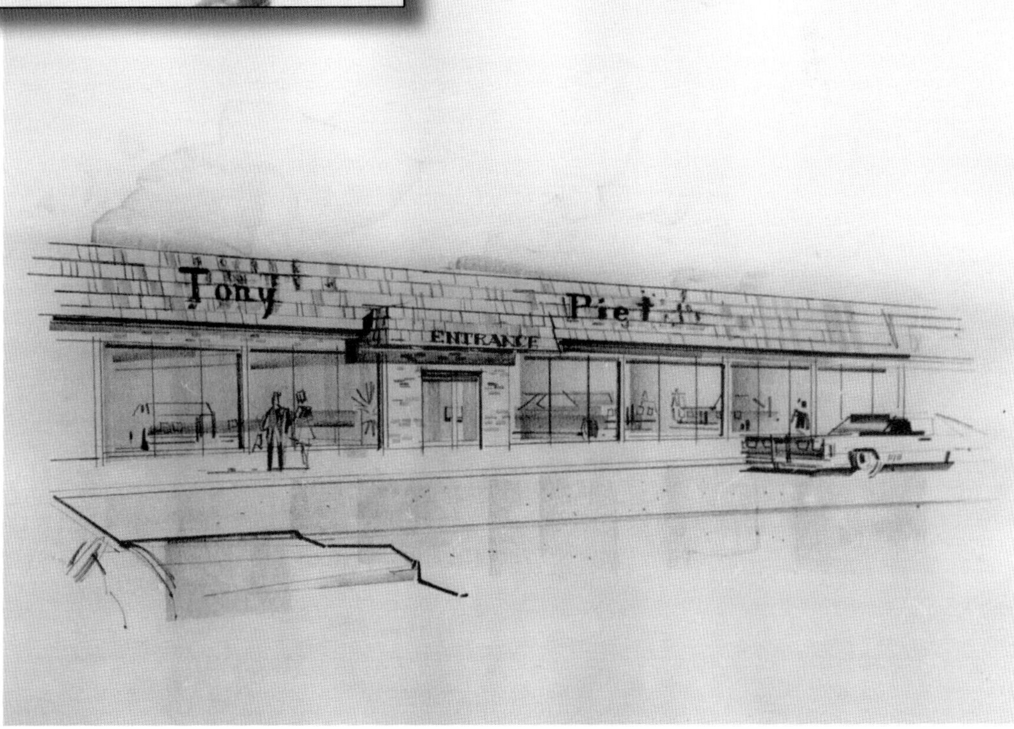

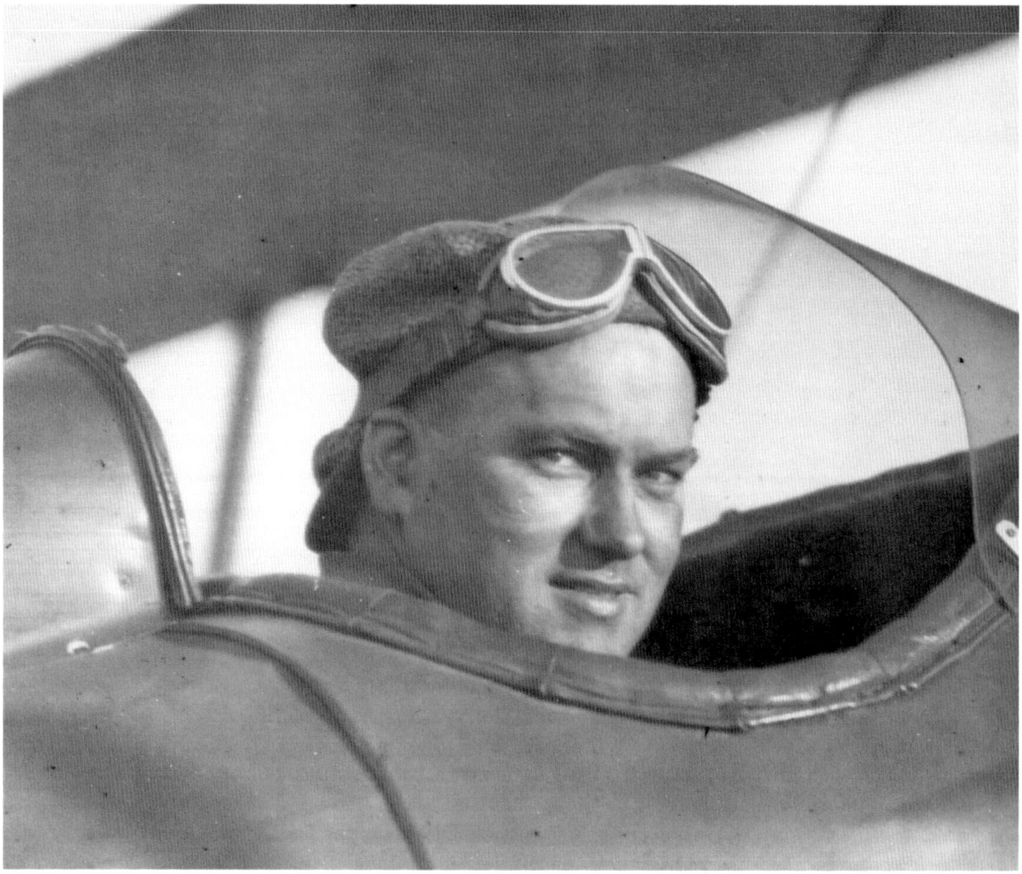

Pierce "Scotty" O'Carroll

A native of County Leix, Ireland, Pierce "Scotty" O'Carroll came to Chicago as a young man in 1924. In the beginning, he worked as a bus driver, but flying a plane was his dream.

In his book *Chicago's Midway Airport, the First 75 Years*, Christopher Lynch, Scotty's grandson, relayed, "He enjoyed the sensation of flying so much, he made arrangements to have another lesson the day after his first one. When he arrived for his second lesson, the instructor was not yet there. Being a bit of a daredevil, O'Carroll decided to take the plane up anyway."

Lynch goes on to say when the instructor arrived he saw the aircraft sailing overhead with Scotty at the controls. When he finally brought the plane down, the instructor strolled over, looked him in the eye, and said, "Pierce . . . you passed." And from that day on, flying would be his career for the next 40 years.

In 1929, he founded Monarch Air Service, an aviation business with headquarters at Municipal Airport, now Midway Airport.

Flying was a very expensive mode of transportation in the early days. Quite often Scotty's charter flights were movie stars going from one engagement to another. They could afford the convenience of having a plane all to themselves, and Scotty was happy to oblige.

By the 1950s, if one had the money, one could take a 30-minute aerial sightseeing tour in Scotty's twin-engine Cessna for $3.50 a ride.

Scotty and his wife and daughter made their home in Chicago Lawn on Sixty-Seventh Street and Spaulding Avenue, but the airport two miles away was definitely their second home.

Scotty was only 62 when he suffered a fatal stroke in New York City. His grandson related, "The plane carrying his casket back to Chicago landed in the dark; the tower had dimmed the runway lights for the pilot's final landing at Midway Airport." (Courtesy of Christopher Lynch.)

CHAPTER THREE

Taking It to a New Level

Never doubt that a small group of thoughtful, committed citizens can change the world.

—Margaret Mead

As chapter 3 begins, World War II has ended, and the community continues to grow and prosper.

John Madigan, the young man from St. Rita Parish with the flaming red hair, was making a name for himself in newspapers, radio, and television. Another St. Rita graduate, Marilyn Olsen, would become the first woman lieutenant in Chicago Police Department history.

Lifelong resident Myrtle Kemp had become the predecessor of today's cooking experts and moved on to part-time work as the judge of Pillsbury Bake-Off contests.

Chicago Public Schools teacher Arthur Silhan created Musichorale. Originally founded as a way to keep his high school choir singing together after graduation, it has remained a popular attraction.

John Korosa, known as Chicago's "Mr. Polka Man," opened the Club Irene on Sixty-Third Street, broadcasting from the club on Chicago radio for 15 years and then on television with his *Hoya Hoya Polka Party* program.

Locals such as Arthur and Virginia Carlson, Mary Leonard, and Rev. Walter McNicholas were making a difference in the lives of the young people. Tom Pilafas and Steve Poulos were perfecting the Gertie's ice cream recipe. And when the Yesutis brothers bought the place, they went for the Guinness Book of World Records.

Ed and Daisy Vondrak were building the *Southwest News-Herald* into the largest ABC-audited community newspaper of its time.

Pat Albergo and Joe Pierri opened a new Italian restaurant on Sixty-Third Street, and Jurgis Janusaitis was turning his small butcher shop on Sixty-Ninth Street into a Lithuanian supermarket.

Rev. Stanley Rizner was assigned the task of building a new church and school for the rapidly growing section of West Lawn south of the golf course.

Also in West Lawn, to much neighborhood acclaim, a fourth-generation physician broke ground for a new hospital. However, before it reached its 20th year, the facility was shuttered, and the doctor had surrendered his license.

And down the street, Michael Rzeminski was building a new kind of business that would keep expanding for several years to come.

John Madigan

Chicago Lawn native John Madigan, a fixture at CBS and WBBM Newsradio, was a member of a very elite group of reporters that worked for newspapers, television, magazines, and radio.

He began as a newspaper copyboy in the 1930s at age 16. In the early days of his career, he picked up the nickname "Red" for his crimson hair. During World War II, he served in the US Navy and worked as the ship's press officer.

When he returned, Madigan went to work as a reporter for the *Chicago American*, wrote for *Newsweek*, and then accepted the job of news director for CBS. He was the first moderator of *Face the Nation* and the first panelist on *What's My Line?*.

During his radio career, he became known for his signature sign off: "WBBM - Newsradio Sssssseventy-Eight." He explained he adopted the signoff as a reminiscence of the drawn out S he employed when shooting craps in the Navy and his luck in banking on a number starting with that letter.

Madigan was a hardnosed reporter, known for his tough questions. He wore black-rimmed glasses and had a penchant for formal suits and a strong dislike for people who parked illegally. One of his pet peeves was newscasters, especially those from out of town, who mispronounced the word "Chicago," insisting they pronounce it correctly—(Chi-CAW-go) if they were going to refer to his city at all.

Before he died, he explained what was important to him as a newsman, "I get exercised when I see or hear things that are unfair or sloppily done or are what I consider unfair attacks. All I hope they put on my tombstone is: 'He was fair.' That's all I want." (Courtesy of St. Rita High School.)

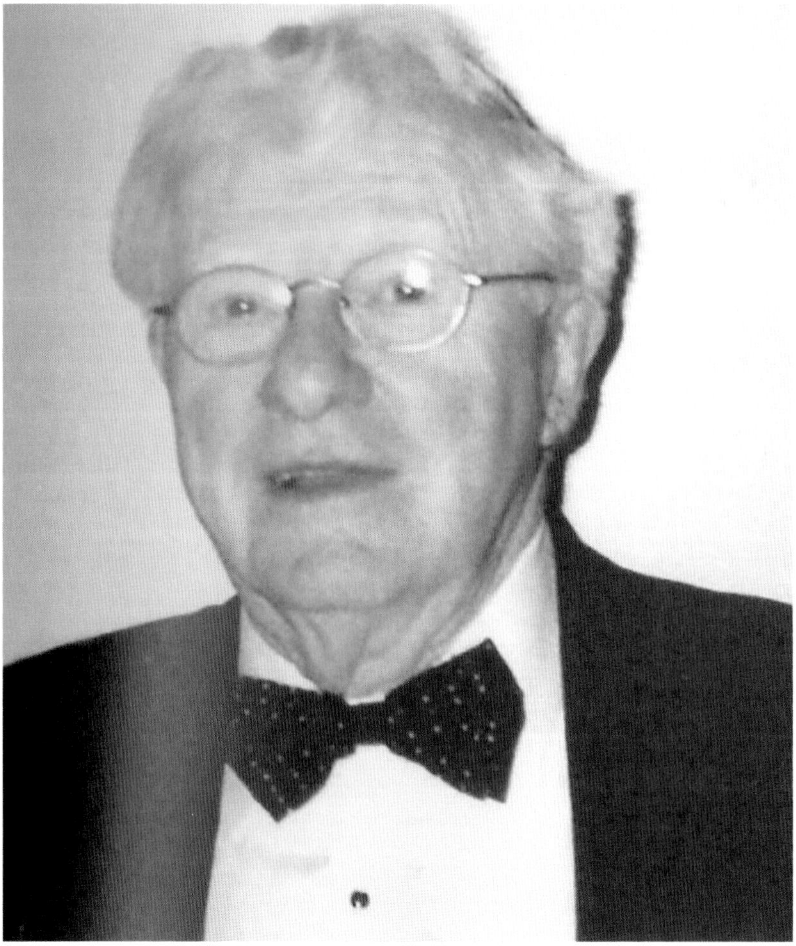

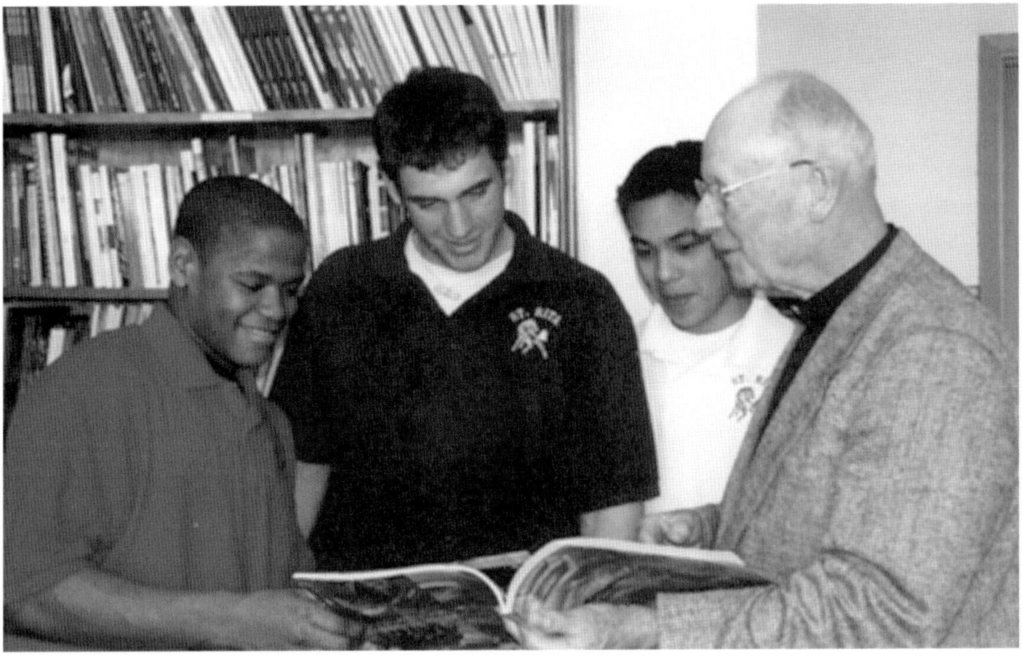

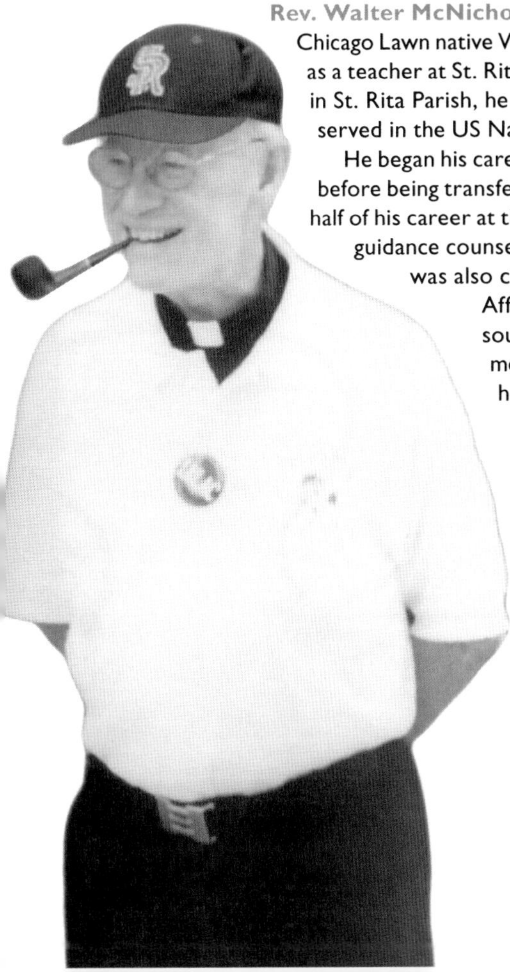

Rev. Walter McNicholas, OSA

Chicago Lawn native Walter Francis McNicholas spent much of his 58-year ministry as a teacher at St. Rita High School, where he is considered a legend. Growing up in St. Rita Parish, he graduated from St. Rita High School, attended college, and served in the US Navy before joining the Augustinian formation program.

He began his career as a priest at his alma mater, remaining there for six years before being transferred. He would come back three more times, spending over half of his career at the school. At various stages he took on the roles of teacher, guidance counselor, vocations director, and alumni-association chaplain. He was also chaplain at Holy Cross Hospital for a time.

Affectionately known as "Father McNic," students frequently sought his guidance. He attended wakes of every St. Rita family member and was known for checking the obituaries daily. It is said he never missed a wake in the family of any St. Rita student.

The much-loved priest frequented the St. Vincent DePaul resale shop, purchasing belts and other items for boys that came to school without. It is said his office looked like a garage sale. (Both, courtesy of St. Rita High School.)

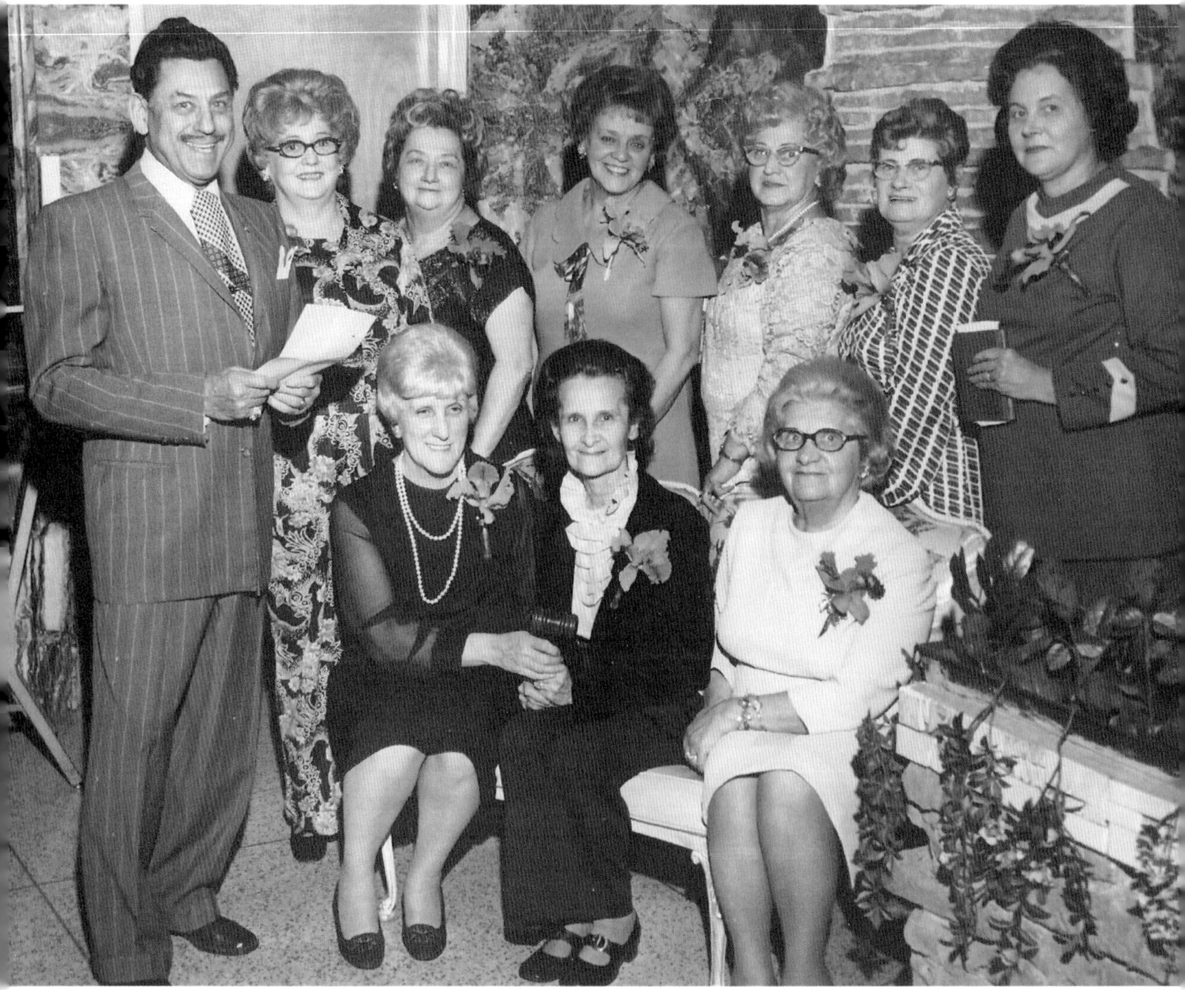

Dr. Charles R. von Solbrig

In 1958, Dr. Charles R. von Solbrig was breaking ground for a new hospital in West Lawn that would bear his family's name, and by 1975 he was answering questions concerning information uncovered by a *Chicago Tribune* taskforce.

The doctor's affiliation with the area began as far back as 1934 when he opened an office at Sixty-Fifth Street and Kedzie Avenue. In 1937, he built a home in West Lawn and moved his practice there. During World War II, von Solbrig enlisted in the US Army and served in the 41st Evacuation Hospital unit. Attaining the rank of major, he often performed as many as 25 operations a day under battle conditions in the European theater.

Upon his return home, the former student of Notre Dame University and the University of Louisville set about the task of realizing his dream of building his own hospital.

In 1958 that dream was fulfilled when he broke ground for his new 83-bed hospital at Sixty-Fifth Street and Pulaski Road. A huge endeavor with a price tag of $2 million, it was a much-anticipated addition to the area.

Officially opening in 1959, the fourth-generation physician named the hospital for his late grandfather Karl, a professor of medicine at Chronik University in Munich Germany.

Things went well at first. The facility was fully staffed, residents were happy to have a second hospital in the area, and soon a ladies auxiliary was even in place.

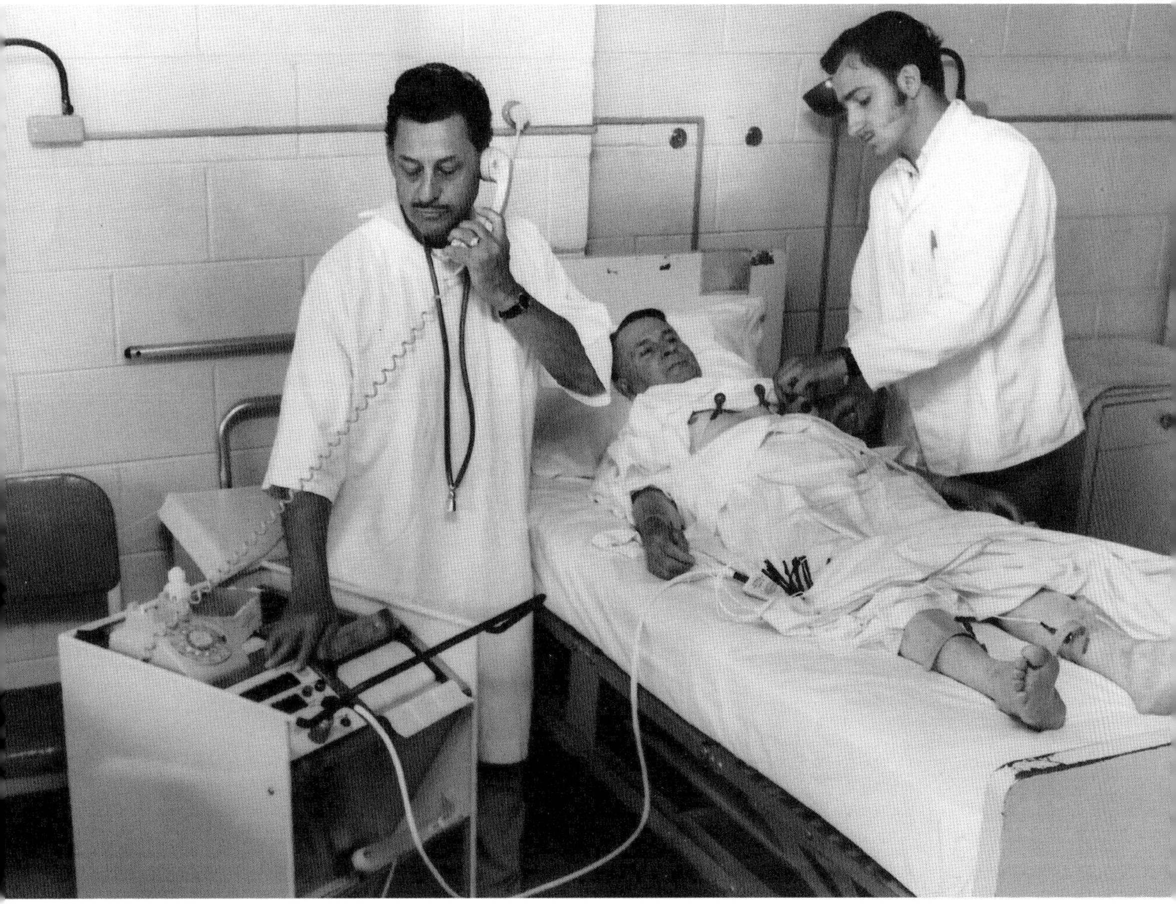

Fourth-Generation Physician

But after only a little more than a decade, the hospital's reputation seemed tarnished. A complaint here, a complaint there, and then questions started to arise. Was this procedure necessary? Why the infection? Five children in one family needing tonsillectomies at the same time? Patient stays extended without justification?

As more accusations came to light, investigative reporter William Gaines went undercover as a janitor for two months at von Solbrig Memorial. He wrote his notes on paper towels, stuffing them in his pockets, passing them to other reporters on his team to follow up.

As a result of the investigation, Algis Augustine, then-chief regulatory officer for the Illinois Department of Registration and Education, filed a complaint against von Solbrig that included allegations that nurses' aides were in charge of the recovery room and performed duties of a nurse during surgery, and a janitor assisted in the operating room and performed functions of an x-ray technician. The complaint also contended that there was no full-time physician on duty evenings and weekends in the emergency room.

The taskforce also found that of the 50 doctors listed as being on staff, some were dead, some had moved a great distance away, and some had never even been on staff. In fact, only 18 of the 50 actually practiced at the hospital.

Dr. Charles von Solbrig was president, medical director, administrator, and chief of surgery at the 83-bed hospital, the only for-profit general hospital in Chicago. He was accused of running the facility as his own personal kingdom.

Amid allegations of unnecessary tests and treatments, and with the possibility of revocation of his license ahead, the 69-year-old doctor agreed to surrender his medical license on November 30, 1976.

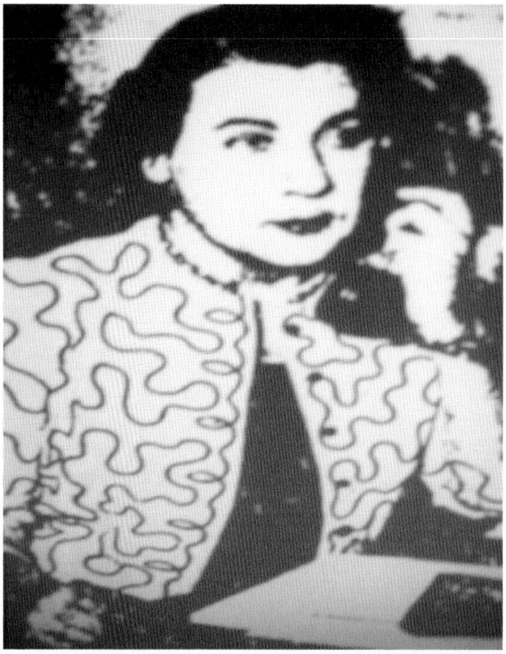

Marilynn G. Olson

In 1956, Marilynn Olson became the first woman in Chicago Police Department history to attain the rank of lieutenant. A graduate of St. Rita Grammar School, the Chicago Lawn native grew up at Sixty-First Street and Whipple Avenue. She was also the first policewoman to become a sergeant.

In her role as lieutenant, she would direct and supervise the work of 84 policewomen and 40 police matrons.

She married Deputy Commissioner Charles O'Regan in 1959 and eventually became the assistant police department superintendent of traffic. She passed away in 2007.

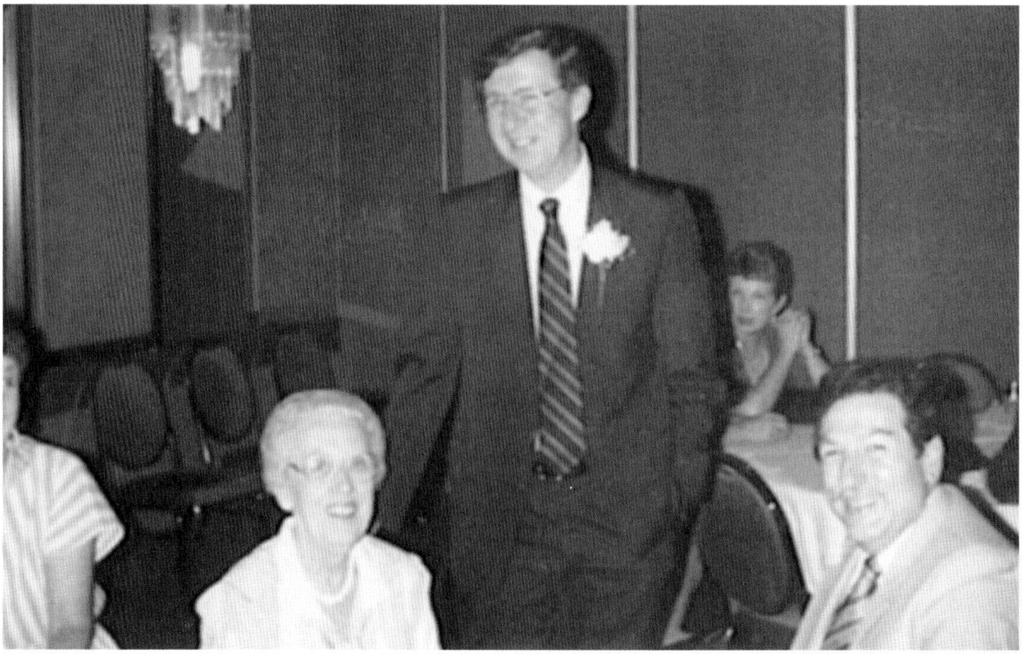

Mary S. Leonard

Mary Leonard spent 33 of her 44 years teaching at Eberhart School. She was called the consummate teacher—intelligent, demanding, dedicated, warm, and loving. Her career was recognized by principal George N. Kulles: "Her high standards, ideals, and vision left a stamp on all of us. Because she has a special place in our hearts, we feel that it is fitting to recognize the legacy that she leaves. In deep gratitude for her labors to that end, it is my pleasure to announce that as of this moment, this auditorium is officially Mary S. Leonard Hall." (Courtesy of Alan Pelt.)

Myrtle Kemp

A lifelong resident of Chicago Lawn, Myrtle Turney Kemp, who died at the age of 92 in the same house on Lawndale in which she was born in 1905, was a predecessor of today's cooking experts on television. After graduating from college, she traveled the country for 13 years, demonstrating cooking for the Hotpoint Electric Appliance Company.

In 1935, her cooking classes were featured on the front page of a Honolulu newspaper. Once word got out about the classes, the plantation owners would get her to go out to the islands to teach American cooking methods to their household help, many of whom were Japanese.

In 1939, she married Leonard Kemp and began raising a family. She left Hotpoint but did not stray far from the cooking business. She began working part-time by becoming a judge in the Pillsbury Bake-Off contests.

Active throughout her life in community affairs, she was a founding member of the Chicago Lawn Historical Society, a board member and treasurer of the Chicago School Children's Aid Society, which primarily provided clothing for needy students, a longtime member of the Chicago Lawn Women's Club, and affiliated with a host of other clubs and organizations.

Myrtle is pictured here in July 1947, right in the center of a group called the Shutterbugs, which met at the first Chicago Lawn Branch Library. From left to right are Lucille Shimek, Kathryn Reilly, Sylvia Street, Myrtle Kemp, Mrs. Wilms, Blanche Walker, and Vila Schueller.

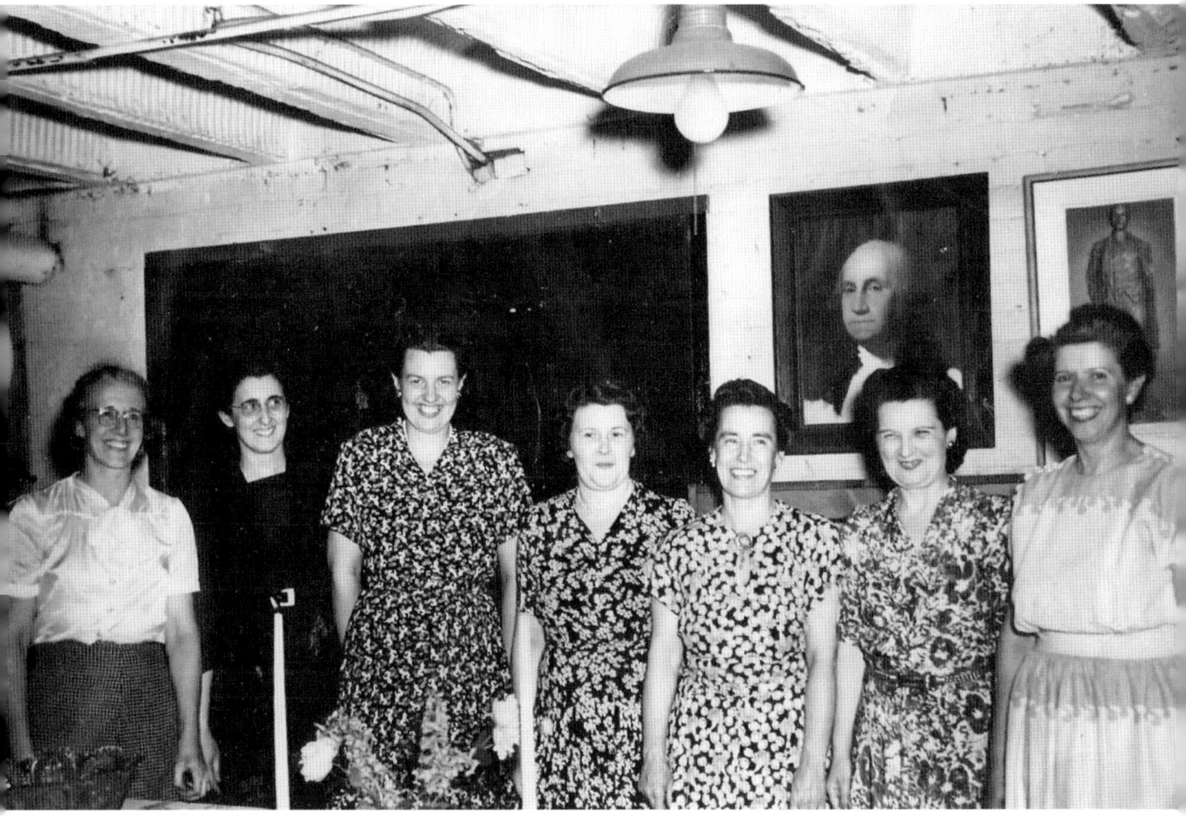

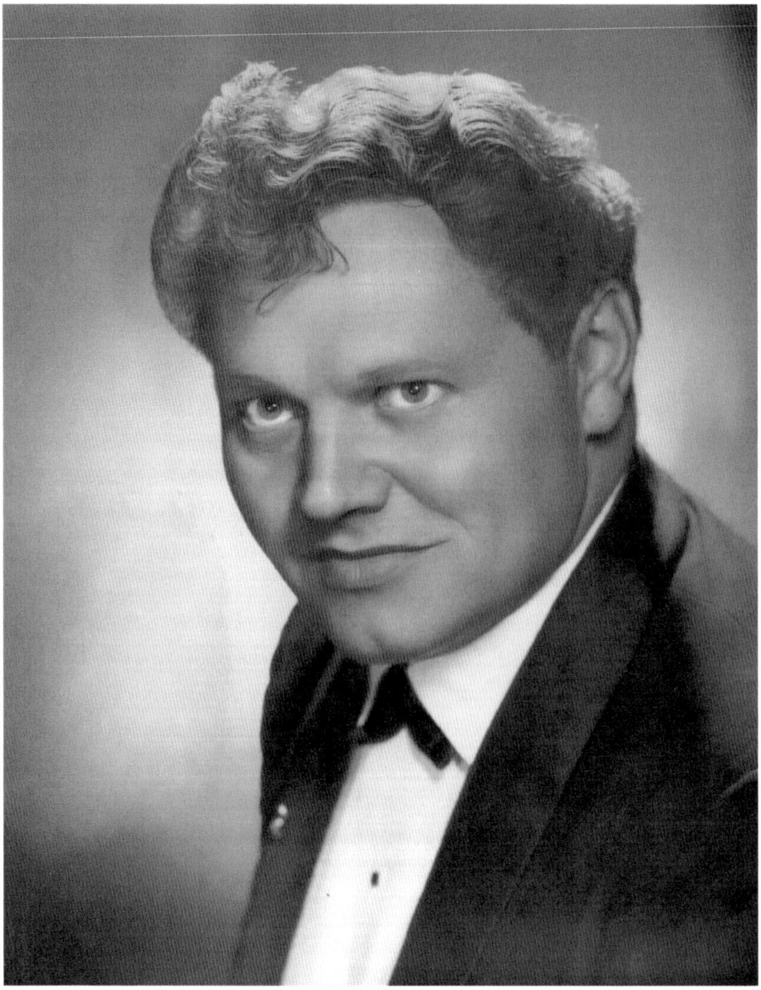

Arthur and Phyllis Silhan
Arthur Silhan was a schoolteacher for 44 years, the founder and director of Musichorale for 58 years, a 32-year member of the Lyric Opera Chorus, and, for 60 years, he directed Southwest Side Chicagoland church choirs.

Born in Chicago in June 1925, he was one of two children of Frank and Ida Silhan. Art grew up in the Chicago Lawn and West Lawn neighborhoods.

He met Phyllis Ballin while they were both at Lindblom High School. They dated through their years at Chicago Teacher's College and even commuted by streetcar together. Two years after Phyllis graduated, the couple got married.

Musichorale began in 1947 as a way to keep his high school choir together. At first they called themselves the Lindblom Alumni Accapella Choir, then the Chicago Choral Club, and finally in 1951 changed the name to Musichorale. In the beginning, they rehearsed at Ogden Park, then the Marquette Park field house, and then moved over to Fifty-Ninth Street and Sacramento Avenue.

He directed several local church choirs, including Lutheran Church of the Cross and Calvary Lutheran. He was a member of the Lawn Lodge, the Masons, and the Shriners.

For 35 years, Phyllis was always there as his accompanist. An accomplished musician herself, she also was the organist at several churches in the area, beginning with Chicago Lawn Methodist in the 1950s. (Courtesy of Linda Silhan.)

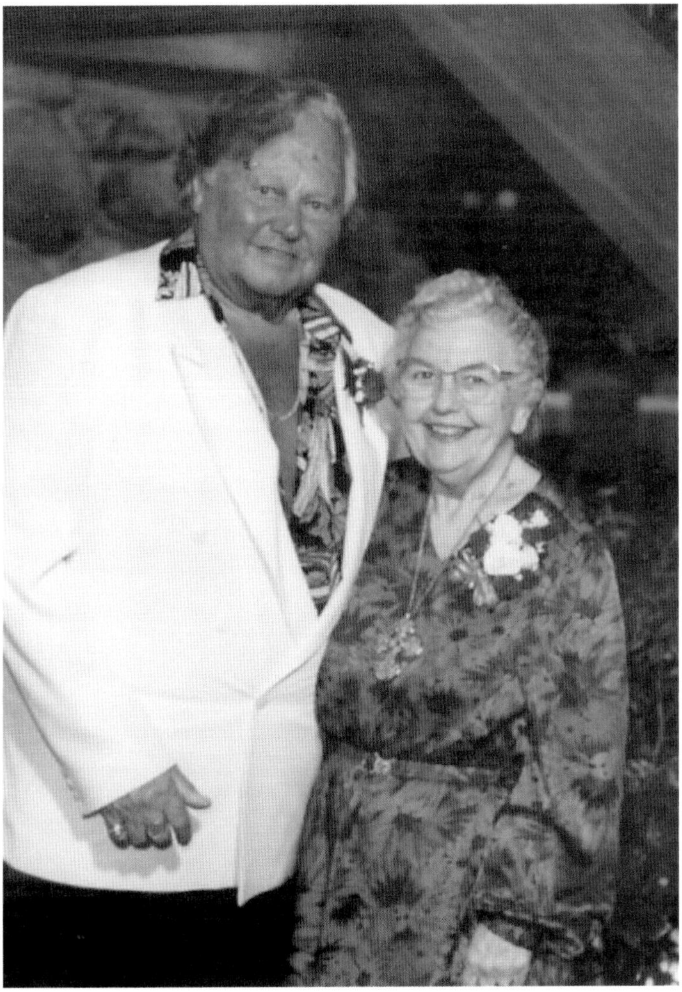

The Silhans
Art was a longtime teacher at McKay Grade School in Marquette Manor, teaching eighth grade there for many years and running the school's music program as well. He directed the McKay choir and brought them to Ford City and Midway Airport to entertain.

A tall large-boned man, he commanded respect in school and was known as a tough but well-loved teacher. He had many sayings that he repeated over and over to his classes through the years. And years later, his former students still remembered them and talked of them on their school website: "Self control is a sign of the civilized; a tattoo reflects a low IQ; don't touch your face when singing."

Both the Silhans always loved music. A retired teacher herself, Phyllis has played the piano at Midway Airport for more than two decades during the holidays. She noted that Mayor Richard M. Daley once called her "Chicago's Best Ambassador."

And Art loved children. He founded the Musichorale Miniatures and Musichorale Mini-cherubs to start them out early.

Known as a real stickler for promptness and tradition, he began each concert at 20 minutes past the hour, and oddly enough, Art died at 2:20 pm.

At his memorial service, 100 current and past members of Musichorale sang six numbers, concluding with the song with which he had closed every concert, "The Lord Bless You and Keep You." (Courtesy of Linda Silhan.)

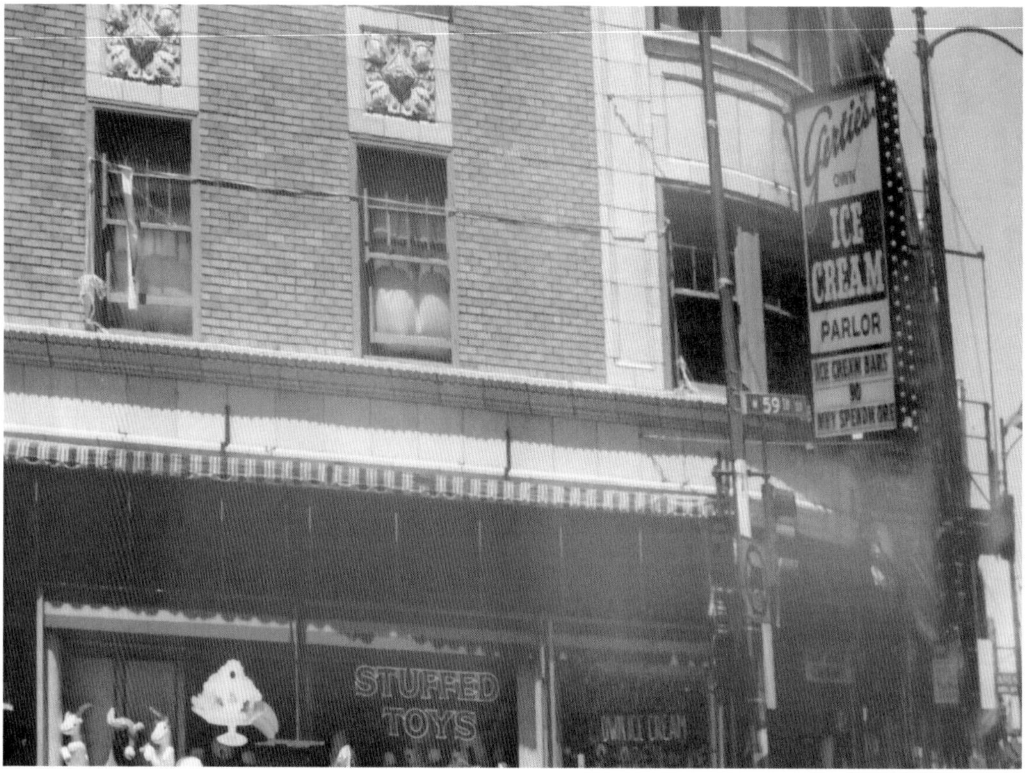

John Sr., Joseph, and Robert Yesutis

In waxing nostalgic about Gertie's Ice Cream Parlor, it is hard to decide which of the folks associated with the legendary shop on Fifty-Ninth Street and Kedzie Avenue should be singled out in one entry. Is it the soda jerk that attempted to put Gertie's in the Guinness Book of World Records? Is it the owners who refused to put any artificial ingredients in their ice cream? Is it one of the managers of the store that was just as excited to be there as if it were his own?

John Yesutis Sr. and his brother Joe bought the popular neighborhood gathering place from Tom Pilafas and Steve Poulos. Pilafas purchased it from the original owners in 1942. The Yesutis brothers kept the wooden booths with velvet cushions, the art deco chrome countertop, and the maroon-and-cream-colored soda fountain. And they insisted on using all natural ingredients in their delectable creations.

Robert Yesutis was the manager of the store when chief soda jerk Art Kyriacopoulos built the world's tallest soda in 1979 and the world's largest ice cream cone in 1981.

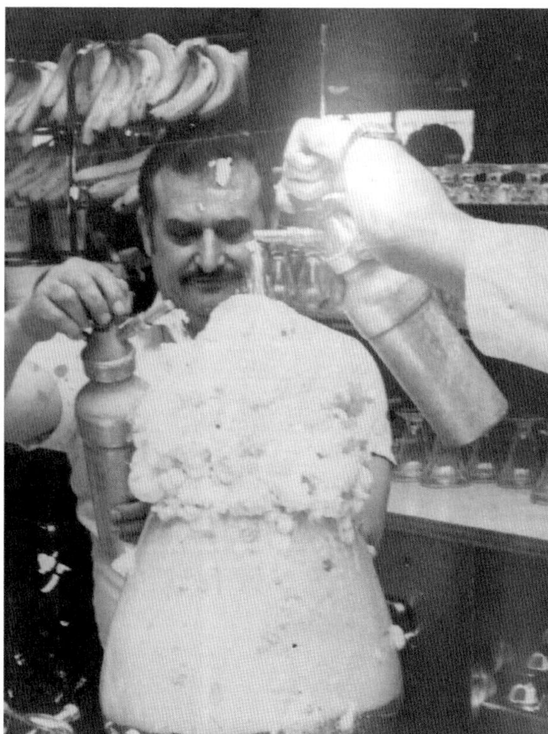

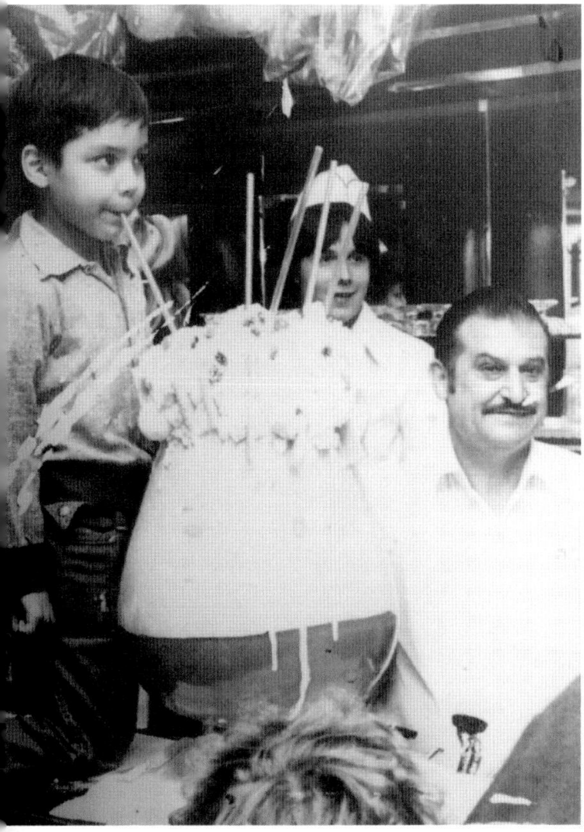

Arthur Kyriacopoulos and Stephen Heimberg

Yesutis and Kyriacopoulos hoped to make it into the Guinness Book of World Records for the huge concoction. The soda was in a special 820-ounce glass and contained 20 pounds of vanilla ice cream, 400 ounces of lime-flavored seltzer, eight pounds of Brazil nuts, five pounds of cashews, one gallon of whipped cream, and 100 cherries.

Art Kyriacopoulos worked at Gertie's on Kedzie Avenue for several decades, beginning in the early 1950s, and earned the title of city's fastest scooper.

Steve Heimberg was an enthusiastic and welcoming manager. During his tenure he was overseeing the creation of 150 to 200 gallons of homemade ice cream a day, which took six to seven hours to blend the cream, eggs, and milk with the flavorings. And they made their own whipped cream and toppings and ground their own Brazil nuts as well.

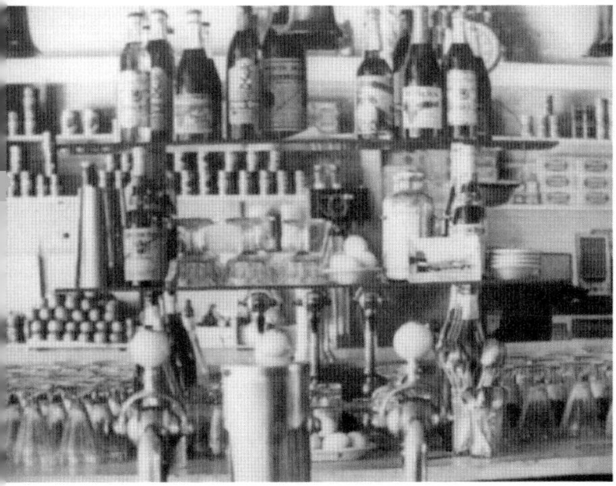

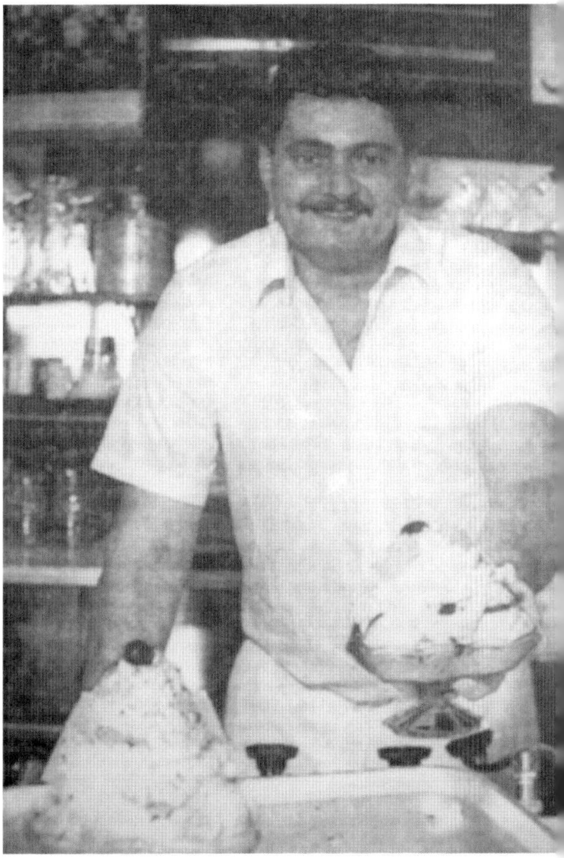

Pat Albergo and Joe Pierri

It was on September 19, 1953, that Pat Albergo and Joe Pierri opened their new restaurant at 2921 West Sixty-Third Street. They named it Little Joe's Pizzeria and Restaurante. And coincidentally, the doors opened on the same day that Albergo's daughter Suzi was born. Pierri became her godfather.

For 33 years, the friends and business partners welcomed folks to their popular spot on Sixty-Third Street for dinners or as an after-club meeting place. In the 1970s, Albergo and Pierri brought in Aldo Nelli to entertain diners evenings Thursday through Sunday. (All, courtesy of Susan Vazquez.)

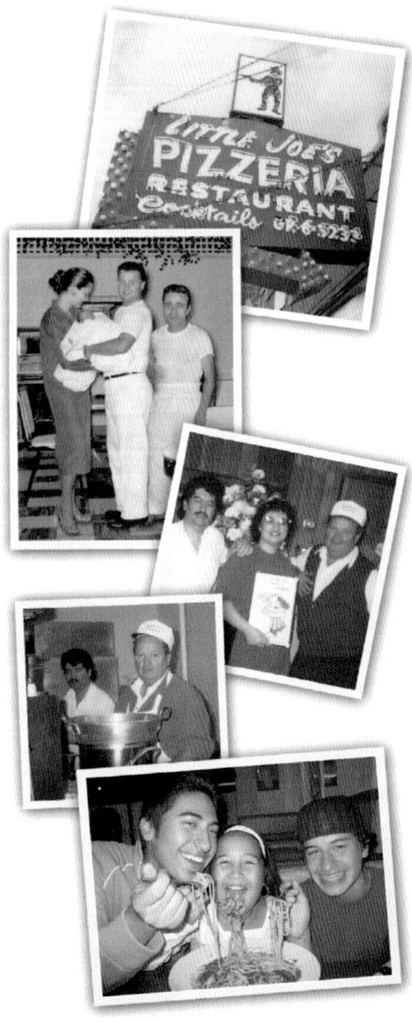

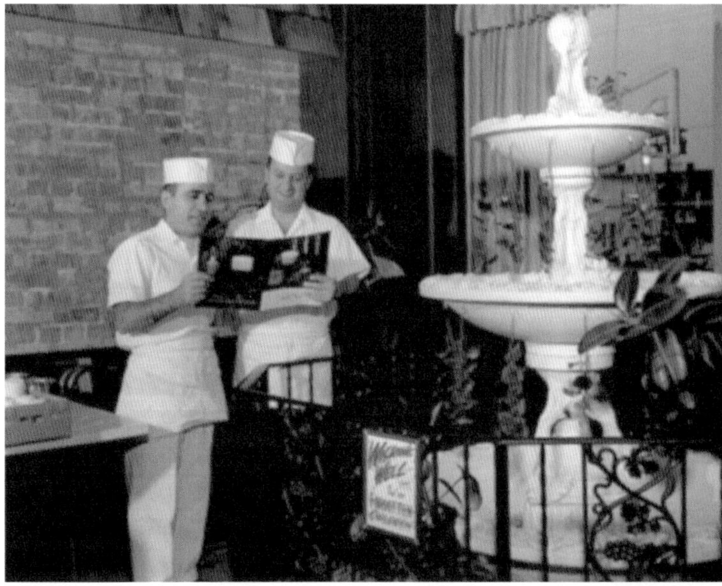

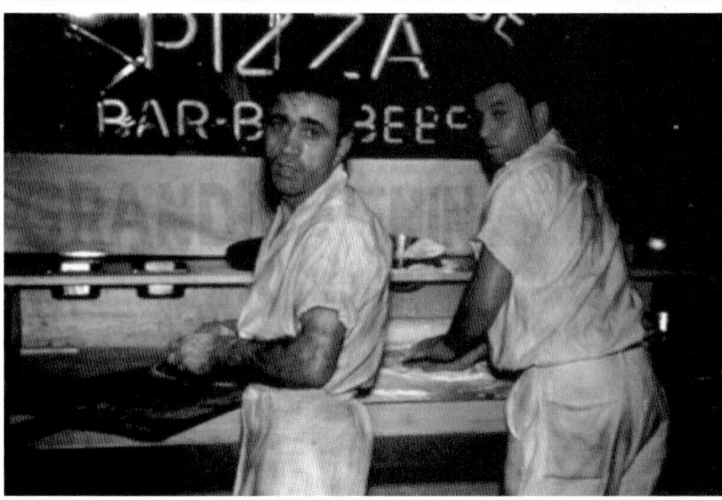

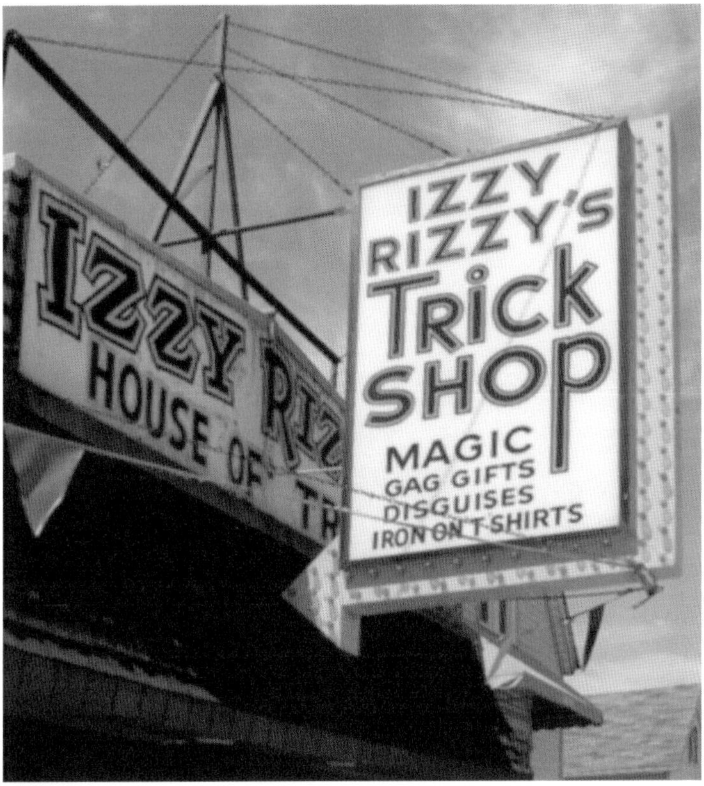

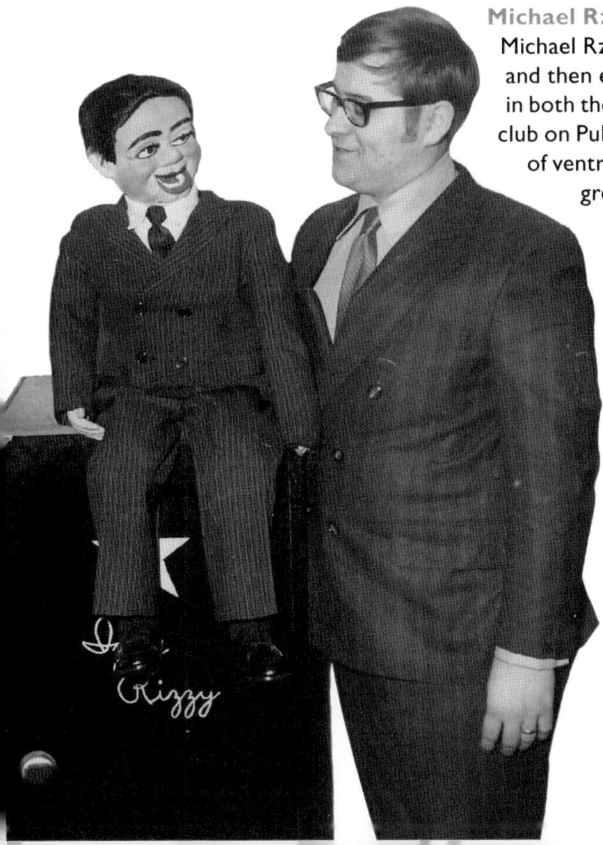

Michael Rzeminski

Michael Rzeminski took ventriloquism lessons at the YMCA and then embarked on a successful career as an entertainer in both the Midwest and Las Vegas. He performed at his own club on Pulaski, A Little Bit o' Magic, and established a school of ventriloquism in West Lawn in 1970. The school quickly grew into Izzy Rizzy's House of Tricks, specializing in ventriloquist dolls, marionettes, novelties, costumes, and magic accessories.

As his customers' interest in magic and novelties increased, so did his sales, and it was not long before the business outgrew its first location on Sixty-Third Street. He moved the store to a new location on Pulaski Road where he had room to expand, and then in March 1974, an even larger building on Pulaski Road was acquired.

Rzeminski's reputation spread quickly, and he eventually purchased land around Izzy Rizzy's, continuing to build on. A well-respected entrepreneur, he was awarded a Certificate of Commendation by Greater Southwest Development Corporation for his contribution to the business community.

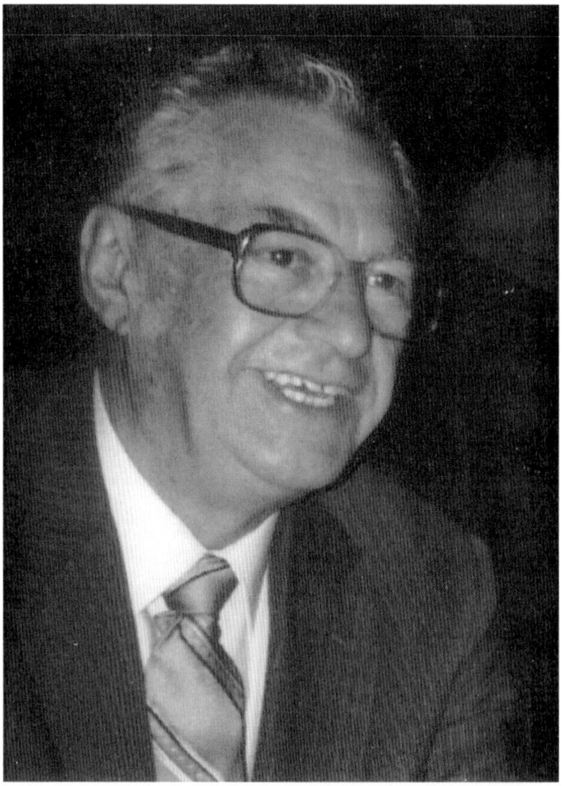

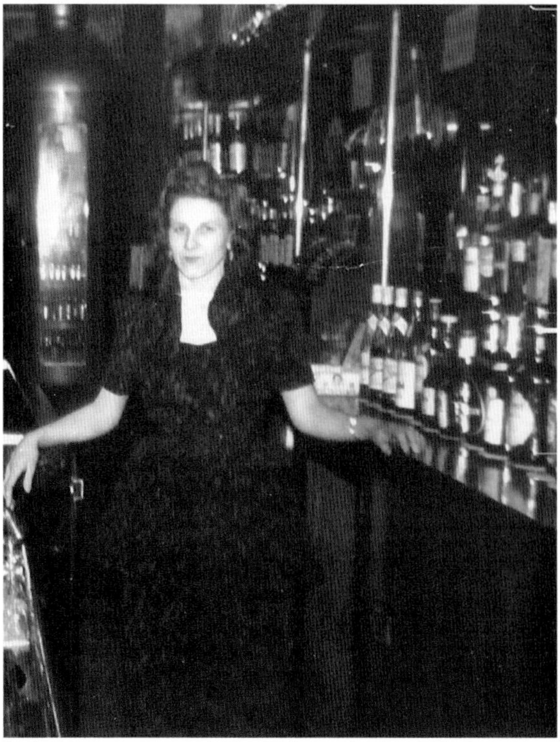

John Korosa

"Chicago's Mr. Polka Man" John Korosa was a gifted musician, and as the proprietor of the Club Irene Lounge on Sixty-Third Street and Sacramento Avenue, he brought polka music to Chicago radio and television. Every Sunday from 1951 to 1965, he broadcast from the Chicago Lawn nightclub he named for his wife. The radio programs that aired on WTAQ, WOPA, and WAIT featured the club's live Slovenian polka music as well as interviews with the bands and plenty of fun with Big John, or as people referred to him in the Lawn—the King of Polka.

Korosa was the first to bring big-name polka bands to Chicago to play at his club, names like Frankie Yankovic from Ohio and Lil' Wally from Florida. In the late 1950s, his television show *Hoya Hoya Polka Party* aired on WGN-TV.

A talented musician, Korosa played the button box, accordion, harmonica, guitar, piano, and violin but was best known for his banjo playing. He started his own band in 1951. John Korosa and the Melody Boys recorded the hits "Over Three Hills," "Girl in My Dream," "Sweetheart Don't Be Sad," and "Irene's Polka." He received a silver record for "Over Three Hills."

John's wife, Irene, is pictured behind the bar at the club named for her. (Courtesy of Cheryl Korosa.)

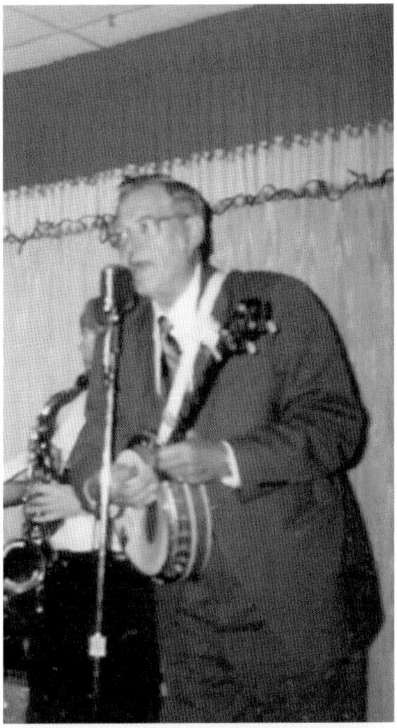

Mr. Polka Man

Club Irene was always crowded. Adding to the fun atmosphere, Korosa liked to take movies at the club, which he showed on the weekends. He also sponsored many parades and parties for children at Christmas and Easter along with the cerebral palsy telethon.

Korosa coined the phrase "Hoya, Hoya," which is still widely used throughout the polka field today.

In 1990, Korosa had a role as a banjo player in the 20th Century Fox movie *Men Don't Leave* with Jessica Lange.

In addition to being named Chicago's Mr. Polka Man by the International Polka Committee in 1956, he and Irene were awarded the Frank Duda Award from the United Polka Association in 1985 for their contribution to the polka industry, and he was elected posthumously to the National Cleveland Style Polka Hall of Fame in 1998. His banjo and records are on display in the Polka Hall of Fame Museum in Euclid, Ohio. (Both, courtesy of Cheryl Korosa.)

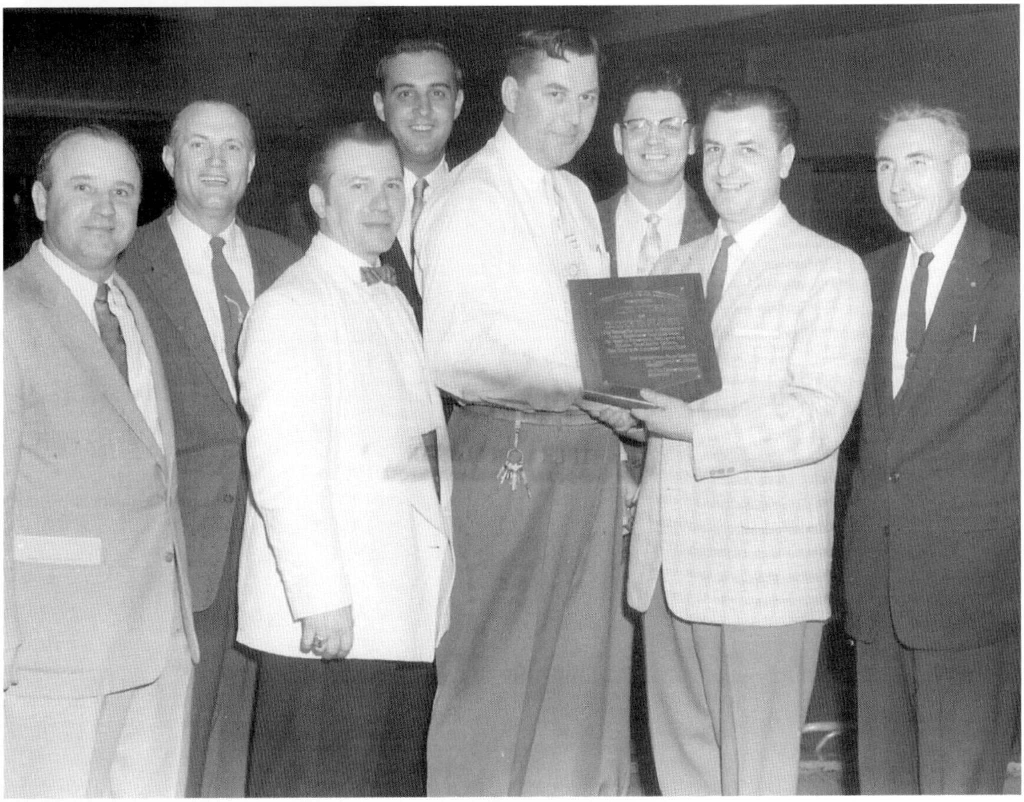

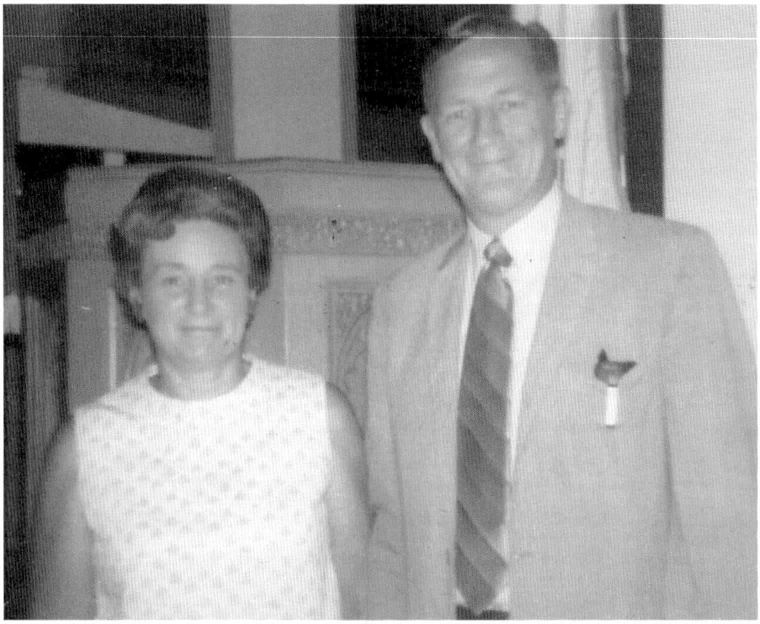

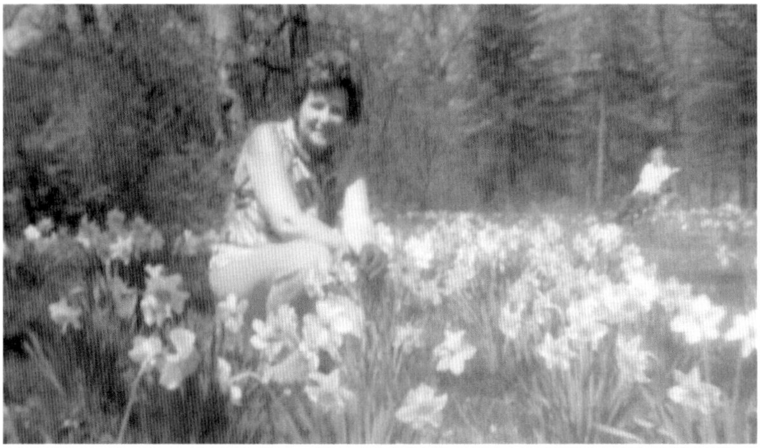

Arthur and Virginia Carlson

Throughout their lives, the Carlsons devoted their free time to helping wherever they saw a need. Both grew up in Chicago Lawn and attended Eberhart School. When they married, Art bought his boyhood home at Sixty-First Street and Homan Avenue, where they raised their family of four children.

Lifelong members of Thomas Memorial Congregational Church, both served as Sunday school teachers. Art did everything at the church from being a Boy Scout leader to monitor and janitorial work. No job that needed to be done was too big or small for Art. Virginia was the superintendent of Sunday school and also chairman of the deaconess board.

The Carlsons were early members of SCOPE (Southwest Community on Peaceful Equality), a community group working toward making the neighborhood more open and welcoming to newcomers of varied backgrounds. When asked about his involvement in the organization, Art explained it as "recognizing his neighbor's problems and seeing them as his own."

Two of the Carlsons' sons suffered from muscular dystrophy and attended Christopher School for the Handicapped. Art started a Boy Scout troop there and after he retired became a teacher's aide at Christopher. (Courtesy Shirley Williams.)

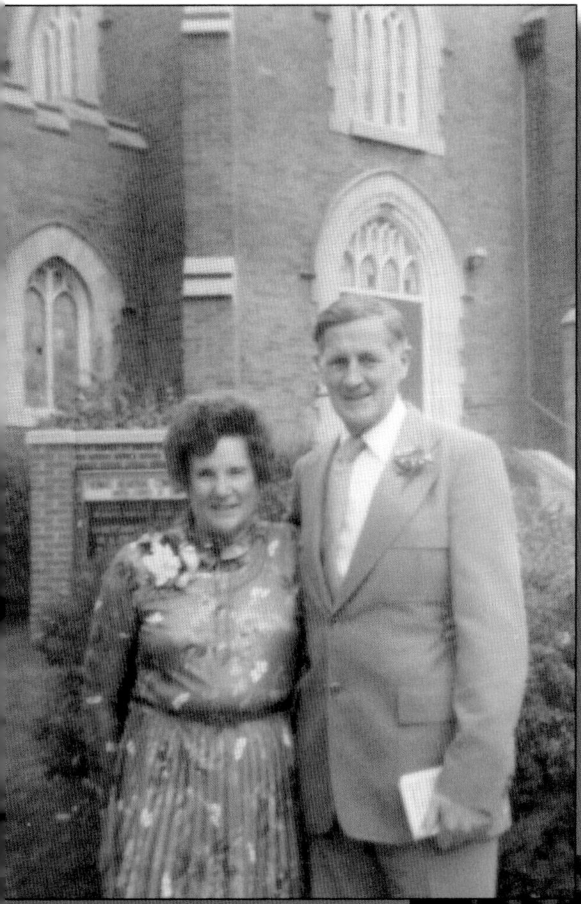

The Carlsons

In the late 1960s, Virginia devoted much of her time to helping her youngest son, who was confined to a wheelchair, attend the University of Illinois. She drove him to class and helped him take notes. Sadly, he died before completing his degree.

For over 25 years, hundreds of mentally and physically challenged children looked forward to regular visits every week from the "Flower Lady," as Virginia was known.

Visiting their classrooms several times a week armed with flowers obtained from funeral homes, containers collected from friends and neighbors, seeds, and a wealth of green projects, Virginia took their minds off their challenges as she taught them about plants and flowers, calling her program horticultural therapy.

For this and her work in establishing the handicapped garden in the Chicago Botanical Garden she was awarded the prestigious Hutchinson Medal. A plaque remains at the Chicago Botanical Gardens in her honor.

"My parents loved Chicago Lawn and they were dedicated to making it a better place," said daughter Shirley. "They taught us by example how to give of yourself." (Both, courtesy of Shirley Williams.)

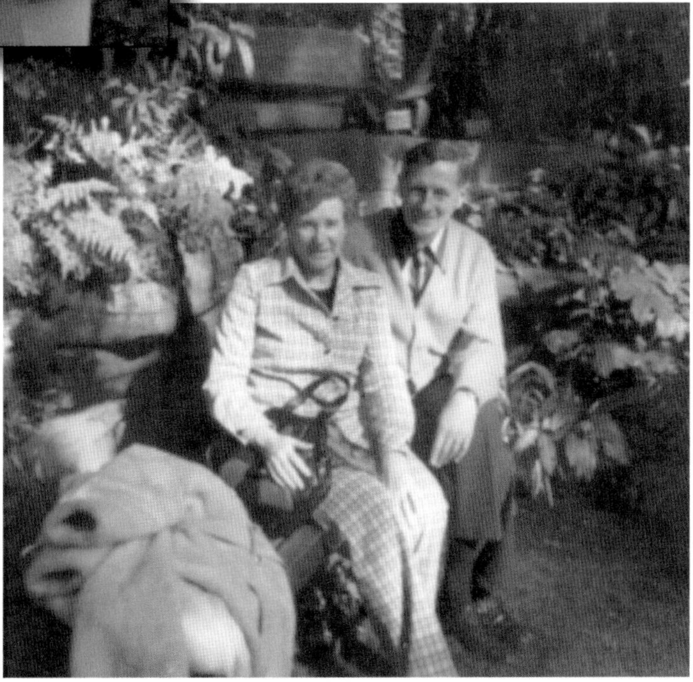

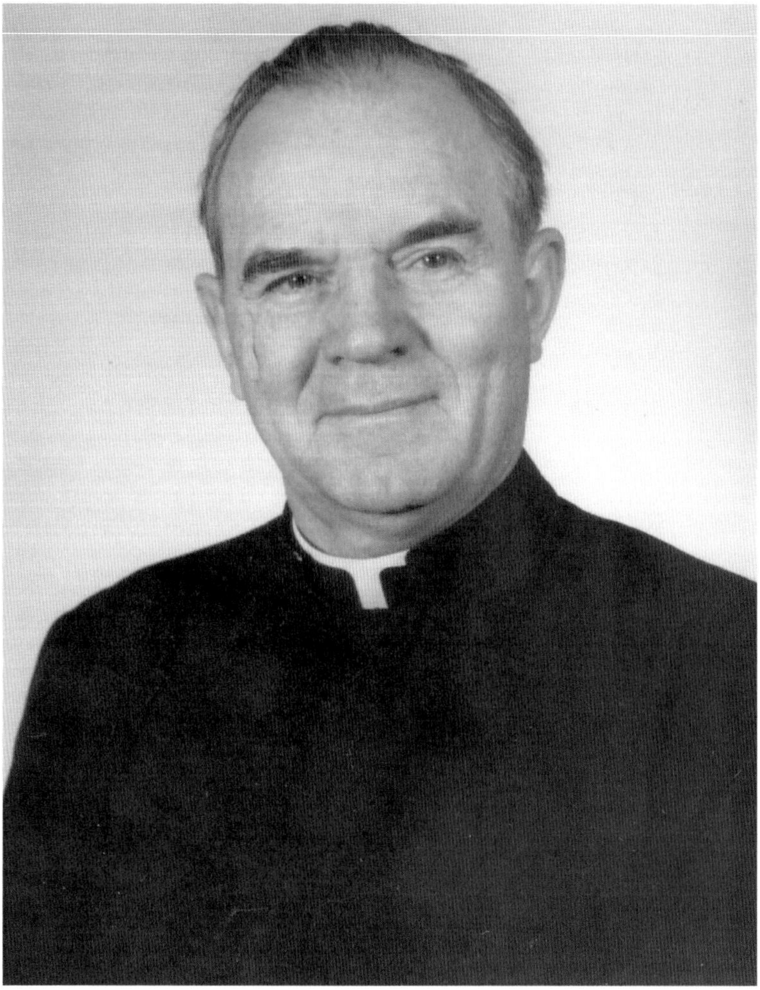

Rev. Stanislaus L. Ryzner

Rev. Stanley Ryzner, one of eight children born to Mr. and Mrs. John Ryzner, residents of Chicago, inherited from his father the taste for hard work and from his mother the ability to see a thing through despite numerous difficulties. Both of these qualities would serve him well as founding pastor of Queen of the Universe Parish.

Ryzner's first assignment after ordination was as an assistant at St. Wenceslas. In addition to his parish duties, he was charged with professorship responsibilities at the seminary in Mundelein.

It was during those years that he risked his life for his master when he courageously entered the smoke-filled church, which had caught fire from an overheated boiler, to save the blessed sacrament.

In 1955, Cardinal Stritch assigned Ryzner the job of building a new parish for the rapidly growing area of West Lawn on the south side of the golf course. Under his able leadership, the dream became a reality in just a few short years. He became an innovative leader and a favorite of the school children.

An advocate of the numerous possibilities of television, when Queen of the Universe School opened in 1957, it was the first grammar school in the Midwest to employ closed-circuit television in every classroom. He also equipped each hallway, and even the church, with television outlets explaining that this way overflowing crowds could view special church services on screens placed in corridors.

With a twinkle in his eye, Ryzner said, "You can bet your life the children will love our closed-circuit television."

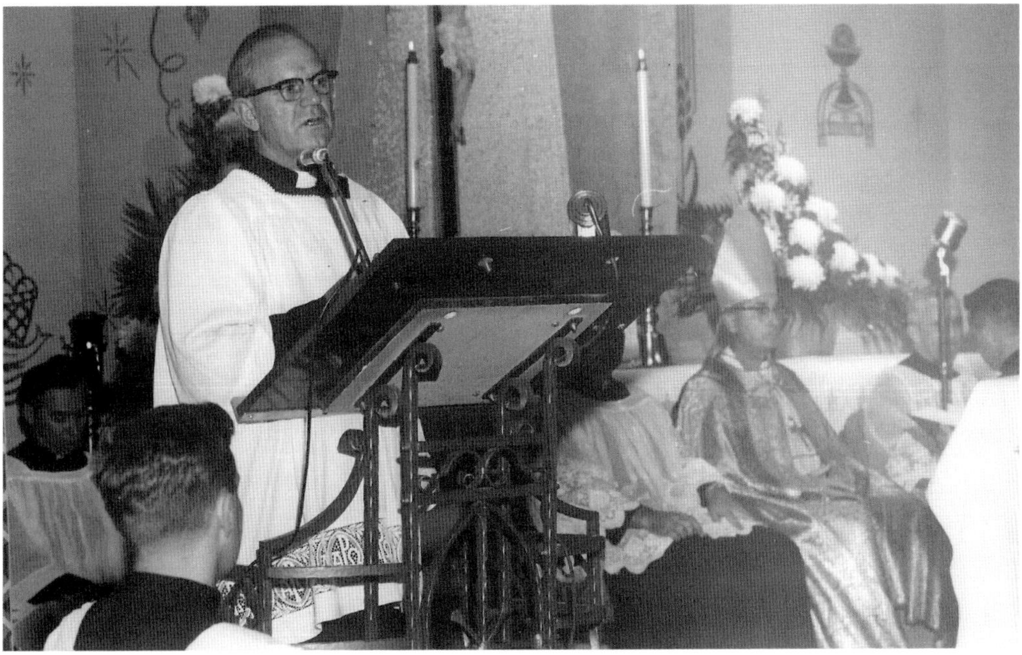

Father Stan

The enterprising pastor invited Jewish leaders to Queens to "light a path of understanding." The traditional menorah of the Jewish festival of Chanukkah is performed at Queens (below) so parishioners "could try and get closer to our Jewish neighbors and friends." While Gino DiVito, the shamus representing congregation, and Eileen Cocco light candles, prayers are read by Reverend Ryzner. Rabbi Gershon Rosenstock is in the center, and Rev. John Hurley to the far right was an assistant at Queens. Much to the liking of parishioners young and old, Father Ryzner remained at the helm of Queen of the Universe until his retirement in 1970. (Both, courtesy of Queen of the Universe Parish.)

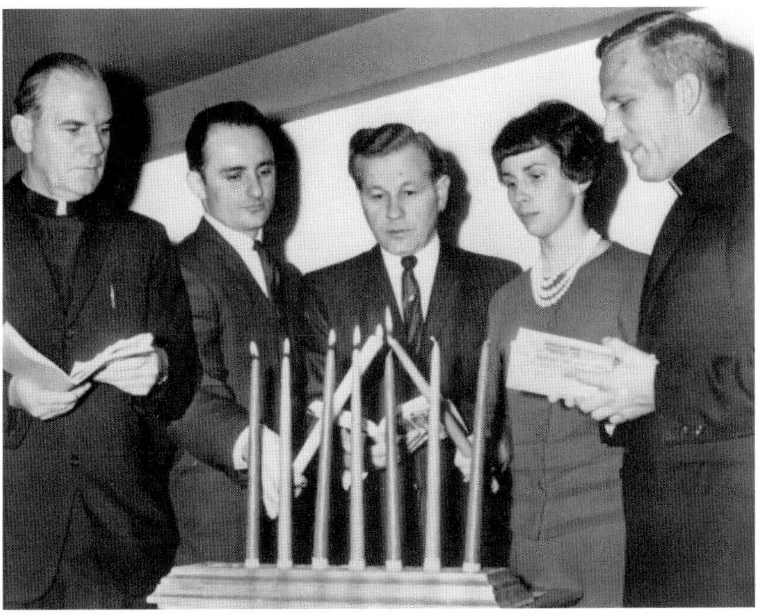

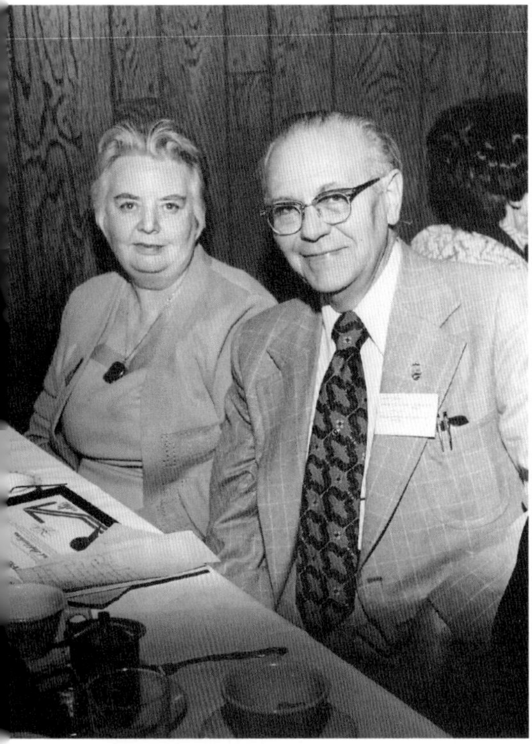

Edward and Daisy Vondrak

Piece by piece, Edward and Daisy Vondrak put together a newspaper that would grow to be known as the *Southwest News-Herald*, the largest ABC-audited paper of its time. Always community-oriented and willing to lend a helping hand, the Vondraks were loved and respected in the neighborhood.

After graduating from Lindblom High School, Ed began working as head soda jerk in the family's candy store at Fifty-Third Street and Kedzie Avenue. Within two years, his mother decided the store would be more profitable if Ed left the soda counter, for he loved ice cream and had already gained 40 pounds.

After a brief stint with the Kraft Cheese Company, the literary field called to him. He wrote short stories and poems, over 500 actually, but Ed said, "I developed a new hobby—collecting rejection slips."

Nerve kept him trying, and on April Fool's Day, 1935, Ed went to work as a script writer for WLS radio. His entry into the community newspaper field came in December 1935, when he joined the *Brighton Park Life* as editor for $6.50 a week.

In October 1936 he married Daisy Ellen Webb. And what Ed and Daisy did was amazing.

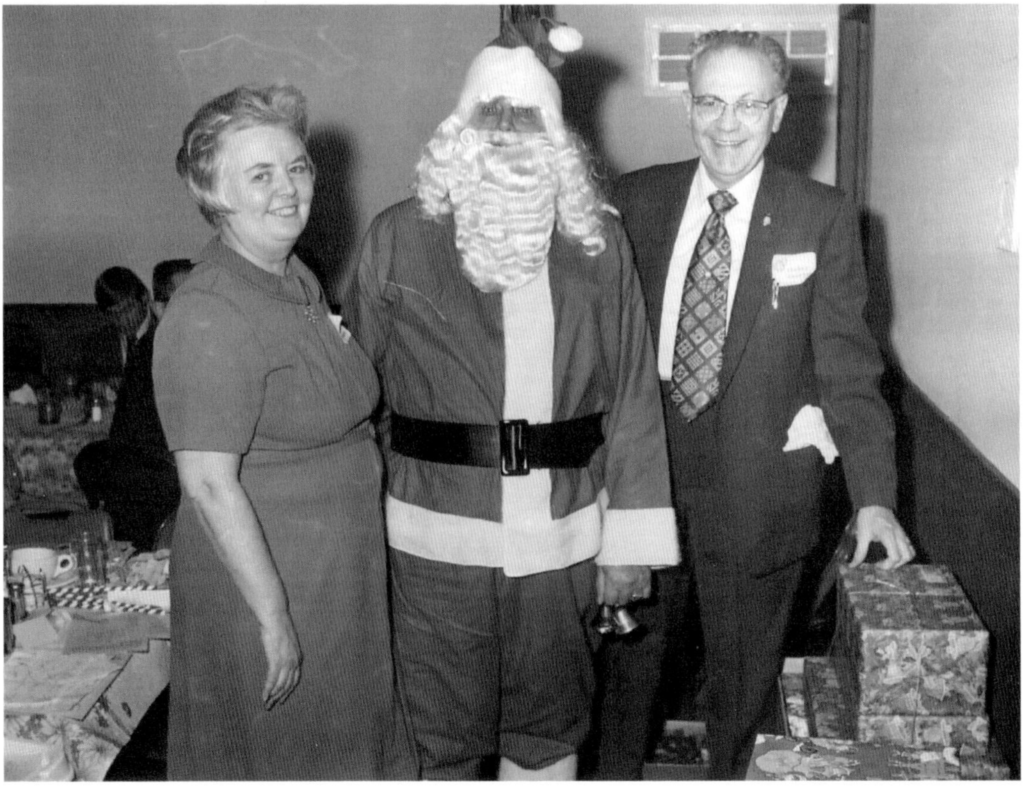

Vondrak Publications

Records show in October 1945 they bought the *Gage Park Herald* from Jerry Pech, who published it monthly (circulation 8,000). In two months they expanded it into the *Southwest Herald*, published twice a month (circulation 20,000), and by April 1946, the Vondraks made it a weekly. Six months later, they purchased the *Southwest News* and merged the two into the *Southwest News-Herald*.

Daisy remembered that after borrowing all they could from relatives and friends, they found themselves still $500 short with two hours to their purchase deadline of the *Southwest News*.

"The hardware store man came in. After we told him the story, he told us to wait a while. He came back with the rest of the money," she recalled. "We were just a couple of punk kids. We started out with just the two of us and ended up with 52 employees."

When the Vondraks opened a large office on Fifty-Eighth Street and Kedzie Avenue, veteran journalists credited it with being "an important step in lifting the community press up and placing it on a dignified professional level."

And then they went one step further, with help from their son Jim, who had returned from the service and joined the operation. They purchased and remodeled a former Jewel Food Store, turning it into an even bigger home for their paper. Daisy handled the bookkeeping and finances of the newspapers, watching the books closely, which got them through the difficult early days.

Daisy and Ed had two sons and raised their boys in Chicago Lawn. Throughout the years, the Vondraks added and subtracted banners from their newspaper family. They stayed focused on the neighborhoods they served and not only wrote about the concerns and problems facing the neighborhood but also stood at the forefront of community issues and worked toward solutions themselves.

Pictured below are Ed and Daisy with their son Jim, checking out the plans for their office on Sixty-Second Street and Kedzie Avenue.

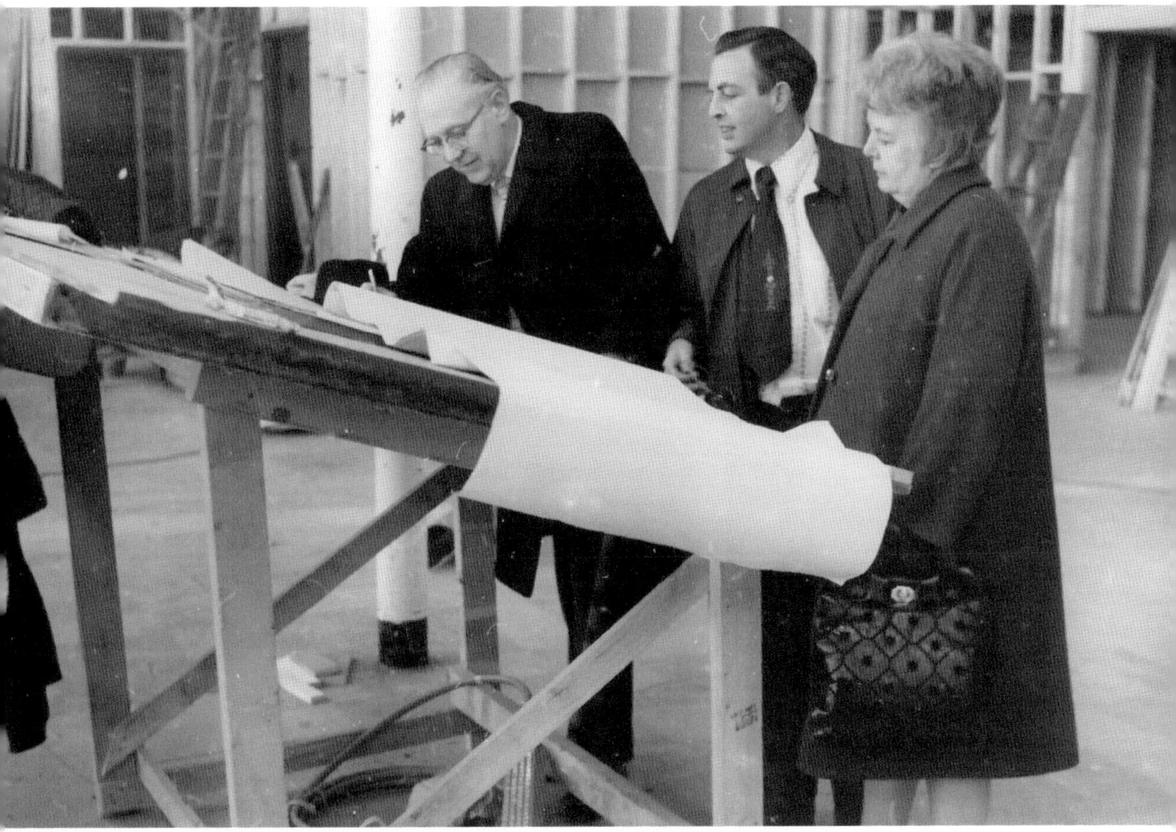

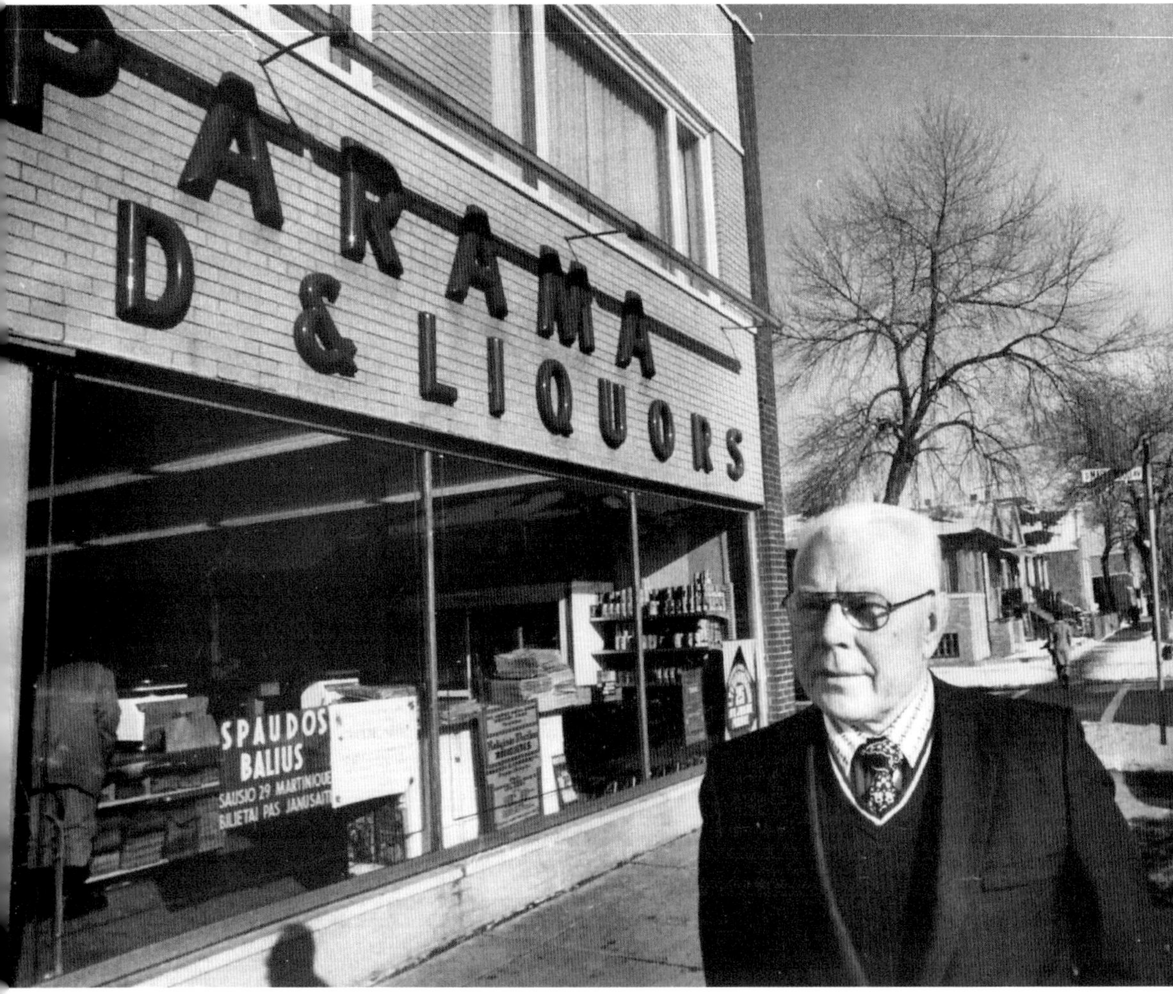

Jurgis Janusaitis

Like so many others at the time, Jurgis Janusaitis left Lithuania in 1949 following the Russian takeover, and immigrated to the United States under the Displaced Persons Act. He escaped with his wife and later learned his brother had been deported to a concentration camp in Siberia, where he died.

Janusaitis came to Chicago looking for work. He found his first job in a chocolate factory working for 95¢ an hour. Next he unloaded railroad cars and then worked as a janitor. His goal, just like so many of his fellow Lithuanians, was to save up enough money to move to Marquette Park, where already a national Lithuanian church had been established, along with grammar schools, a high school, and a hospital.

When Janusaitis earned enough to settle in Marquette Park, he opened a small butcher shop on Sixty-Ninth Street, which grew into the grocery store Parama.

Janusaitis built Parama into a big impressive store for its time. He stocked frozen Lithuanian foods and the miniature supermarket had an amenity not usually found in local ethnic shops—shopping carts.

Parama sat on the northwest corner of Sixty-Ninth Street and Maplewood Avenue, and every morning like clockwork, Janusaitis could be seen sweeping up around the front and side of his store.

Janusaitis collaborated with the Lithuanian press and also became a board member of the Lithuanian Journalists Union.

CHAPTER FOUR

Carrying the Torch

Don't buy the house, buy the neighborhood.

—Russian proverb

As communities grow and prosper, they can only be as successful as the people that live within them. Businesses contribute to the success of the neighborhood, and the neighborhood's residents contribute to the success of the businesses.

Henry Bianco Sr., Chicago fireman turned restaurateur, grew his Club El Bianco into a vehicle for bringing celebrities into Chicago Lawn. At the same time, photographer Michael Rotunno was in the middle of his 34th year at Midway Airport, where he photographed stars and dignitaries stopping in Chicago, many times on their way to El Bianco.

Eddie Korosa, dubbed the "Prince of Polkas," opened his Baby Doll Club on Western Avenue, which would become the broadcast home of his long-running television show. Frances Loepker created the Welcome Wagon for the neighborhood.

West Lawn resident Barbara Hummel helped lost pets and lost owners find each other. At a time when animal shelters were quite often the beginning of the end for lost pets, she took it upon herself to become the intermediary.

Elizabeth King was at the middle of her long career as the children's librarian at the Chicago Lawn branch. On the eastern end, Fr. Francis Lawlor, OSA, became a controversial alderman of the 15th Ward, the first Catholic priest to do so.

In the world of politics, Michael Madigan, Frank Savickas, and Ray McDonald had become household names. Adeline Paplauskas was operating her long-running Chicago Lawn gift shop. Ray and Rose Groth were the proprietors of a favorite neighborhood corner store. Tony DiNolfo's Sparkle Food Center was attracting attention on Fifty-Ninth Street.

Greek immigrant Leo Stefanos had opened a candy shop in West Lawn and was developing an ice cream bar that one day would be known across the nation. And on Seventy-First Street, a new group was setting up shop under the leadership of Frank Collin.

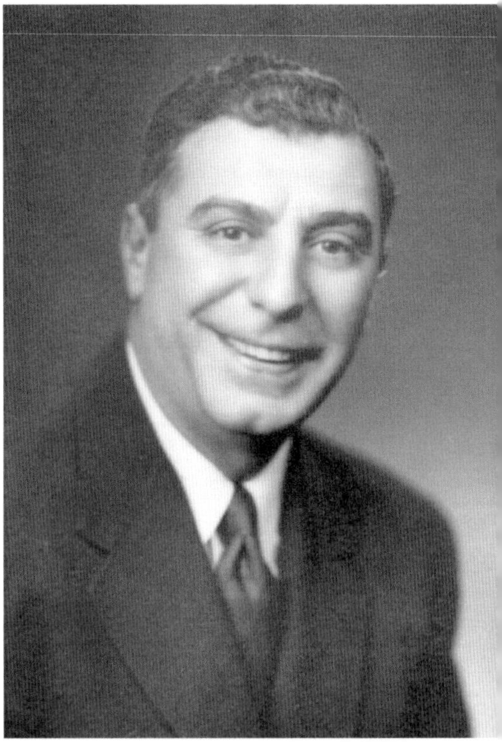

Henry Bianco Sr.

Club El Bianco was the vehicle for bringing celebrities into Chicago Lawn, and its owner, the congenial and hospitable Henry Bianco, was more than happy to be their host. He turned his restaurant into a gathering place for politicians, businessmen, and celebrities for more than 30 years.

Bianco started out as a Chicago fireman. In his 10-year career with the department, he became a lieutenant and was stationed at Midway Airport. In 1946, he opened a small grocery store at 6312 South California Avenue. Occasionally he would take lunch and pop into a tavern at 2747 West Sixty-Third Street. There he marveled at the price of a glass of beer. At his store he sold a quart of beer for 25¢. That same quarter only bought him an eight-ounce glass of beer at the tavern. The profit margin was certainly better in the tavern business.

Bianco kept his store for two years. Then he bought the tavern. He began serving food, cooked by his wife, Mildred, from family recipes. Soon people were coming in just to eat. When he realized the food was taking off, Henry closed the tavern, remodeled it, and Club El Bianco was born. (Both, courtesy of Henry Bianco Jr.)

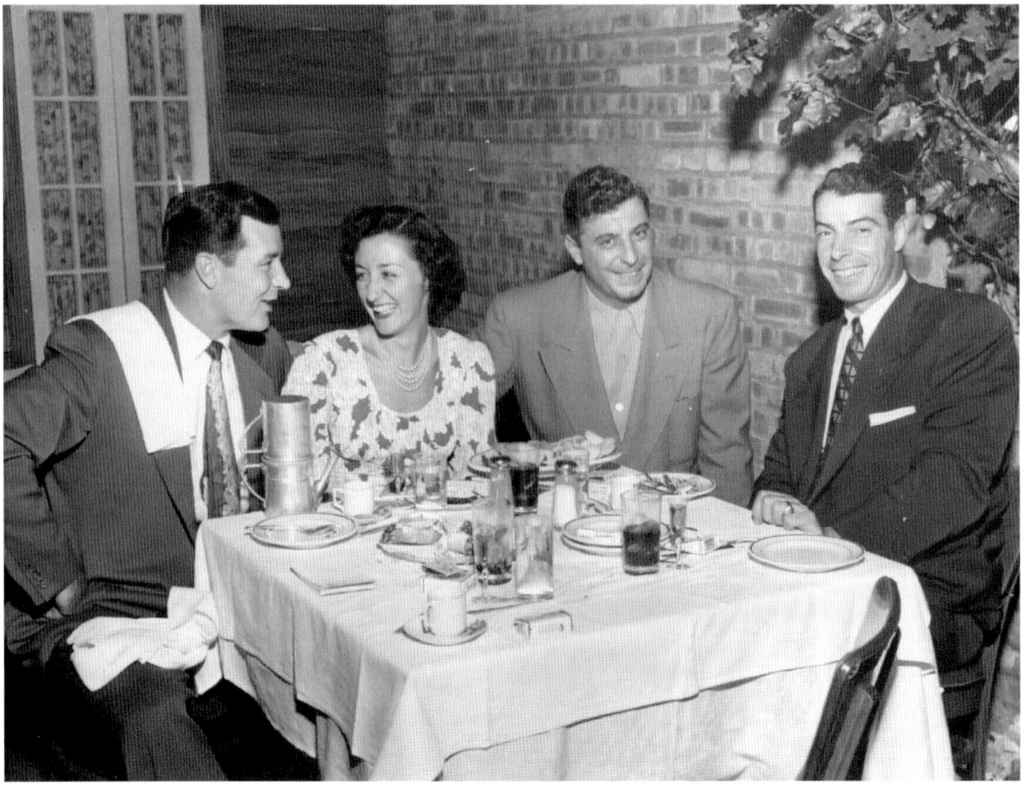

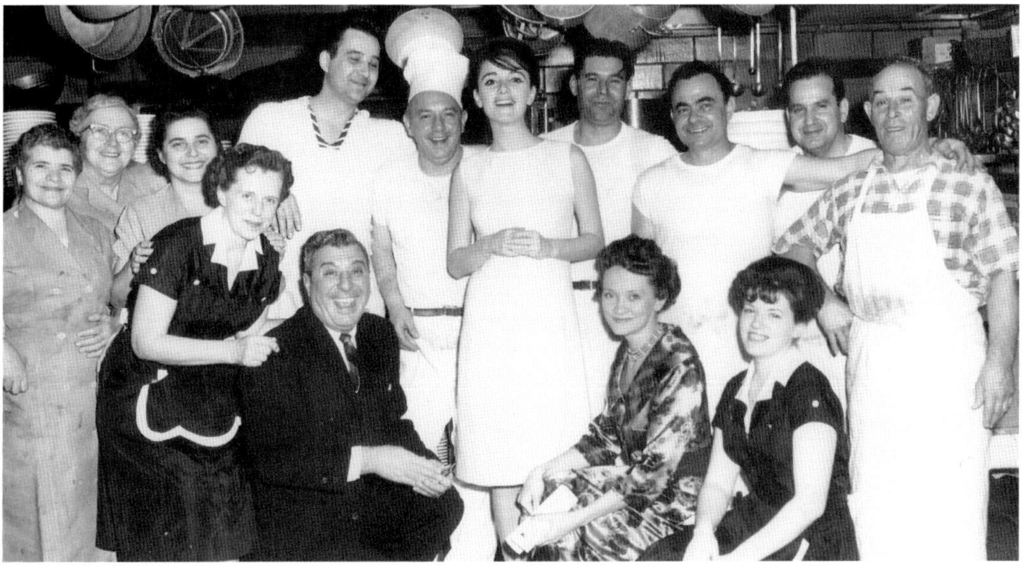

The Host

Several factors figured into Henry's success. The host and his philosophy that every meal should be a fiesta certainly, and then there was Midway Airport, which was coming into its own as a major hub. With no transatlantic flights yet, layovers sometimes three or four hours long were common. And, with few other fine-dining restaurants around, limousines brought celebrities to El Bianco. AP photographers caught on quickly and waited at the club. Snapping photographs and giving the images captions like "Dean Martin enters El Bianco restaurant in Chicago," they developed the negatives hastily, wired them to major newspapers, and brought El Bianco national notoriety.

On the opposite page, Henry sits down with Joe DiMaggio at the club. Above, Henry and his staff took a quick break for a photograph with Anna Maria Alberghetti.

And to add icing onto the cake, often enough the stars were flying to a guest spot on a television show, many times Johnny Carson's *Tonight Show*. Carson would ask what was new, and stars would mention their layover in Chicago and what a great time they had at Club El Bianco. (Both, courtesy of Henry Bianco Jr.)

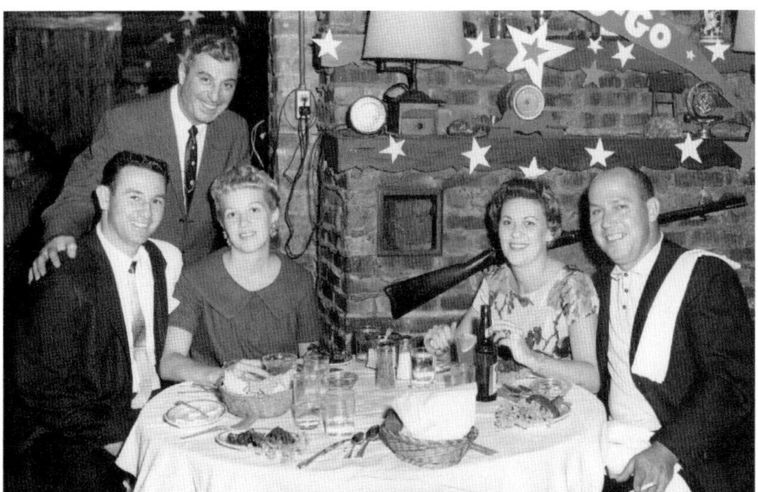

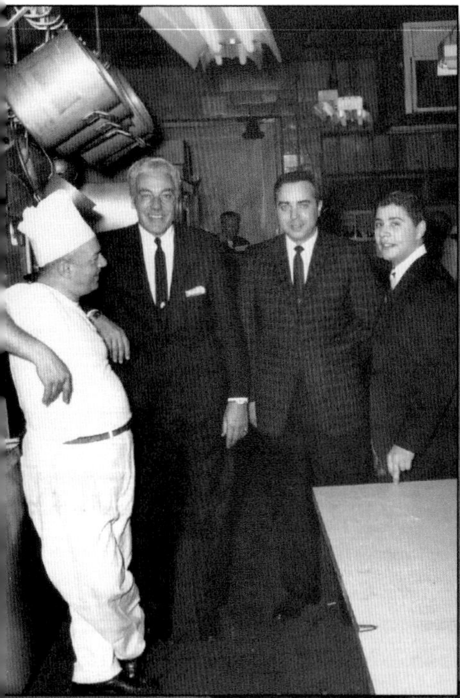

Henry Bianco Jr.

Henry "Butch" Bianco grew up with Club El Bianco and learned the business daily from his father. He became adept at making his guests feel welcome and at home. Henry Sr. had purchased the building next door to the club. The former barbershop was remodeled into the club annex. All the pastries and cookies were made in the kitchen, and the Biancos made their own spumoni ice cream. Under Butch's leadership, the fiesta dinners continued.

Butch was also active with the Marquette Manor Chamber of Commerce, serving for many years with folks such as John Pakel and Stan Evans. He was and still is as of this writing faithful to his alma mater, St. Rita High School, cooking up several hundred pounds of his signature Italian sausage under a tent before the Friday-night homecoming football game.

In January 1981, Butch was named a Chicago ambassador by the Chicago Convention and Tourism Bureau. The plaque presented to Butch was in recognition of his hospitality in serving many world-famous celebrities. Here he is pictured with Ziggy LaParta, Cesar Romero, and Ed Montgomery and with Pat O'Brien and Dennis Morgan. (Both, courtesy of Henry Bianco Jr.)

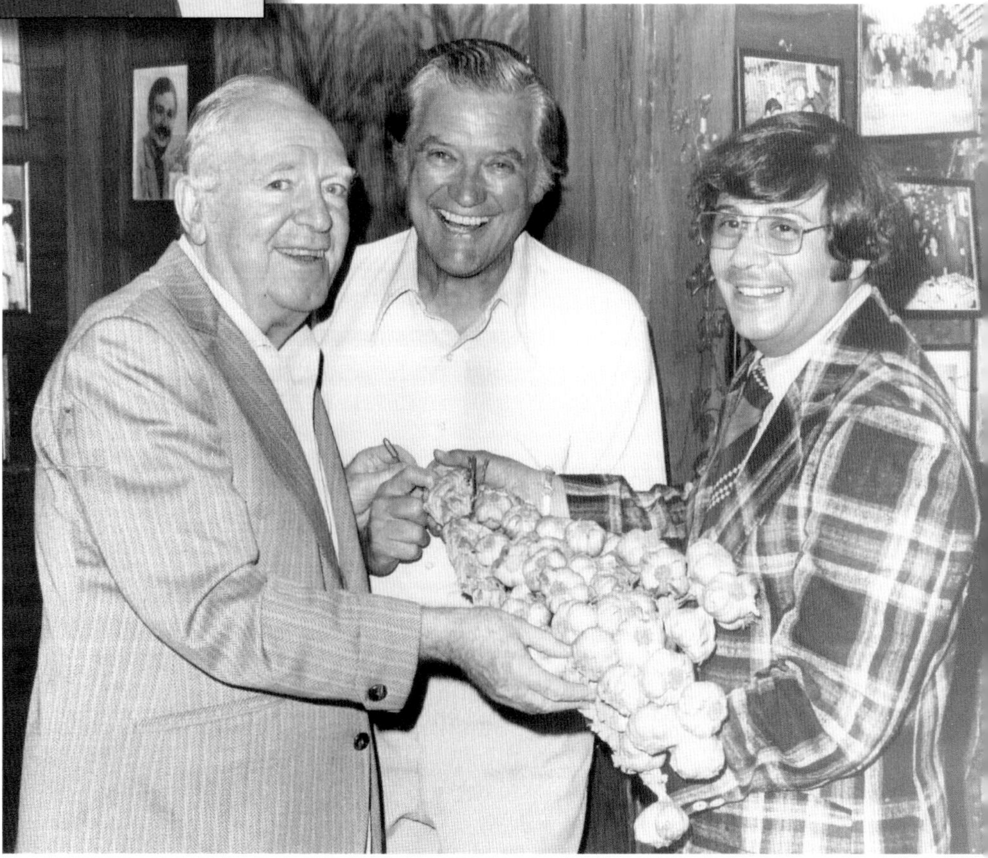

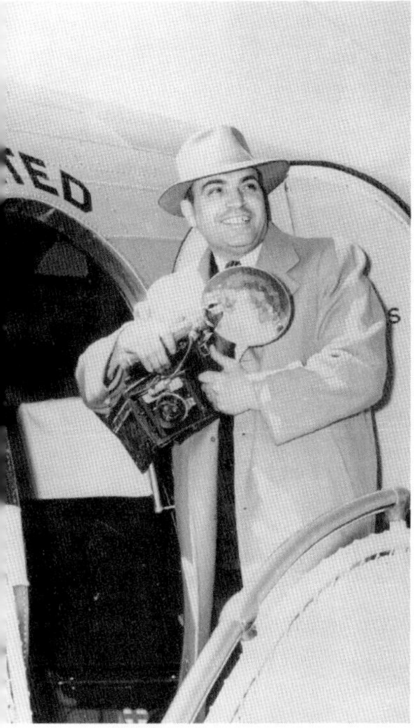

Michael Rotunno

Michael Rotunno, Chicago's unofficial greeter with a camera, was named the Chicago Press Photographer of Goodwill in 1959. He was already starting his 34th year as a photographer at Midway Airport, where he photographed visiting and departing celebrities.

He gained experience working with newsreel companies as a young man, and in 1926, when Municipal Airport was first opening, he started what would be his dream job.

For the next 50 years, Rotunno lived at the airport, either at his Metro News Service counter or on the tarmac. He would shoot the photographs, quickly develop them, and wire them to newspapers.

Pictured below, Winnie Rotunno, Les Lear, Mimi Rotunno, Henry Bianco, Joe E. Brown, Fran Roberts, Butch Bianco, unidentified, Dottie Lear celebrate at El Bianco.

In his 2012 book, *When Hollywood Landed at Chicago's Midway Airport*, Christopher Lynch relayed this story: "Al Capone, once hit the deck as Rotunno captured him on film in an explosion of flash powder, followed instantly by Capone's bodyguards pulling their guns out of their coats, ready to fire."

Lynch said that for every celebrity that ran from his camera, many more stopped to have a drink or a meal with Rotunno. (Below, courtesy of Henry Bianco Jr.)

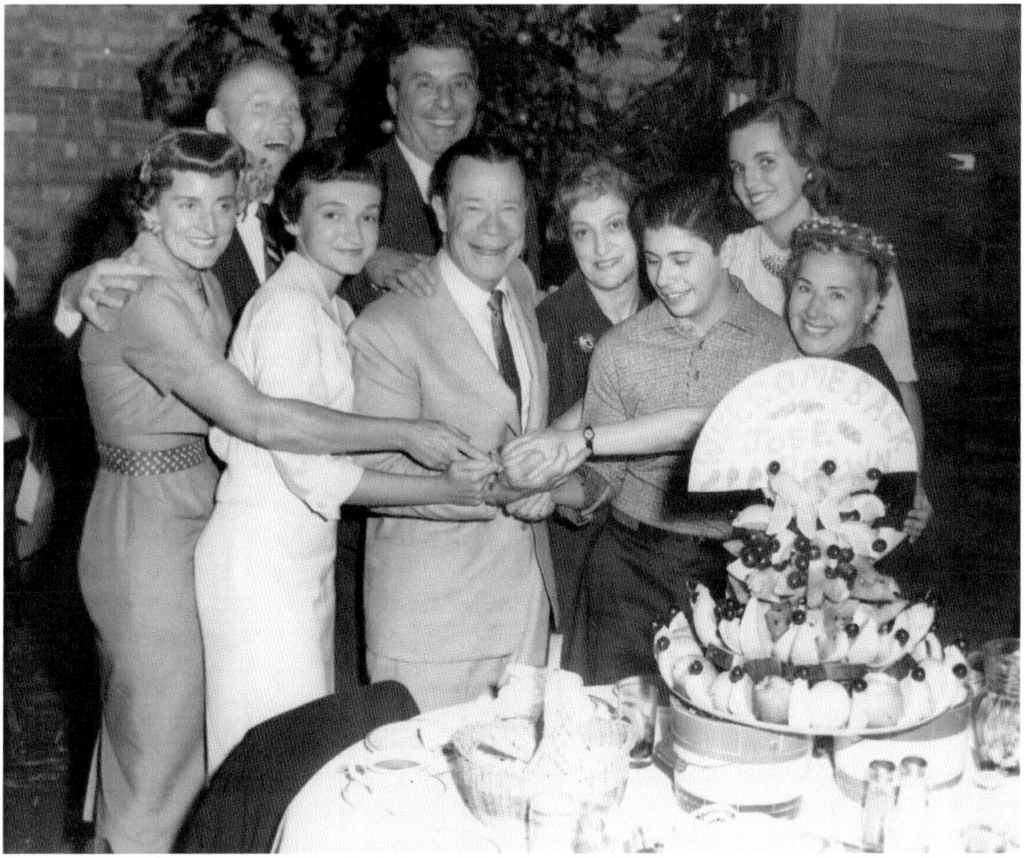

Rev. Francis X. Lawlor OSA

A high school biology teacher for 22 years, Francis Xavier Lawlor became alderman of the 15th Ward in 1971, the first Catholic priest to do so in the Archdiocese of Chicago.

The son of a policeman, Francis Lawlor was born in 1917 to Martin and Margaret Lawlor and raised in the Bronx section of New York. After ordination, he was sent to Chicago, where he taught sociology and biology at St. Rita High School from 1946 to 1968. During that period of time, he was active with the Christian Family Movement, the Knights of Columbus, and, beginning in 1950, he served as citywide moderator of Chicago Inter-Student Catholic Action (CISCA)

In 1969, Lawlor was a delegate to the Constitutional Convention. He made the decision on a Thursday to run, and by Friday he had 3,000 signatures on his petition. He believed in home rule and the voice of the individual. He opposed the Crosstown Expressway. At that time, he stated he would support a school system that would be a neighborhood system that guaranteed everyone a quality education in his or her own community.

Signs began popping up in windows in the 15th Ward: "Pray for Father Lawlor." In 1971, he ran for alderman. Leading marches and giving impassioned speeches added to his appeal and a victory over his opponent with a 2-1 margin. Lawlor organized block clubs to prevent blockbusting—186 in three years—and formed alliances for orderly neighborhood change. He led campaigns against indecent bookstores and charged the government with allowing permits for shoddy construction that damaged neighborhoods. Many colleagues acknowledged his policies as wise suggestions, but his controversial tactics put him in hot water with his superiors and he declined reelection to a second term.

Leaving office, he changed his focus and began using his passionate approach on other issues important to him, such as the death penalty and abortion.

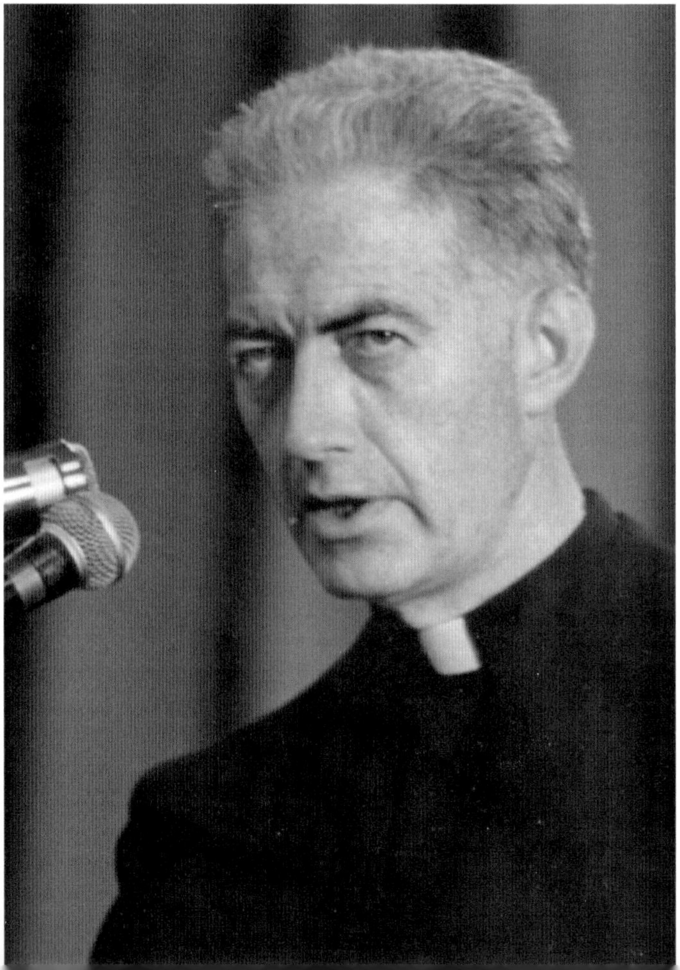

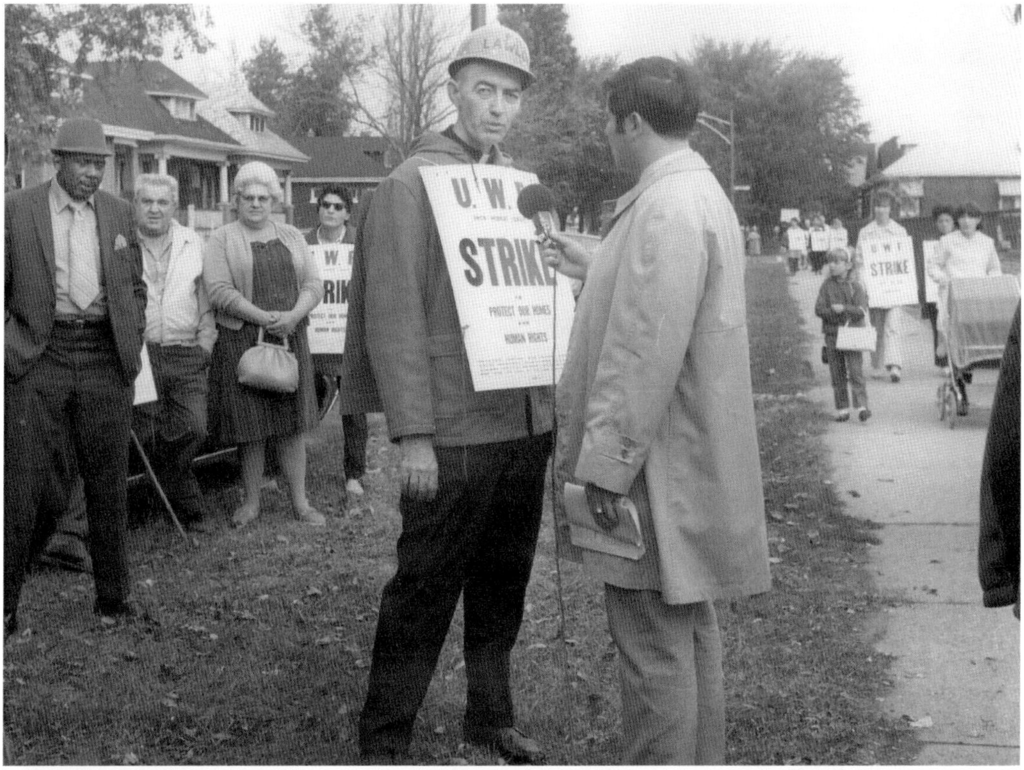
STRIKE
PROTECT OUR HOMES
HUMAN RIGHTS

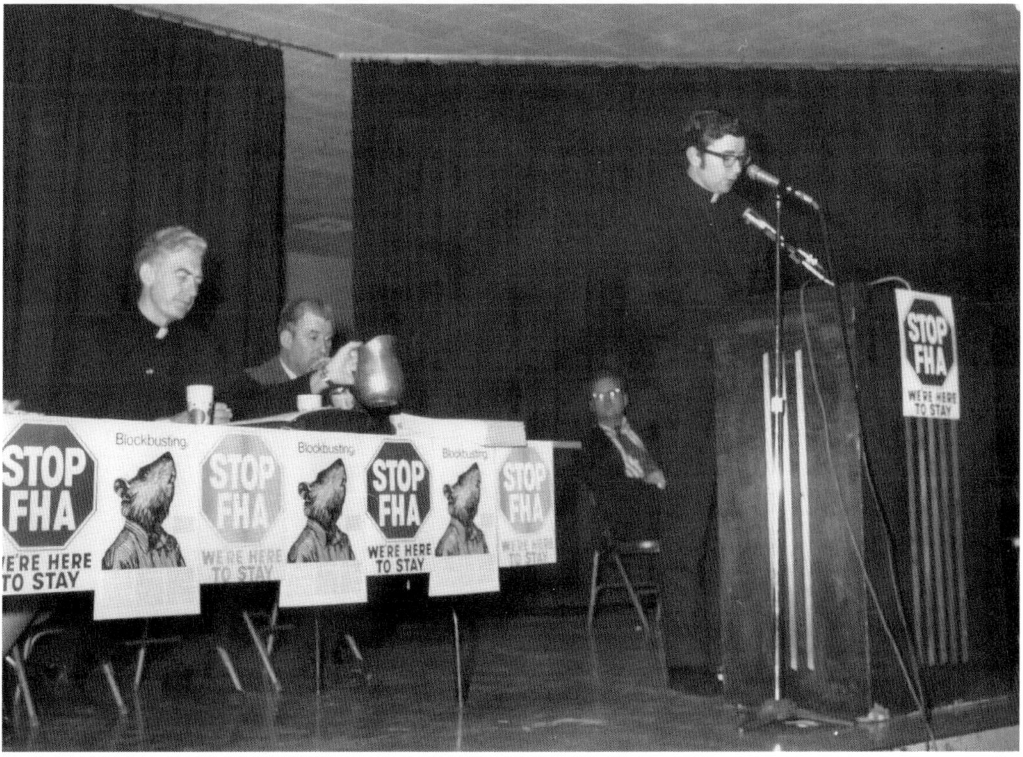
STOP FHA
WE'RE HERE TO STAY
Blockbusting

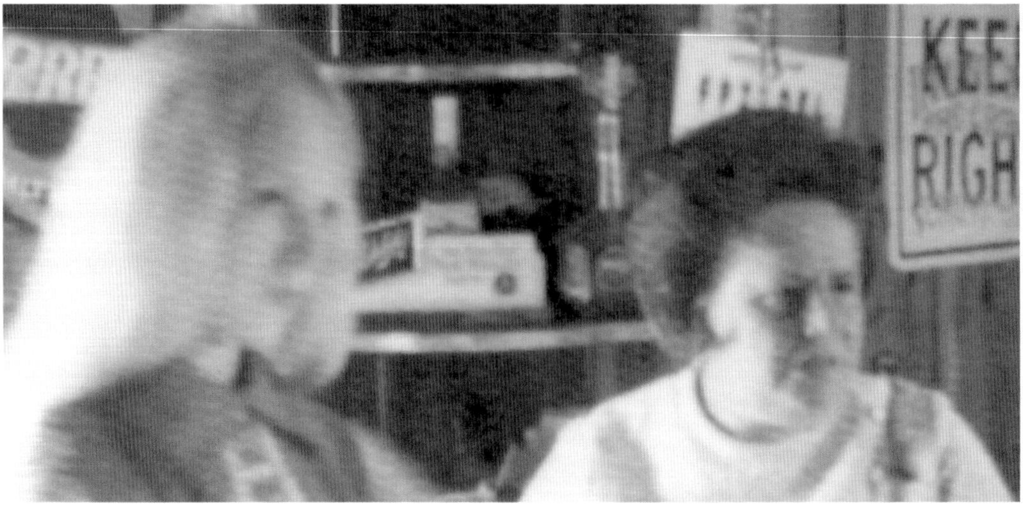

Adeline Paplauskas

For 42 years, Adeline Paplauskas was known in the neighborhood as "Grammy" to local kids. Her husband, Bill, was quite often addressed as "Mr. Adeline." Many is the child that walked into Adeline's Gift Shop at 3456 West Sixty-Third Street, clutching the contents of his or her piggy bank, hoping it would be enough to buy that wonderful birthday gift. And it always was, for Paplauskas could tell when it was a special gift. She asked ahead of time how much they had. The price was always just a little less.

The gift shop in Chicago Lawn opened in 1954 after moving from their first location at Seventy-Ninth and Loomis Streets. Daughter Janice grew up at the store, as a baby taking her naps behind the counter where Bill had built a little bed and later helping out after school.

Generations knew Adeline for her specialty Easter baskets. Parents phoned in their request, and she would get to work creating a basket geared toward the child. When Janice was old enough, she helped with the baskets. One year, Adeline decided it might be fun for Janice to have an Easter bunny costume. Adeline commented to the children in the store that she hoped they had been good because the Easter bunny was in the back working on Easter baskets. Skeptically they looked at her. Adeline called. Out hopped the bunny. And with eyes wide, out ran the kids.

Over 200 people showed up for her surprise retirement party, and they said she knew every single one and their names. (Both, courtesy of Janice Paplauskas.)

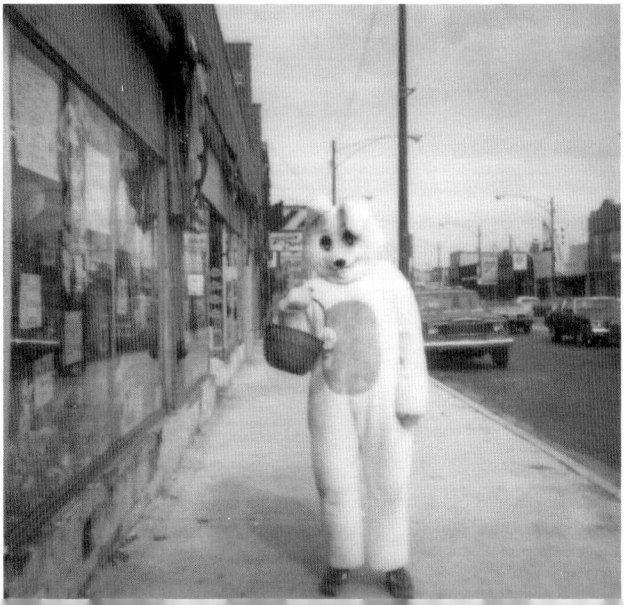

Rose Hodel

Longtime West Lawn resident Rose Hodel won awards at art fairs for her dollhouse interiors, handcrafting furnishings down to minutest details. Her bakery miniature was given to her daughter Rosemary, who with her husband, Ed, owned McDonough Bakery at Fifty-Ninth Street and Albany Avenue. An avid toymaker, Rose's soft toys like Raggedy Ann dolls and clowns made for children at Misericordia were featured on Lee Phillips's show.

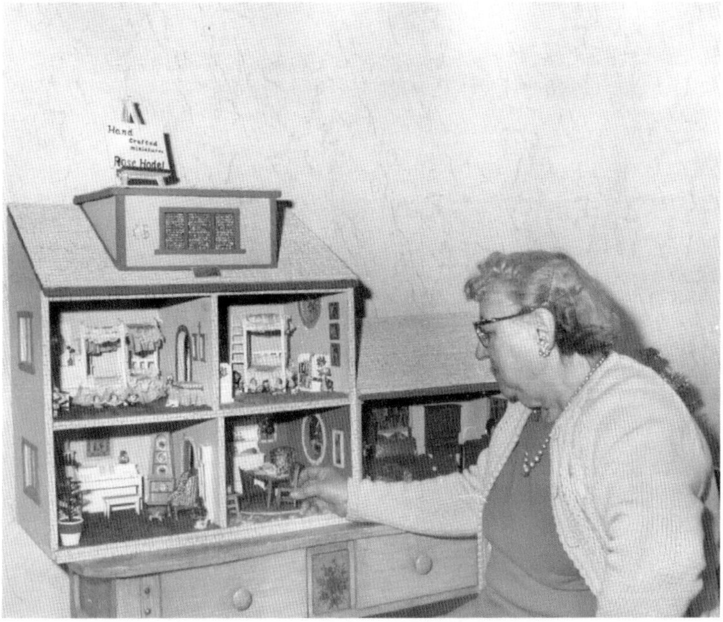

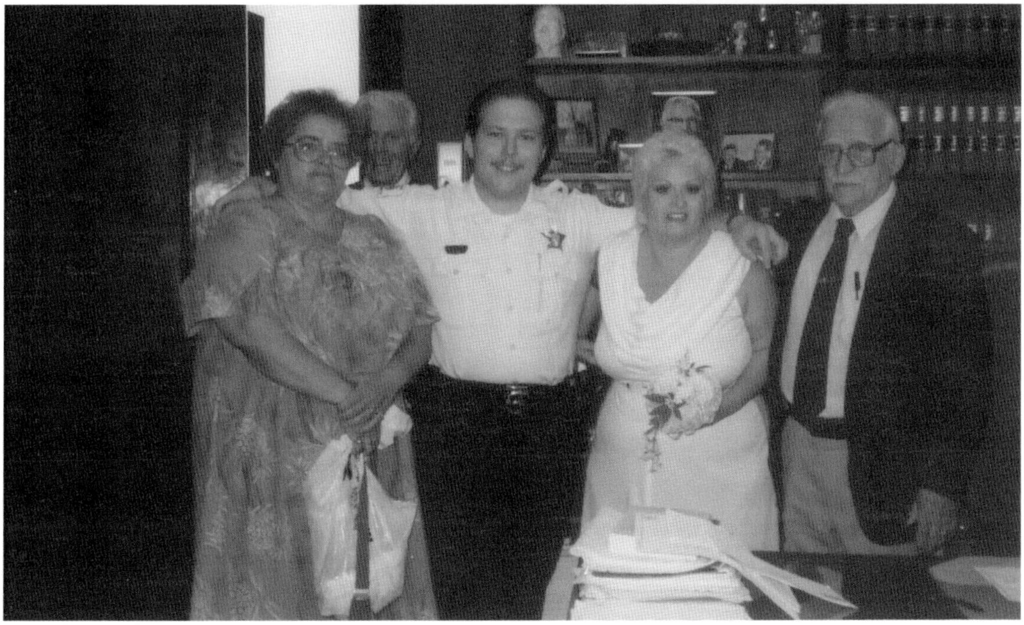

Barbara Hummel

Barbara Hummel of West Sixty-Fourth Street was described by those who knew her as a friendly, personable woman who took it upon herself to circumvent the system and match pets with people herself. She had a big yard and a big heart.

For at least 20 years, whenever she came upon a stray she took it in, checking the lost pet signs and advertisements, and then posting signs herself. For those animals that were not claimed, she gave them away, keeping track of names and addresses just in case former owners turned up. People would often leave a bag of pet food in the yard, knowing Hummel, pictured here with her family, would not put a monetary value on this wonderful service she provided. (Courtesy of David Hummel.)

Raymond and Rose Groth

Reminiscent of every baby boomer's childhood is the proprietor of the corner store. For those growing up in West Lawn around Marquette and Lawndale, it would be the husband and wife team of Raymond and Rose Groth.

Ray knew all the neighborhood kids by name, and they remembered him fondly decades after the store closed. He was the pleasant fellow behind the counter who waited patiently as they gave careful thought to each candy choice.

Ray grew up at Sixtieth Street and St. Louis Avenue. A milkman for Bowman Dairy for 19 years, he made his early deliveries by horse and wagon. In the early 1960s, he worked at a chemical plant on Seventy-First Street and Pulaski Road when an accident caused a permanent injury to his hand. That is when they bought the little store on Marquette Road.

Opening up for business in 1966, Ray put in 15-hour days at the store, seven days a week, but he loved it. And they both loved their customers. When the record snowfall began in January 1967, Rose said, "We didn't feel right just closing up, leaving the neighbors stranded so we stayed open all night." (All, courtesy of Rose Groth.)

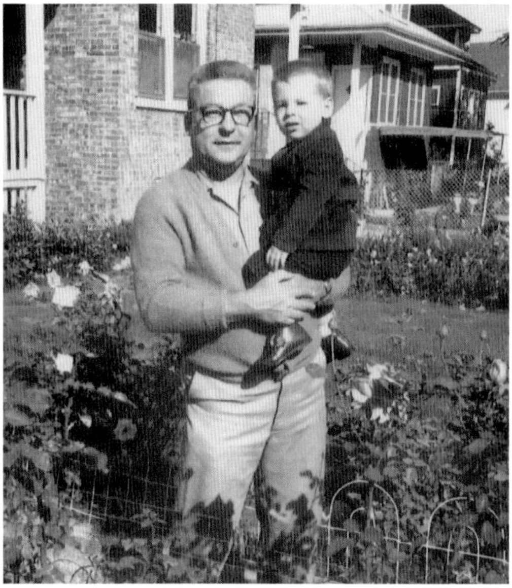

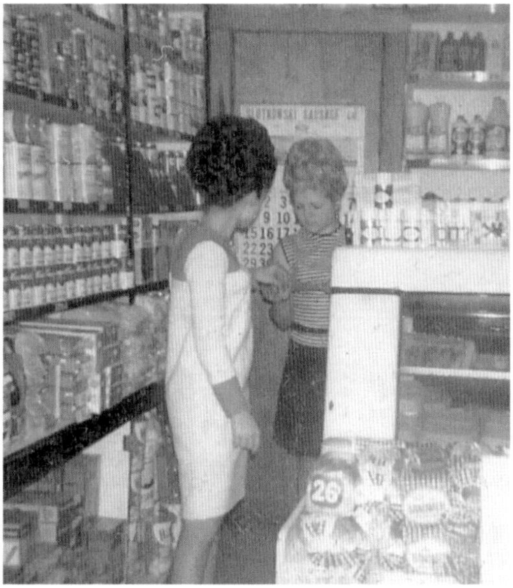

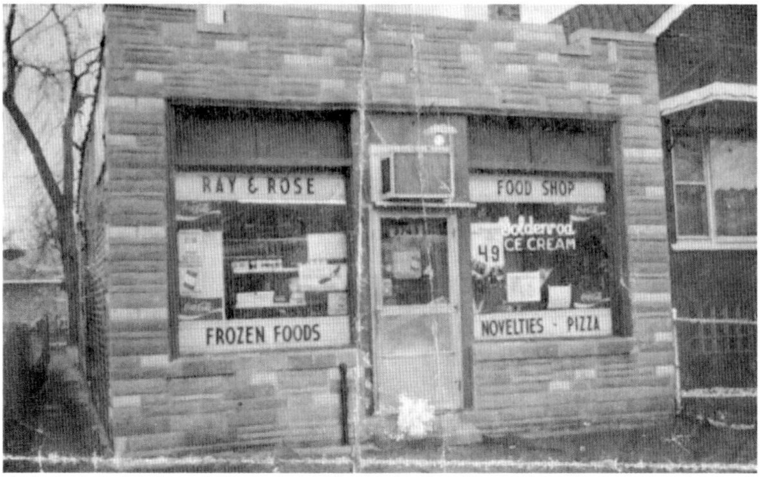

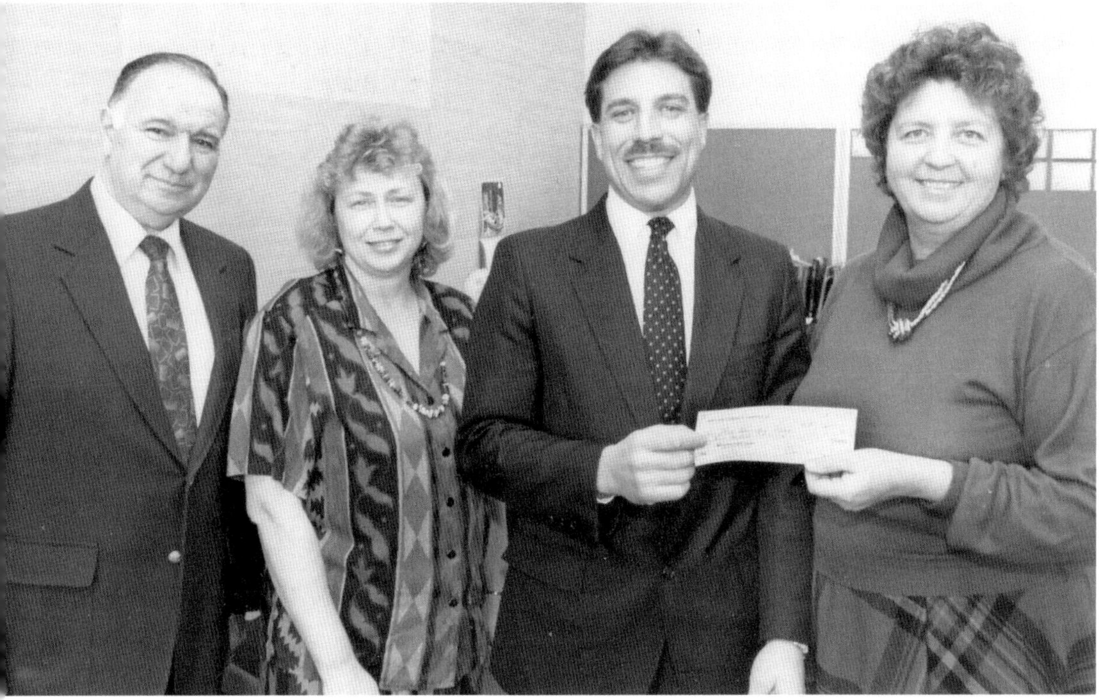

Anthony DiNolfo

As president of the Sparkle Food Center at Fifty-Ninth Street and Pulaski Road, Anthony "Tony" DiNolfo was heralded as a trendsetter in the food industry in 1969 when he created "Return the Shopping Cart," now a national program. At one point, it was estimated that over a million shopping carts were stolen every year. Being a store owner whose carts had turned up in all sorts of places far from where they belonged, DiNolfo began his campaign. Since then, across the nation, February is Return Shopping Carts to the Supermarket Month.

Tony came from a pioneering grocery family. His father owned a store in Bridgeport, and Tony got his early training there, leaving the business only when World War II called. Upon his return in 1948, not only did he marry the former Mary Cacciato, but he also began working at Minicino's Certified at Fifty-Fourth Street and Kedzie Avenue, one of the first supermarkets on the Southwest Side of town.

After 10 years of learning the store operation, Tony opened Tee's Superette at Fifty-Seventh Street and Pulaski Road in 1957. In 1965, he became a partner in the Sparkle Food Center, which was the last Kroger store sold to an independent when the chain vacated the Chicago market.

An active community proponent, Tony was a founding member and past president of the West Lawn Chamber of Commerce. He also served as president of the Southwest Cultural Arts Council, sponsoring art fairs in his parking lot.

He has been on several boards, including the West Communities YMCA and the Certified Grocers of Illinois. An Army veteran and a Fourth-Degree Knight of Columbus, he has also received several Man of the Year awards.

Even with all of his activities and accomplishments, perhaps the one that he will most be remembered for is the creation of Cart Month. Tony retired in 1985 and has since passed away, but his great crusade, the one he began in 1969, goes on.

The West Lawn Chamber of Commerce presented a donation to the West Communities YMCA in this photo taken in 1991. From left to right are Anthony DiNolfo, WLCofC director; Liz Carr, WLCofC president; Joseph Giacchino, executive director of West Communities YMCA; and Elaine Maukus, WLCofC treasurer/secretary.

Elizabeth King

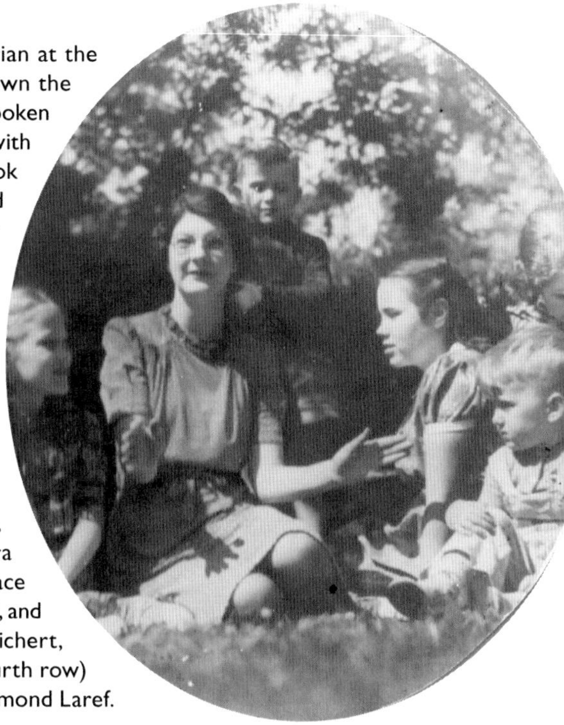

Elizabeth King was the much-loved children's librarian at the Chicago Lawn Branch for decades. She lived just down the street with her parents. Tall with dark hair and a soft-spoken voice, she was helpful and patient. King was very good with children. It was easy for them to get excited about a book when King was there. Sometimes she took them on field trips to the park, and once there, not only would they read but also they would make scientific discoveries about bugs, birds, and trees. She loved the children and they loved her. Elizabeth King died in February 2000 at the age of 91.

In 1949, on the 20th anniversary of the Chicago Lawn Branch Library, past and present members of the staff posed for this photograph: (first row) Florence Richards (kneeling), Vivian McNally, Camille Thornell, Kathleen Dillon holding Jo Ellyn Litts, Patricia Cunnea holding Leanne Ferris, Ruth Walsh, Patricia Litts, and Victoria Mryc; (second row) Marie Moore, Alvira Sullivan, Alfheld Anderson, Stachin Brzostowski, Grace Gatenby, Helga Nielson, Mary Jane Letts, Bessie Smejkel, and Frank O'Brien; (third row) Patricia Hay, Barbara Schleichert, Molly Prendergast, Verna Redman, Virginia Ryan; (fourth row) Bernice Scales, Bennie Brown, Elizabeth King, and Edmond Laref.

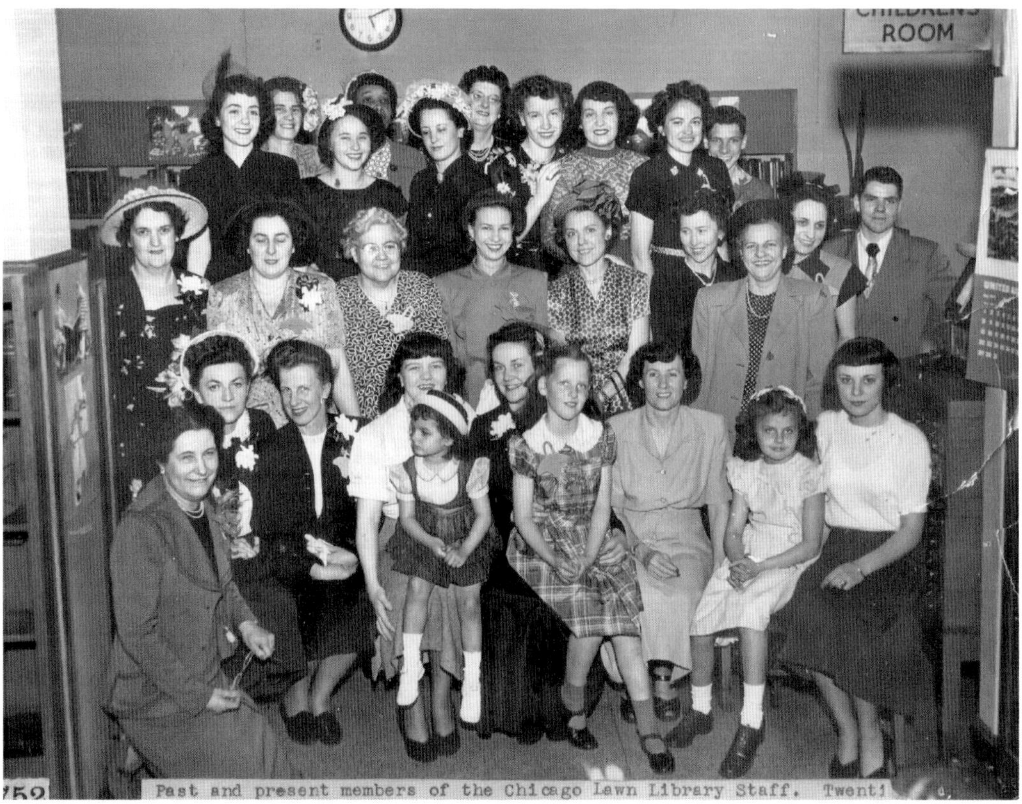

Raymond McDonald

For many growing up in West Lawn, Raymond "Ray" McDonald was their first introduction to the Chicago Park District. Scores of adults remember McDonald as the supervisor at West Lawn Park, Wentworth, and several other area parks; and they all echo the same sort of sentiments. Ray was a mentor, a big brother, and a great example of a man.

Walking into the field house, it would be hard to miss Ray, for he was a big man, and at over six feet tall, he towered over his charges. He had thick white hair and a caring personality, and the consensus is that Ray made one feel important and like he really cared.

In the 1974 Chicago Park District Junior Citizen event, pictured here, Ray McDonald is on the far right. On the far left is Ed Wilke, and in the center is Ed Senka, both also park-district supervisors.

Ray retired after 28 years with the Chicago Park District to become legislative assistant to Ald. William O. Lipinski.

In *My Fall From Grace: City Hall to Prison Walls*, James J. Laski, who met McDonald at Lipinski's office, described him as "one of the kindest, most compassionate, and hardworking individuals you would ever want to meet."

Laski also wrote, "In my political career, I met thousands of people. However, only a small number would really have an impact on my life, and Ray would be one of them."

Ray McDonald passed away when he was only in his 50s.

Walk into the West Lawn field house, and right inside the door there is a hall of fame plaque. Ray McDonald is the first name on it.

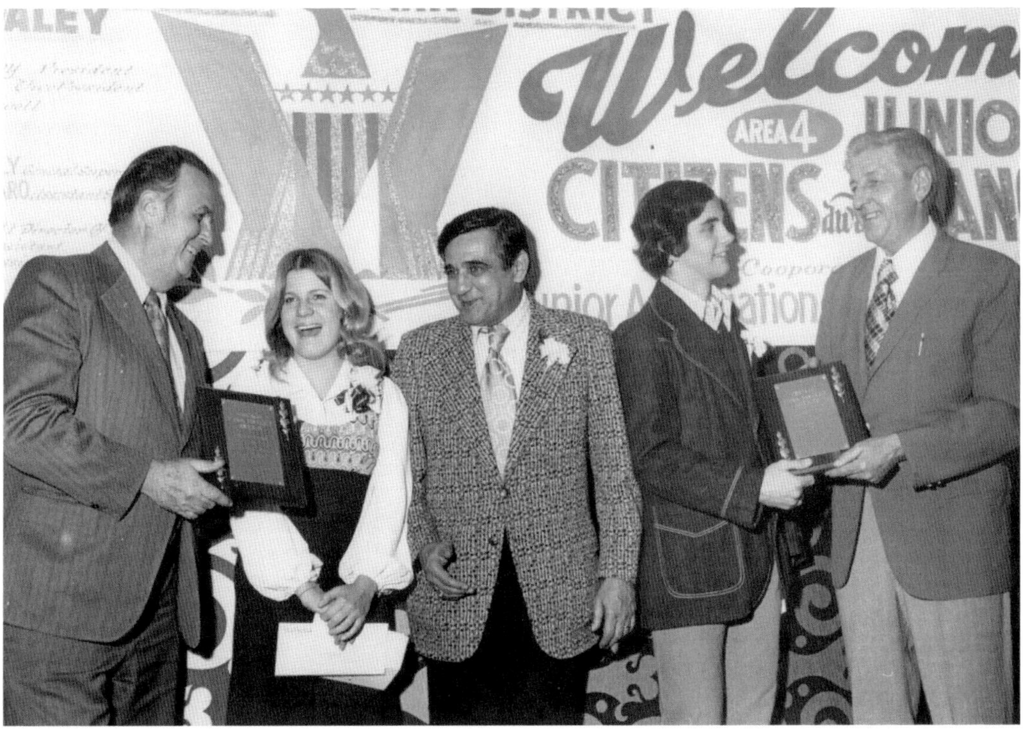

Francis J. Collin

The name Frank Collin is synonymous with the neo-Nazi movement in Chicago in the latter half of the 20th century. And on the Southwest Side, Marquette Manor was his stomping grounds.

As a young man, he had been a member of George Lincoln Rockwell's American Nazi Party but left shortly after Rockwell was assassinated. Collin then founded the National Socialist Party of America in 1970, purchasing a building and setting up headquarters at 2619 West Seventy-First Street. He named the building Rockwell Hall in honor of the fallen commander. Collin and other members of his organization lived in a barracks in the upper floor.

During the next several years, Collin would gain national notoriety as he led his group in organizing marches and demonstrations at Marquette Park. The park would become off-limits to locals during these events, and the streets surrounding the park would be closed off and barricaded by police as well.

In 1975, Frank Collin ran for alderman and garnered a surprising 16 percent of the vote.

As the marches continued, they grew in size and volume as well. The cost to the city in the form of police protection and park cleanup during and after the events was escalating. Concerns of violence heightened. Soon the city of Chicago banned all demonstrations in Chicago parks unless the demonstrators paid an insurance fee of $250,000.

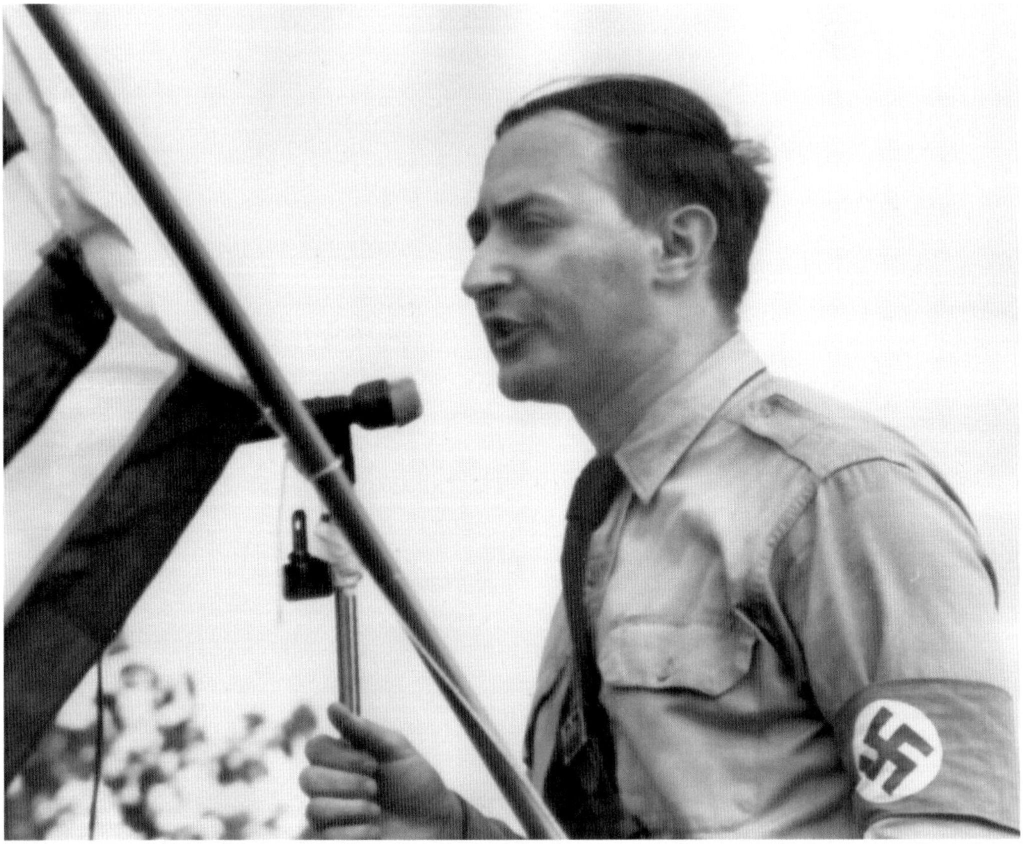

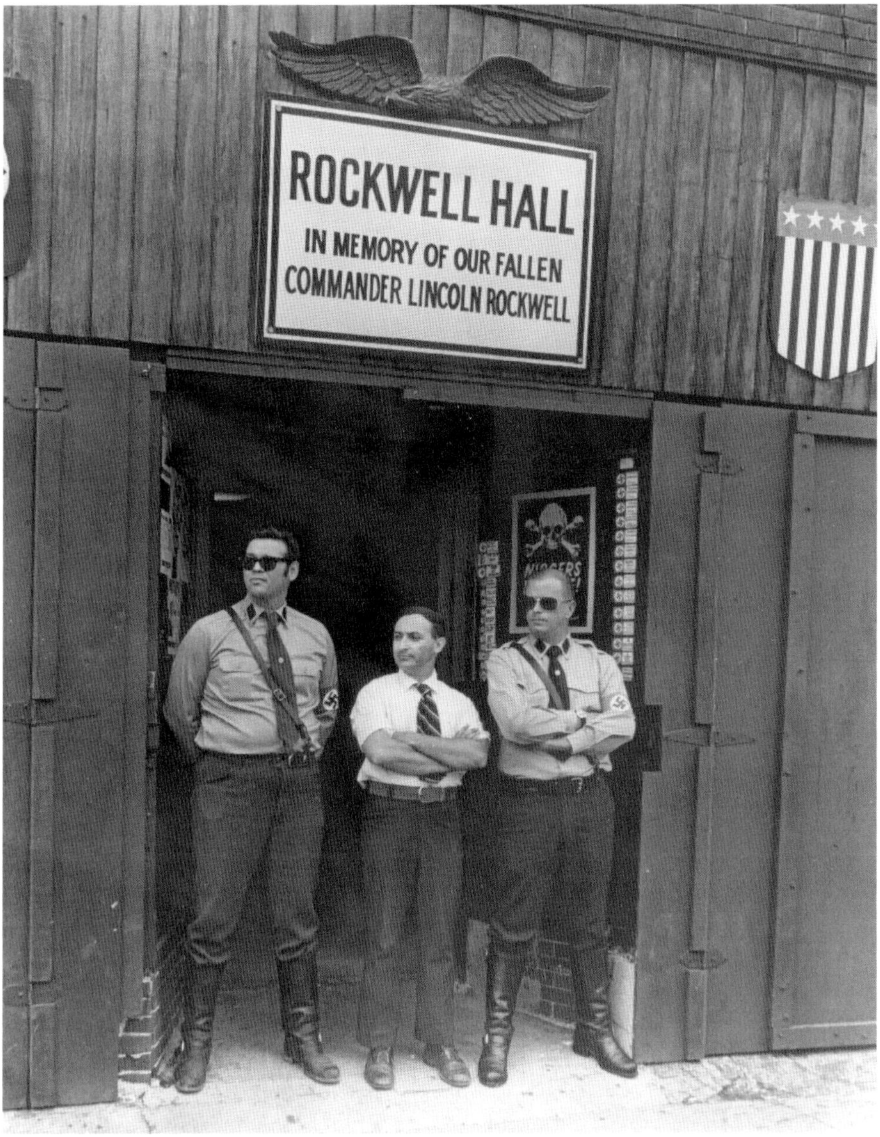

Frank Joseph

In 1977, Frank Collin was acquitted in circuit court of two disorderly conduct charges stemming from a rally and march in Marquette Park in October 1975. That rally attracted about 500 demonstrators.

The judge ruled that Collin, as local head of the National Socialist Party of America, was not guilty because he did not incite the crowd to violence by either his language or behavior. Collin testified that he carried signs and distributed T-shirts bearing swastikas but instructed persons attending the rally to be orderly.

"It was a difficult decision to make—separating my personal feelings from what I believe the law to be," the judge said. "Their message was obnoxious to an overwhelming number of enlightened people, but that alone is not sufficient for a finding of guilty."

In 1979, he was arrested and convicted of child molestation and given a sentence of seven years.

After serving his time in prison, Collin reinvented himself, began going by the name of Frank Joseph, and penned several New Age books.

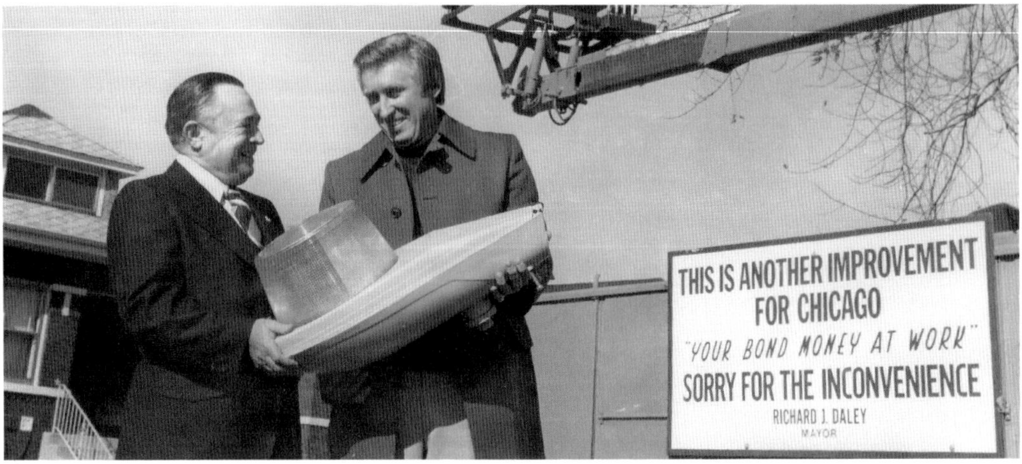

Frank D. Savickas

Frank Savickas was the first person of Lithuanian heritage to be elected to the Illinois Legislature, where he spent four years in the House of Representatives and 21 in the Senate. Throughout his career, he was known as a strong defender and supporter of the communities he represented, which included the Marquette Park and Garfield Ridge areas.

Born and raised on the Southwest Side, he attended St. Rita High School. The 25-year Democratic legislative veteran and 15th Ward committeeman started out in the Illinois House in 1967 and moved to the Senate in 1971.

He rose to become chairman of the Senate labor committee and an assistant majority leader. Wielding significant influence, he became known for his independence during battles over the leadership of the Senate Democrats in the 1980s and did not hesitate to cross the political line if it meant getting things done for his constituents.

He was the recipient of many Outstanding Legislator of the Year awards, including Environmental Legislator of the Year in 1982. But according to his daughter Sherry Brticevich, her father was particularly proud to have received the Man of the Year award from the International Brotherhood of Operating Engineers Local 150.

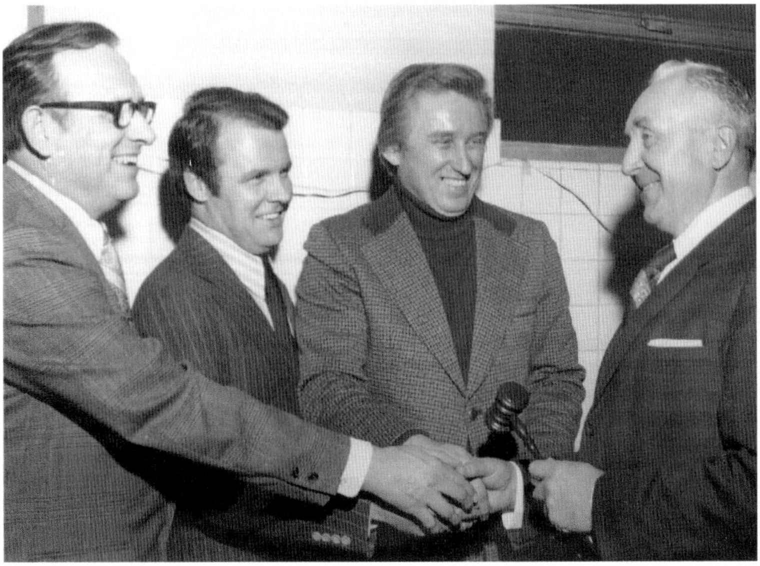

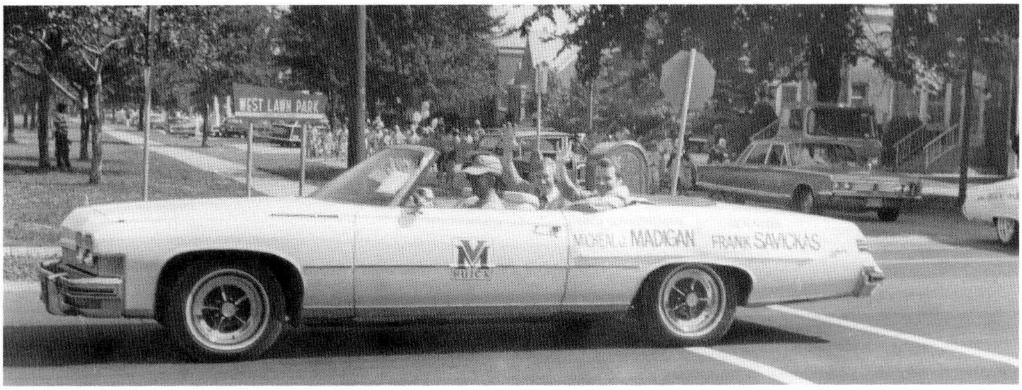

Legislator Savickas

In a legislative career that spanned a quarter century under five different mayors, Frank Savickas remained protective of the communities he served and presented numerous bills directed at the rights of senior citizens and workers, fighting off attacks that would have reduced workers' rights. He was at the forefront of efforts to reintroduce the back to basics curriculum in public schools and preserve Midway Airport.

Savickas was a member of the Lithuanian Chamber of Commerce and the Cardinal Mundelein Council of the Knights of Columbus.

In addition to supporting legislation aimed at assisting laborers, the elderly, and the disabled, Savickas was not averse to teasing the Springfield establishment. In 1985, he sponsored a measure allowing 10-year veterans of the legislature to automatically become lawyers. Savickas's reasoning was that legislators know more about making the laws that others litigate. The bill did not become law, however. Frank Savickas died on his 66th birthday.

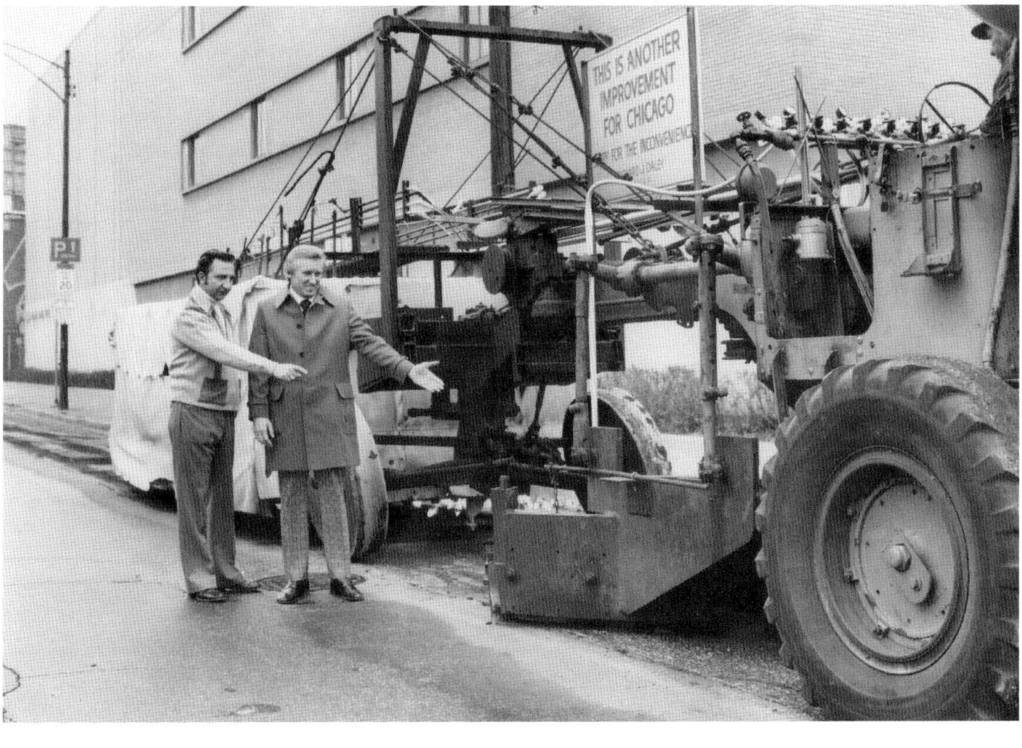

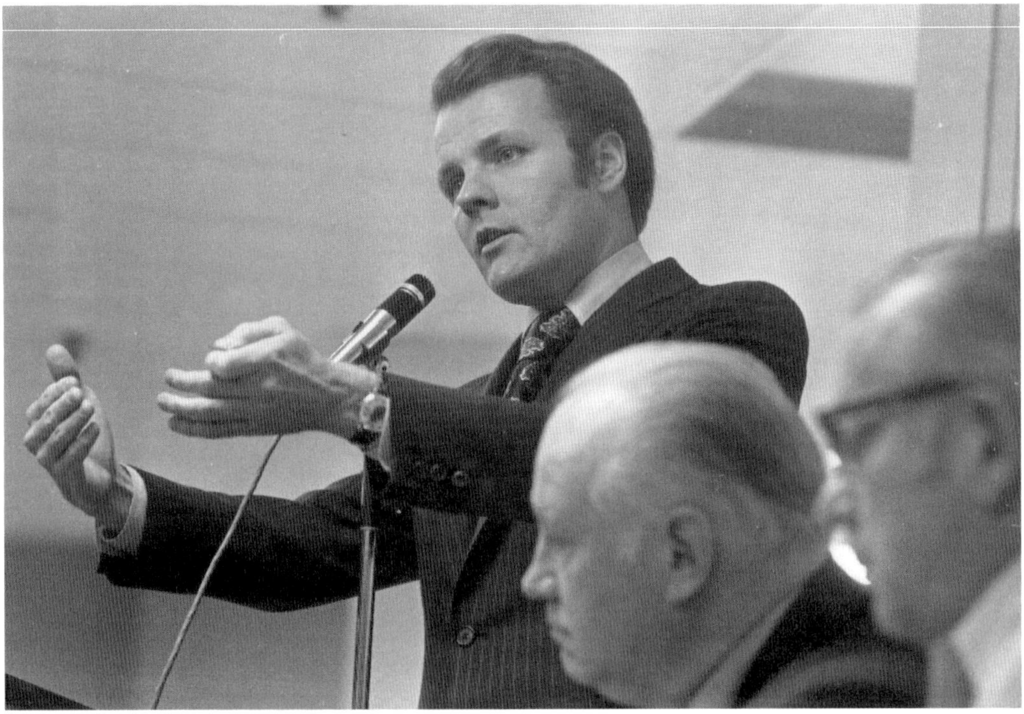

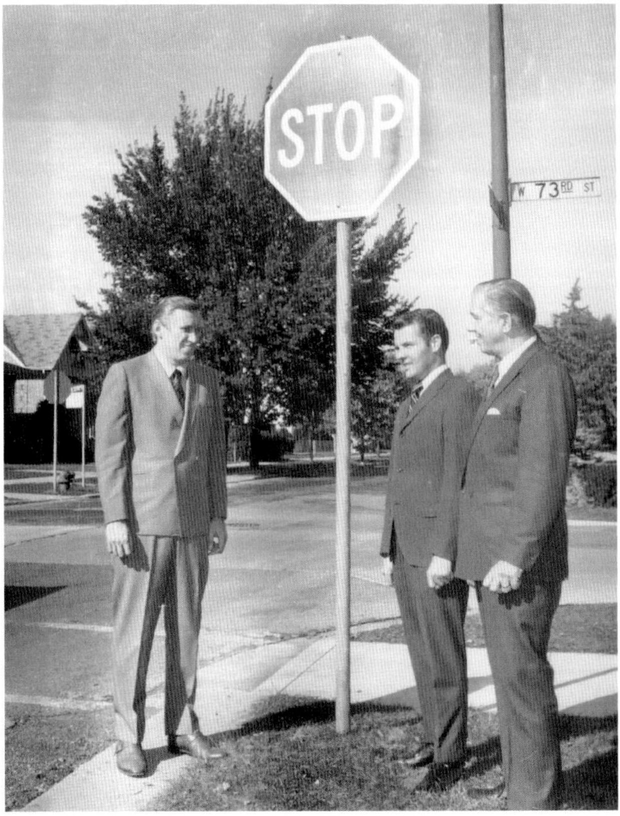

Michael J. Madigan

A lifelong resident of Chicago, Michael J. Madigan was born in the Southwest Side district he has represented. Attending St. Adrian Grammar School, he went on to St. Ignatius College Prep, the University of Notre Dame, and Loyola University Law School.

Voters first elected Madigan as their delegate to the 1970 Constitutional Convention and then later that year as state representative in November. As of this writing, he has won reelection in every election since that time.

When he was reelected as Speaker of the House in January 2015, he had held that position continuously since 1983, with the exception of 1995–1996, when there was a Republican majority. He is the longest-serving House speaker in Illinois history and holds the record as the longest-serving state House speaker in US history.

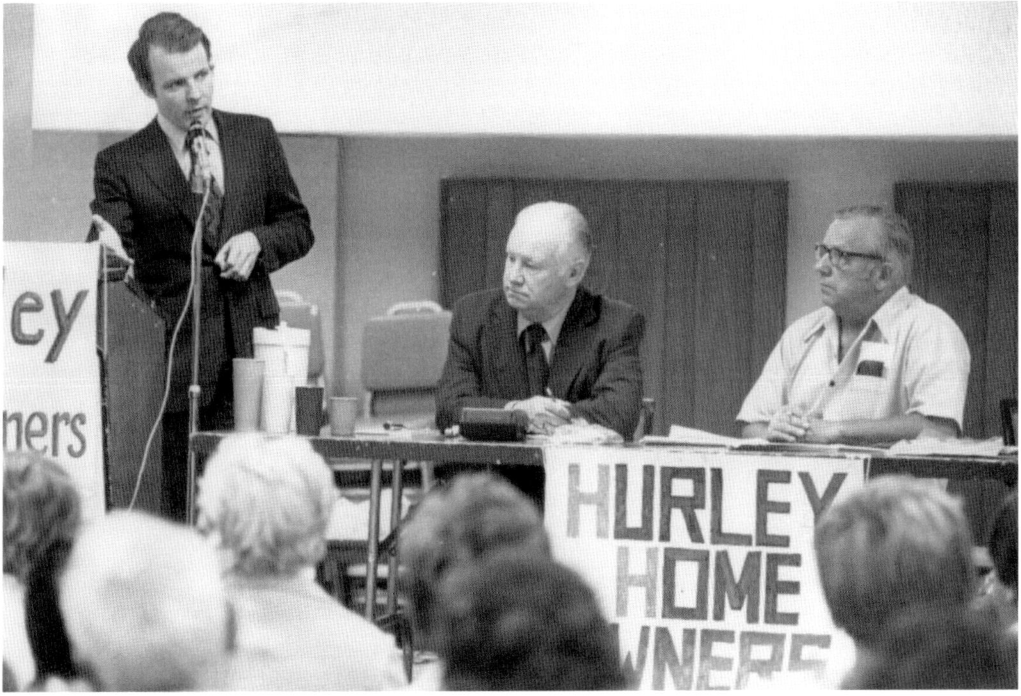

Speaker Madigan

Chicago Magazine rated him No. 2 on their recent list of most powerful Chicagoans. The *Chicago Sun-Times* twice rated him as one of Illinois's Ten Best Legislators. The *Illinois Political Reporter* designated Madigan Most Effective Representative. His work has time and again received honors from civic, community, educational, and business organizations. In a November 2013 *Chicago Magazine* article, Michael Madigan was said to be "as close to a king (in Illinois) as it gets."

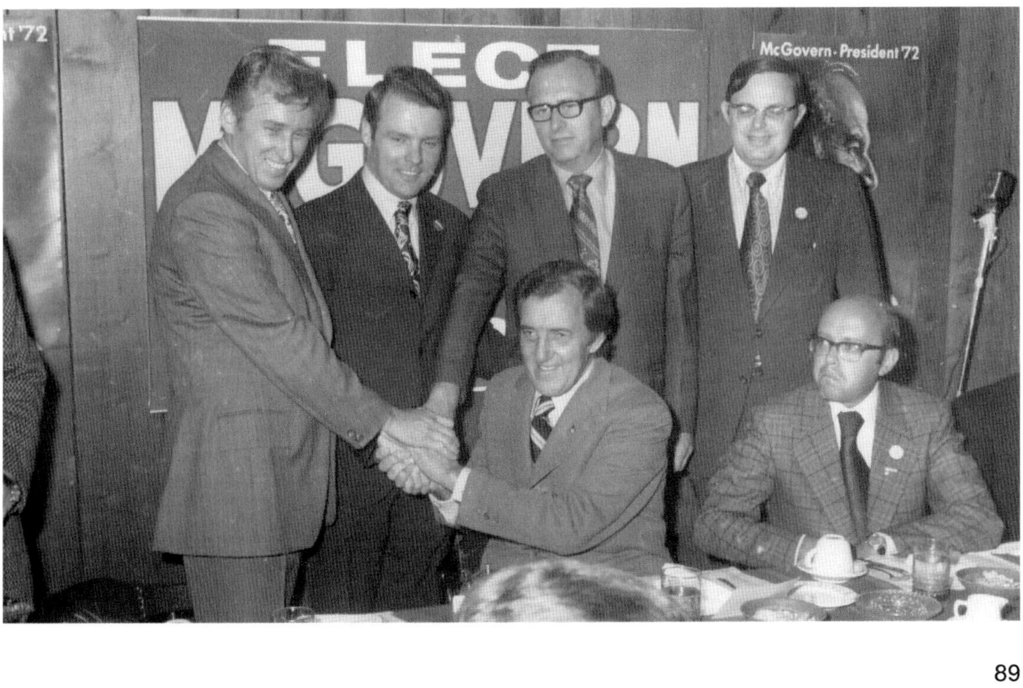

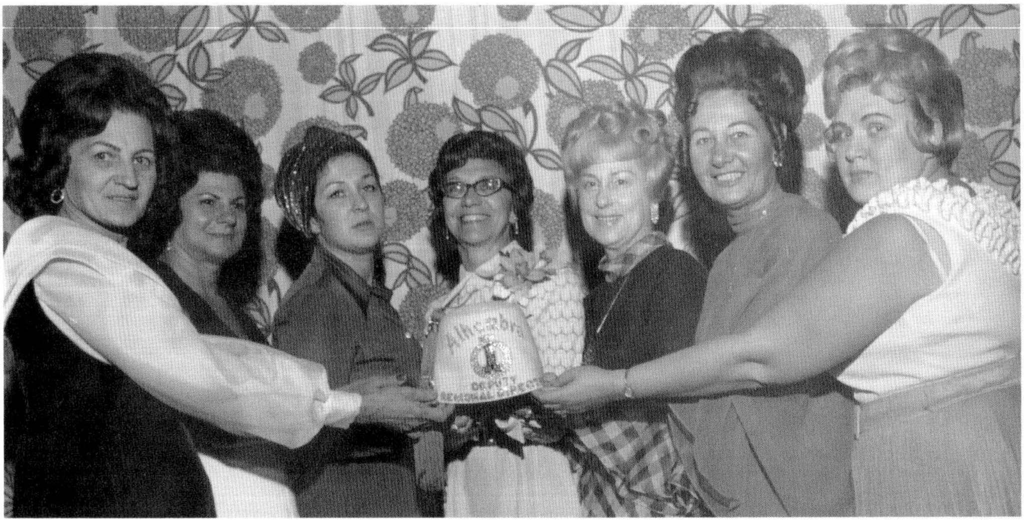

Frances Loepker

Frances Loepker devoted her life to community service and volunteer work. For many years, Loepker was best known as the executive secretary for the Chicago Lawn Chamber of Commerce and in that capacity served as chairperson of many chamber events, including making sure Santa arrived on time and assuring he had a welcoming committee to greet him when he did.

She began the Welcome Wagon in Chicago Lawn in the 1950s and as a complement to the Welcome Wagon, created Loepker Community Hostess Service, which she served as president.

The resale shop of Holy Cross Hospital, known as the Attic, was operated by the Holy Cross Auxiliary under the direction of Frances Loepker. She managed the store and spearheaded fundraisers for several decades.

For almost 30 years, there was nary an event on Sixty-Third Street or one in connection with the hospital in which Loepker did not take part.

And even with all of those activities to keep her busy, she was also active in the Alhambra group, working with disabled children.

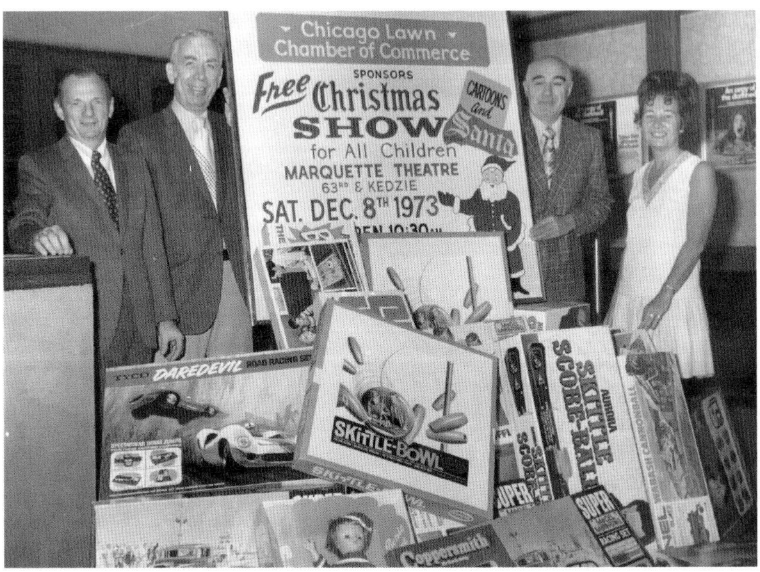

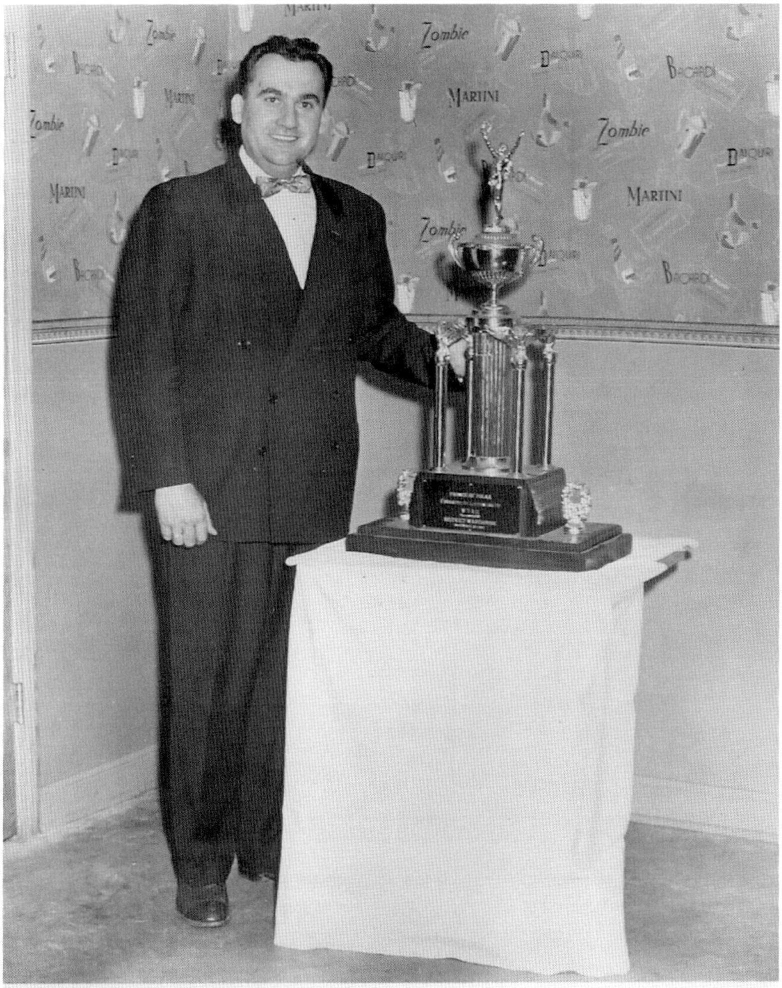

"Chicagoland's Prince of Polka"
EDDIE KOROSA

Adam "Eddie" Korosa

Eddie Korosa, probably best known in Chicago for his Baby Doll Polka Club and his hit song of the same name, started playing his first button-box accordion at the age of eight. By 10 years old, he was playing at parties and then as a teenager in local taverns with his band the Merry Makers.

In 1951, Eddie wrote and recorded "The Baby Doll Polka," which remains a perennial favorite. The following year he was named the "Prince of Polkas" by radio station WATQ.

In 1954, Korosa and his former wife, Irene Bara Korosa, built the Baby Doll Polka Club at Seventy-Third Street and Western Avenue, which became the broadcast home of his long-running television show *The Eddie Korosa Polka Party* and his radio show as well. Here he also gained notoriety for his ability to dance on the bar during his performances playing his button box.

In the next six years, he recorded five albums and then in 1964 had another hit single with "All I Need Is You."

In 1998, Eddie Korosa was inducted into the International Polka Association Hall of Fame in the Pioneer category.

Like his brother John, he loved to entertain. He loved his audience, and they loved him. (Courtesy of Cheryl Korosa.)

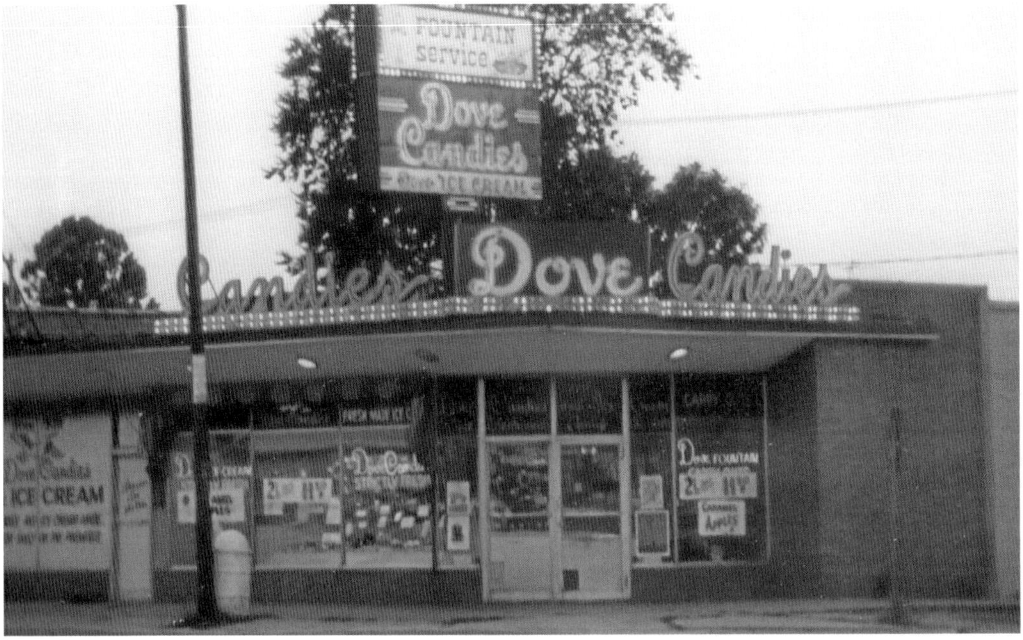

Michael Stefanos

Michael Stefanos, the son of the man that put first-class ice cream on a stick in 1956, took his father's idea, introduced it into supermarket chains, and then integrated products into markets from coast to coast. His father, Leo, was born in Greece, and when he came to America he settled on the Southwest Side. Legend has it that he was alarmed when his son Michael ran hastily down the street in pursuit of an ice-cream truck. And from that incident, Leo decided to create his own ice-cream bars in the back of his candy store.

Leo had opened Dove Candies in 1939, and once he perfected the recipe, he named the big square bars after his shop. The premium quality ice cream hand-dipped in bittersweet chocolate did not take long to catch on at all.

Michael is credited with expanding the business and then later selling it to candy giant M&M/Mars, Inc., which allowed his father's creation to be enjoyed across the United States. (Above, courtesy of Ed Kwiatkowski.)

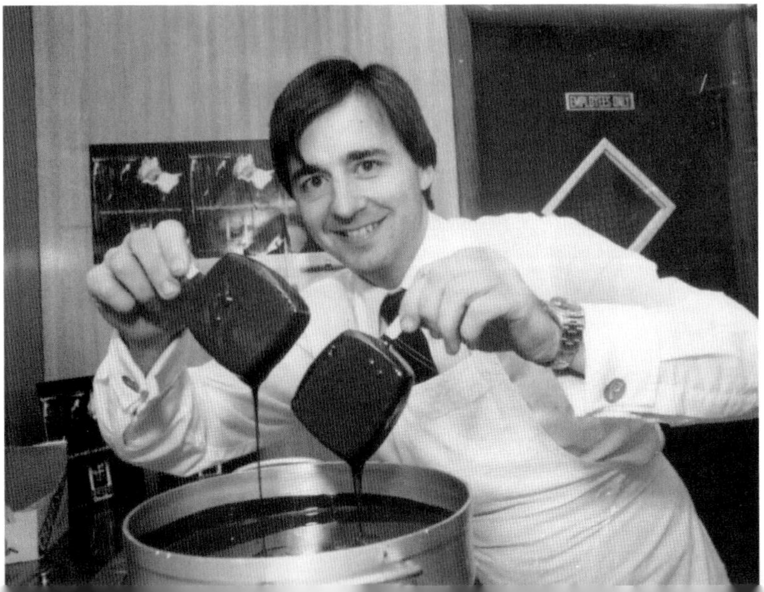

CHAPTER FIVE

Rewriting History

Those of you who say it can't be done are getting in the way of those of us who are doing it.

—John Barnes

Every chapter in a neighborhood's history has positive people who do what they feel is right and in doing so help to change the current of the neighborhood's flow. Sometimes it is by their actions. Sometimes it is by their inaction, their steadiness, which keeps others grounded.

Pat Cronin took a football team with a 0-9 record and within three years produced a state championship team. Andrew Rozdilsky went from his day job as a supervisor at International Harvester to being the unofficial mascot of the Chicago White Sox.

Art Velasquez founded one of the largest Hispanic-owned businesses in the Midwest and continues to give back time and again with his philanthropic donations of time and fortune.

Mike Trost, named the "Founding Father of the Hobby Industry," operated his business for 78 years in the same location. He got his start in his parents' hardware store.

Joe Herbert built his business next to his father's and turned his love of photography into a career that has spanned over seven decades.

Jeffery Silhan took over his father's legacy of Musichorale. Mike Gehant learned the retail business from his father and continued to run his store as the last remaining authentic variety store of its kind for 30 years. Paul McCarthy took over from his father at Marquette Bank and assured that the institution held firmly to its South Side roots.

Jack Klaus was the Hubbard High School teacher and counselor who was always available to help out and keep things running smoothly.

Samir Ibrahim Ahmed Odeh was called a charismatic visionary who actively worked toward bringing people together and helping Arab immigrants adapt to life here. His wife, Camille, was founding director of the Southwest Youth Collaborative.

Seeing unfairness around him sparked Jim Capraro's life work in community development. With his leadership and revitalization, neighborhood reinvestment became the norm.

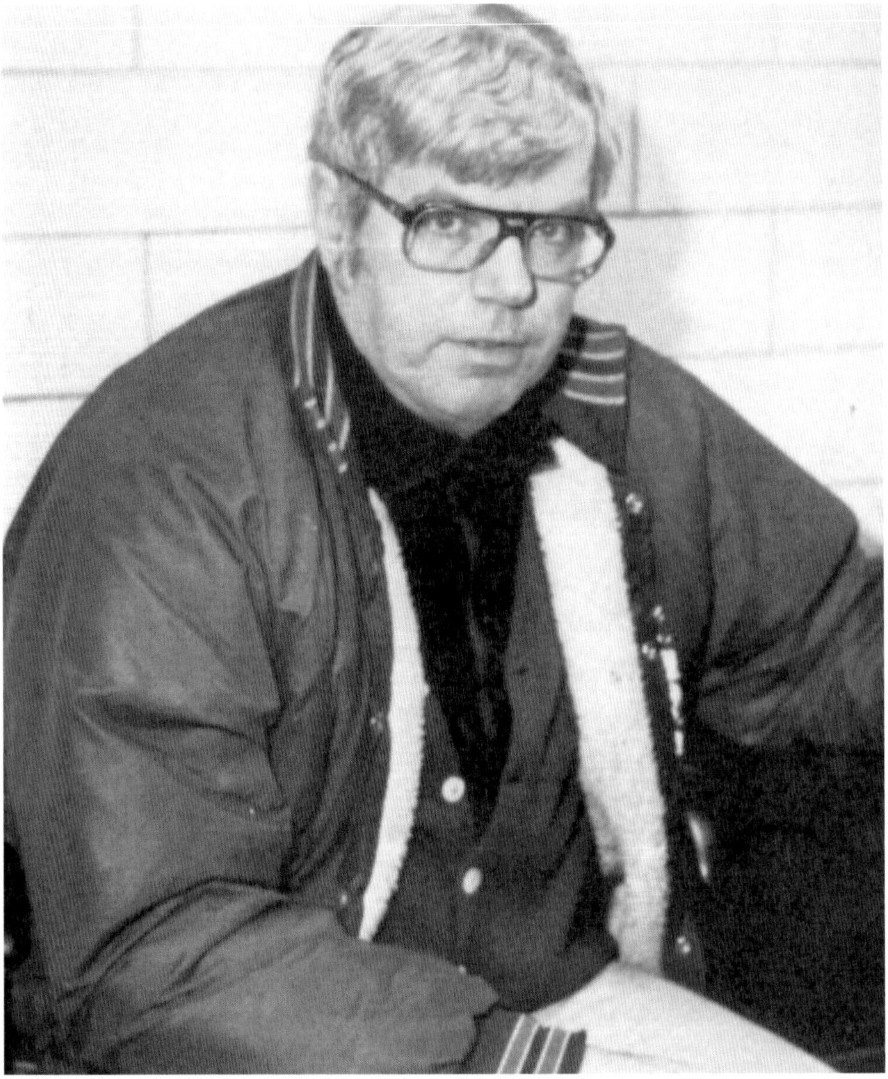

Maurice Patrick "Pat" Cronin

The most successful coach in St. Rita football history, Pat Cronin won 196 games, over 100 of which were at St. Rita, won three city championships (1970, 1971, 1977) and a state championship in 1978, and was Illinois Coach of the Year in 1978 and Missouri Coach of the Year in 1960. He was inducted into the Catholic League Hall of Fame and has also been a three-time league Coach of the Year.

Pat Cronin was the son of a Chicago police officer Maurice Cronin, who was killed in the line of duty. He was born and raised in Chicago. Pat was a tall Irishman, a confirmed bachelor who loved football, books, beer, and Italian food.

He commanded respect from his players and got it. His no-nonsense approach inspired the team and was just a part of his legend. If boys could not pay their tuition, he was known to dig into his own pocket to help out.

Coach Cronin built the St. Rita Mustangs into a perennial state-ranked powerhouse, taking the team from a 0-9 record in 1968 to going 5-4 in 1969, producing an 11-2 prep bowl champion in 1970, and then garnering the state championship in 1971, turning them into an unbeaten championship team. (Courtesy of St. Rita High School.)

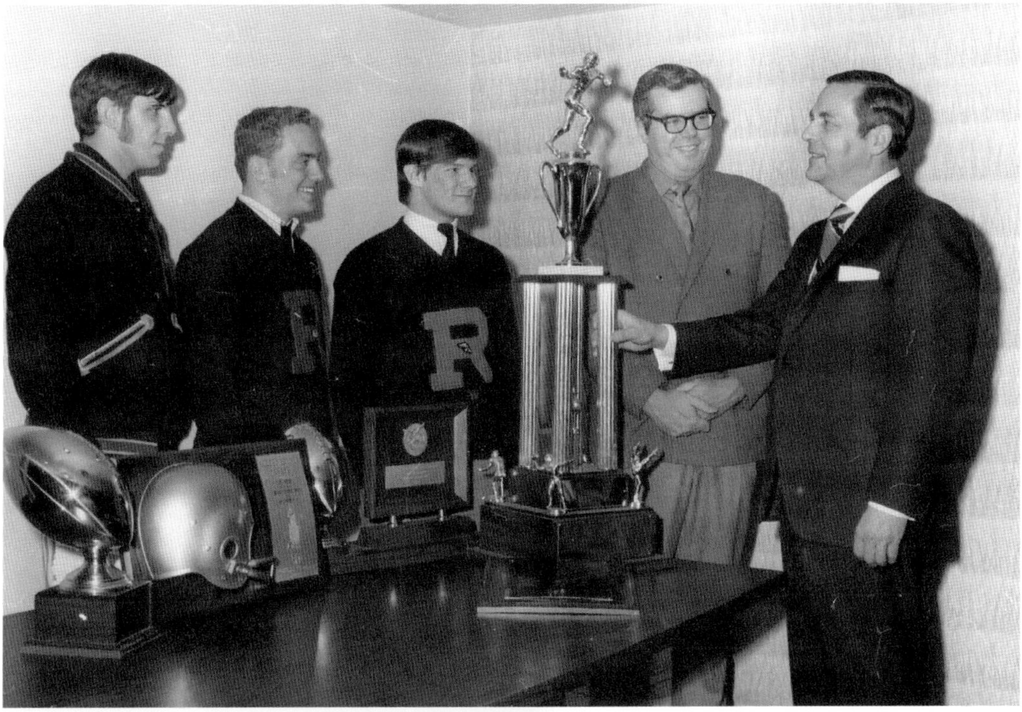

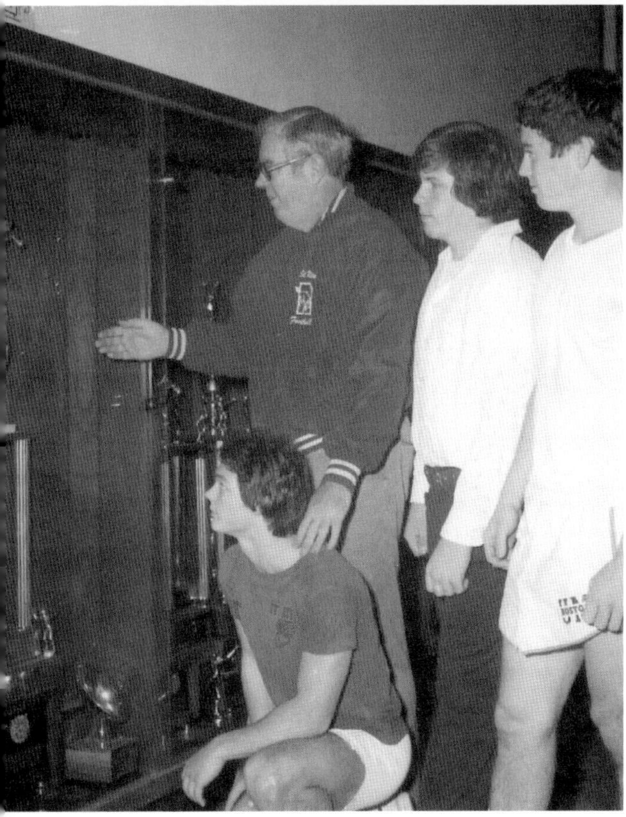

Coach Cronin

Pat Cronin died at the age of 49. In the 12 years prior he had suffered six heart attacks. His doctors had advised him to quit coaching.

In an interview shortly before his death, he said, "I can always sit in a dark room and wait for something to happen but I'd rather be out on the field doing what I love to do."

Just before watching his team win the last game of the season, he was inducted into the St. Rita Hall of Fame.

A plaque to the legendary coach sits in the end zone of Pat Cronin Field in Doyle Stadium. (Below, courtesy of St. Rita High School.)

Marzell "Mike" Trost

In a 1997 profile in the trade magazine *Model Retailer*, Mike Trost was named the "Founding Father of the Hobby Industry." His Trost Hobby Shop, with 78 years in the same location at 3111 West Sixty-Third Street, got its start in his parents' hardware store.

The Trost family entered the Southwest Side business landscape in 1922 when the late Edward Trost began serving local residents as a painting contractor. At the same time, his wife, the late Ernestine, opened a retail hardware and paint store.

In 1928, Mike and his brother Edward opened a hobby department in a corner of the hardware store, making it one of the first hobby centers in the nation. In a *Southwest News-Herald* interview, Mike said the ownership of the new enterprise took a strange turn several years later when the two sons decided to re-divide their assets, which consisted of the hobby shop and a Ford Roadster. Edward took the car, and Mike ended up as owner of the hobby shop.

After he got the retail business well under way, Mike moved into a new field when he opened a wholesale division, which grew into a 40,000-square-foot warehouse. Then he expanded his retail store, adding the next storefront to his in 1965 and then yet another storefront in 1974.

Mike built the hobby shop into the largest in the southwest Chicagoland area. He was assisted in the operation of the business by his wife, Verna, his sister Betty, and manager Edward Transier.

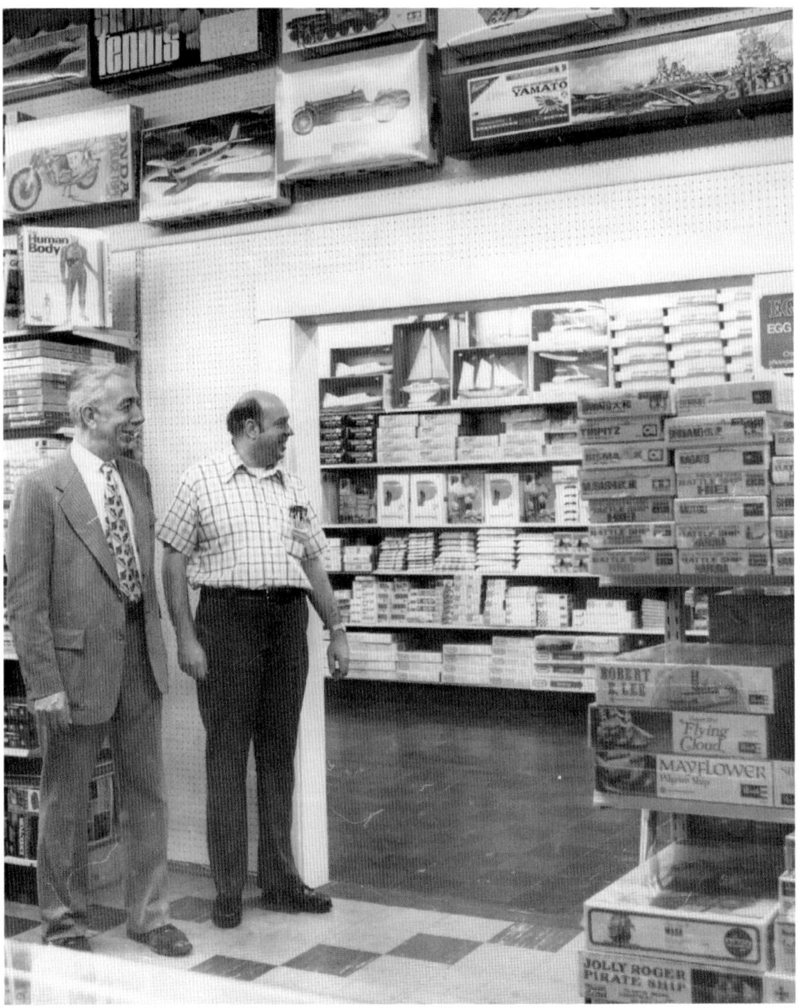

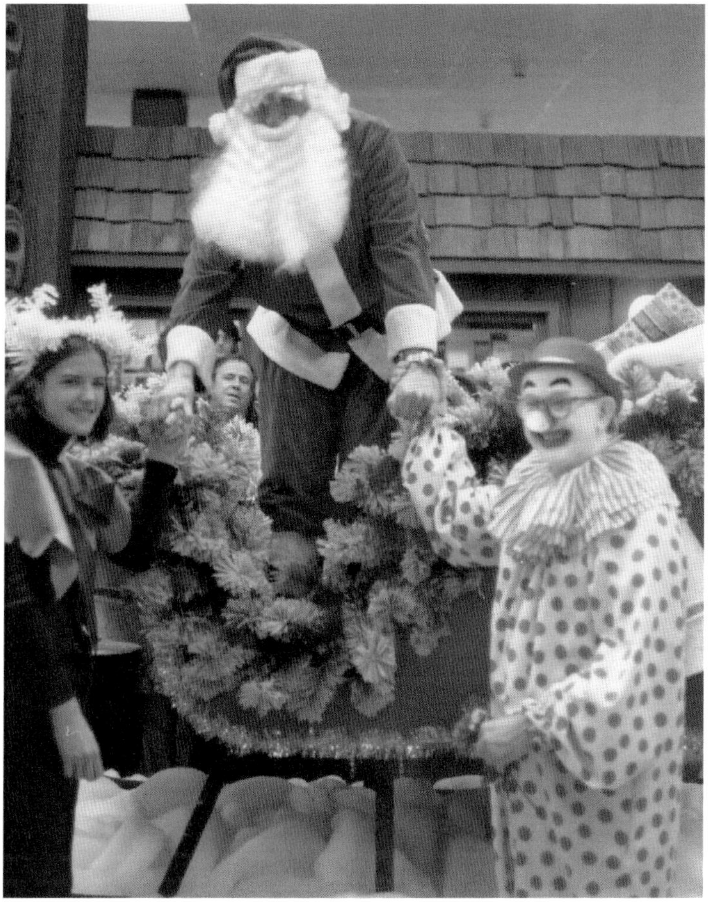

Andrew Rozdilsky

More commonly known throughout Chicago and the Southwest Side as the popular Andy the Clown, Andrew Rozdilsky was a supervisor for International Harvester, a World War II Army veteran, a member of the Loyal Order of the Moose, a member of the Chicago Lawn Sertoma group for children, and the unofficial mascot of the Chicago White Sox for three decades.

In the early 1960s, he began taking a week's vacation every year at Christmastime in order to entertain at local hospitals, where he would spend at least four hours at each one, cheering patients with his clown act and magic tricks, all for free.

While he enjoyed amusing patients of all ages with his jokes and antics, he got the most pleasure from entertaining the children in the pediatrics section.

He often said whenever he could bring a smile; he knew he had achieved something.

His business cards read, "A smile wins friends, chases blues, lightens work, and costs nothing, so keep smiling."

Rozdilsky began playing the Andy the Clown character when he decided to wear the costume to a bowling outing in 1960. Later that evening, he decided to keep the costume on as he and his friends went to a White Sox game. An overwhelmingly favorable response to his costume inspired him to continue to don the outfit at White Sox games at Comiskey Park for the next 30 years. He was a fan favorite with his blinking red nose and long cheers for White Sox players.

In 1985, he was given special recognition by his own home community when he received a plaque from the Chicago Lawn Sertoma Club during the citywide program honoring him at Comiskey Park for 25 years of entertaining baseball fans.

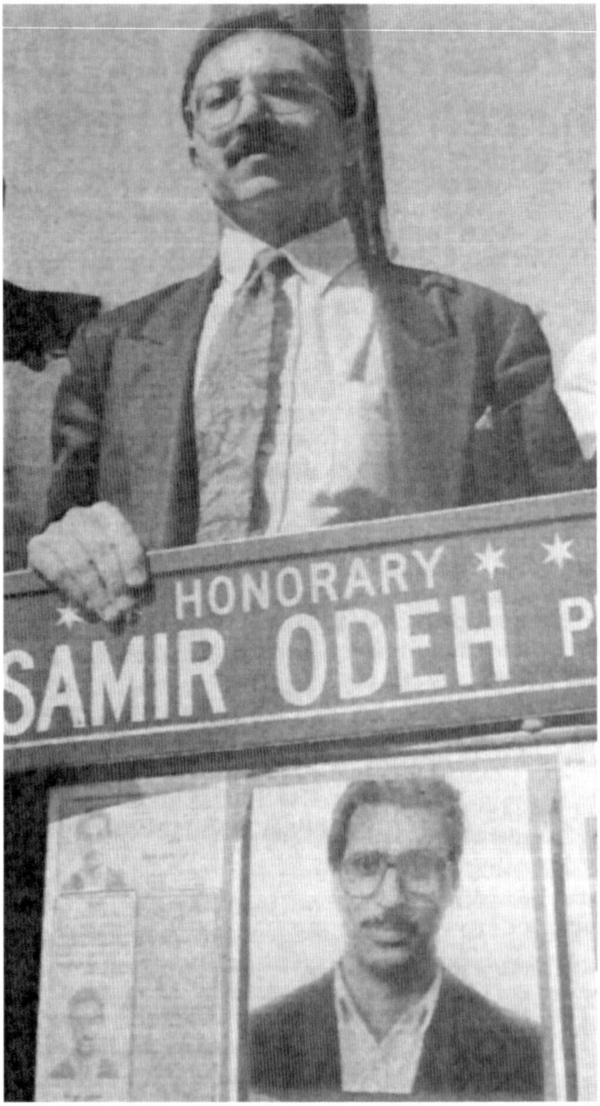

Samir Ibrahim Ahmed Odeh

In 1996, Sixty-Third Street between Troy and Kedzie Avenues was dedicated as Honorary Samir Odeh Place. He died at the early age of 41 in 1994. Called a charismatic visionary, he was instrumental in the formation of the Advisory Commission on Arab American Affairs in Chicago. The former West Lawn resident cofounded the Arab American Community Center with the purpose of helping Arab immigrants adapt to life here. He is also the first Arab American to have a street named in his honor.

Samir's wife, Camile, said his West Lawn café called Random Worlds was a place "where cultures went and borders disappeared." Throughout his life here, he actively worked toward bringing people together. She said he made the world and the Southwest Side a better place.

Pictured here in a *Southwest News-Herald* photograph is Yasine Odeh holding a street sign honoring his late cousin (inset) Samir Odeh.

The *Chicago Tribune* quoted Alfred Rogers, then-president of the Southwest Community Congress as saying Odeh's efforts were valuable in helping to combat the prejudices and stereotypes Arab Americans sometimes encounter.

Camille Odeh

Camille Odeh has been widely known in the community as the founding director of the Southwest Youth Collaborative (SYC), a community-based network of youth and community-development organizations working together to help youth from as young as five years old to 19 unleash their potential and grow into active contributing members of the neighborhood.

Organized in 1992 with support from the Chicago Community Trust, SYC began with three afterschool youth centers in the Chicago Lawn area.

"Our whole mission at that time was as a quality, affordable, after school program. Many kids had no where to go," said Camille. "Our vision was that each kid feels at home here."

Under Camille's leadership, it grew for 20 years, forming partnerships with youth and local churches, schools, and businesses in the area.

The mural on the east side of the Inman building is the work of the collaborative.

Camille has also served as a director of the Chapin Hall Center for Children.

She married Samir Odeh in 1983, and they had two children.

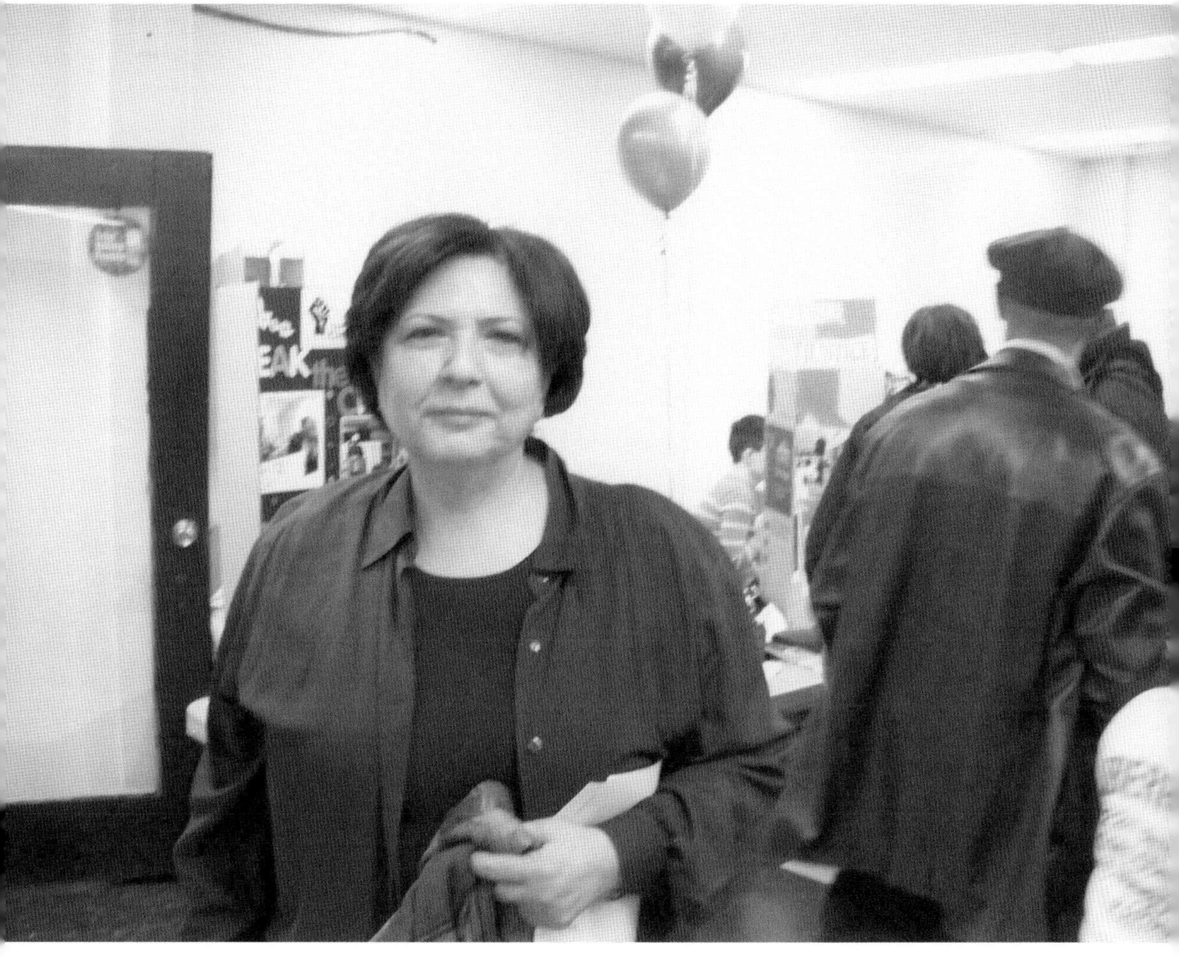

Jeffery Silhan

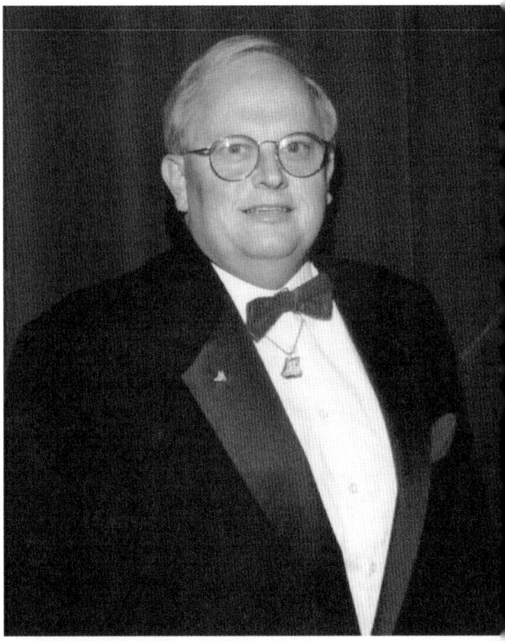

Jeffrey Silhan is well known as a soloist, director, and musician throughout Chicago. Growing up on the Southwest Side in the shadow of Musichorale, it was inevitable that when his father, Art Silhan, decided it was time to retire his baton, Jeff would take over.

At the age of 19, Jeff took on his first directing position in a small Lutheran church in Bettendorf, Iowa. He has been the choir director at both Grace Church and Chicago Lawn Methodist as well as Zion Lutheran and Oak Lawn Community Church. He also directed the Beverly Hills-Morgan Park Community Choir for three years.

He is best known for the job he stepped up to in 1980, that of director of the choir his father started back in 1947, Musichorale. As Art's schedule began expanding at the Lyric Opera, Jeff, who had been mentored by his father from the beginning, started taking over the directing duties. He has also formed smaller groups to perform independently known as the Ensemble and G.Q. (Both, courtesy of Linda Silhan.)

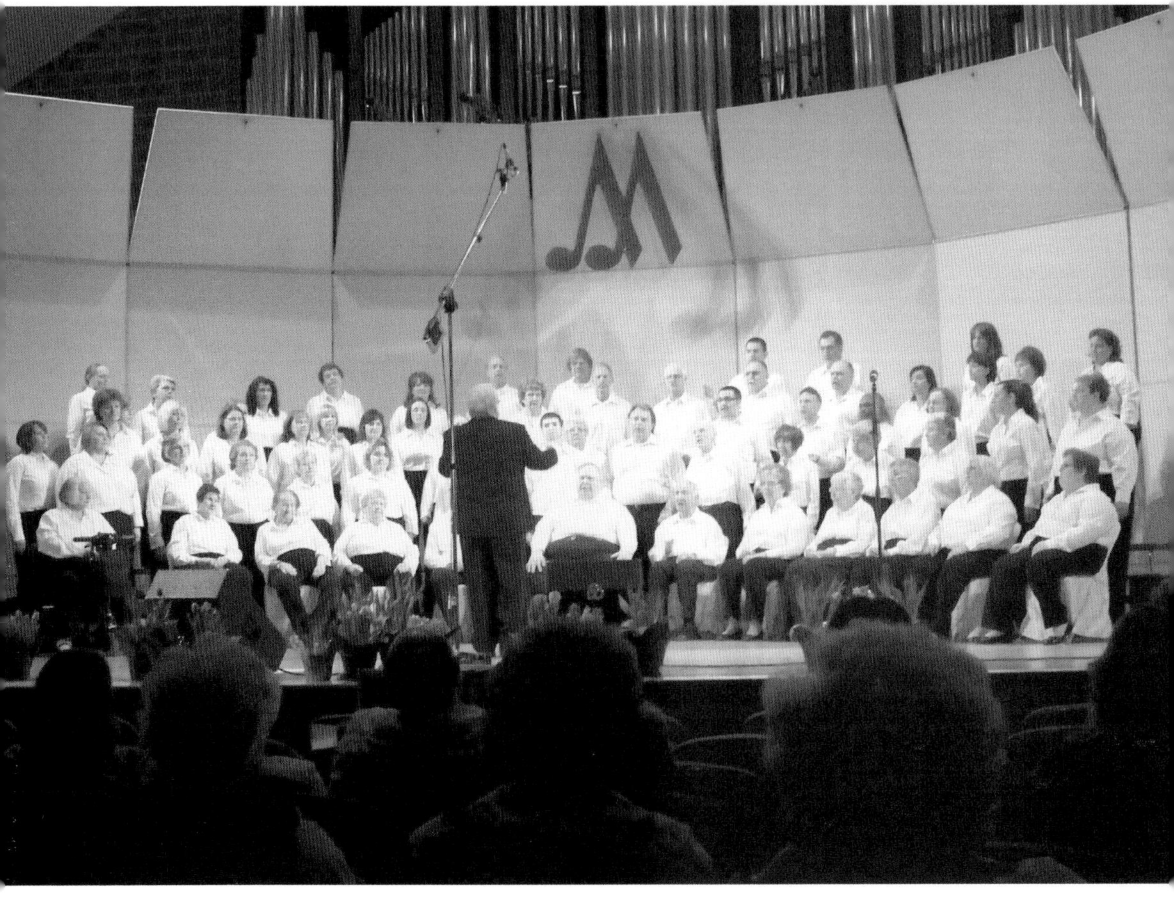

Arthur R. "Art" Velasquez

Arthur Velasquez is a founder and chairman of Azteca Foods, Inc., one of the largest Hispanic-owned businesses in the Midwest. He has appeared in television spots for Crain's Chicago Business as an example of the American Dream and what can be accomplished.

Art and his wife, Joanne, met at Marquette Park when they were 16 and 14 respectively. The couple married in 1960.

He and Joanne raised six children in the West Lawn neighborhood and became active in parish and park activities, with Art serving as president of the Holy Name Society at Queen of the Universe and Joanne working with West Lawn Little League. At the same time, both he and his wife remained faithful to their alma maters, serving on the boards of St. Rita and Maria High Schools.

Art has served on the boards of over 20 different not-for-profits. He sets aside at least five percent of pre-tax profit at his company for charity. Involved in the redevelopment of the Pilsen-Little Village area, he has served as chair and cochair of three capital campaigns related to the Mexican Fine Arts Center. He has been a trustee of the University of Illinois, the Museum of Science and Industry, and the Big Shoulders Fund.

Art earned his bachelor's degree at the University of Notre Dame and his MBA at the University of Chicago. He was awarded an honorary doctorate degree from St. Xavier University and Governors State. (Courtesy of Arthur Velasquez.)

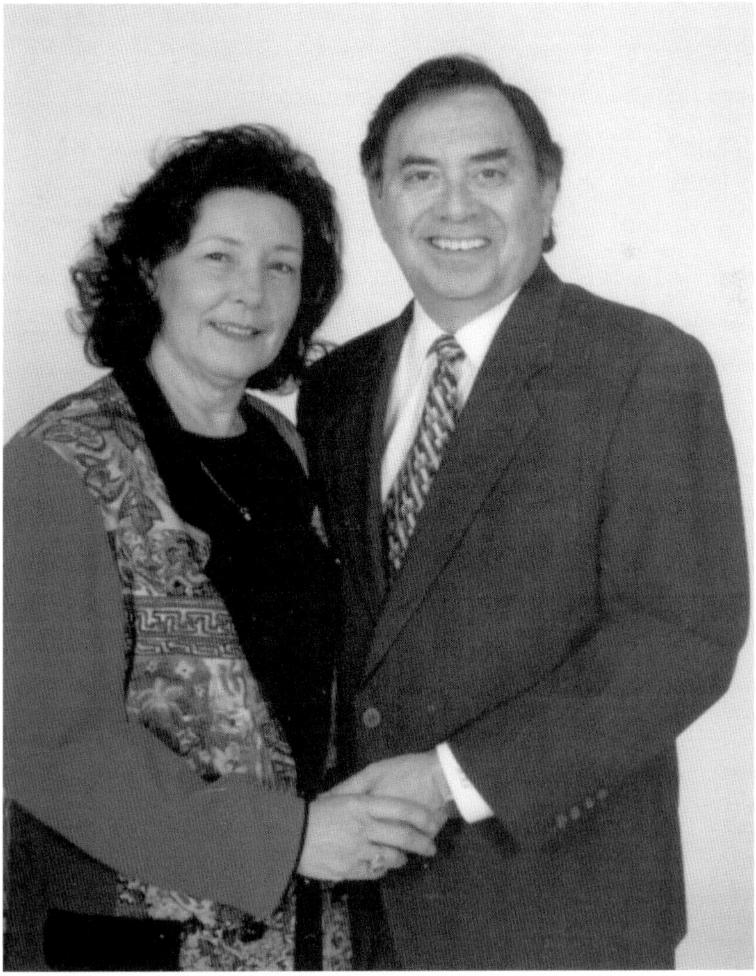

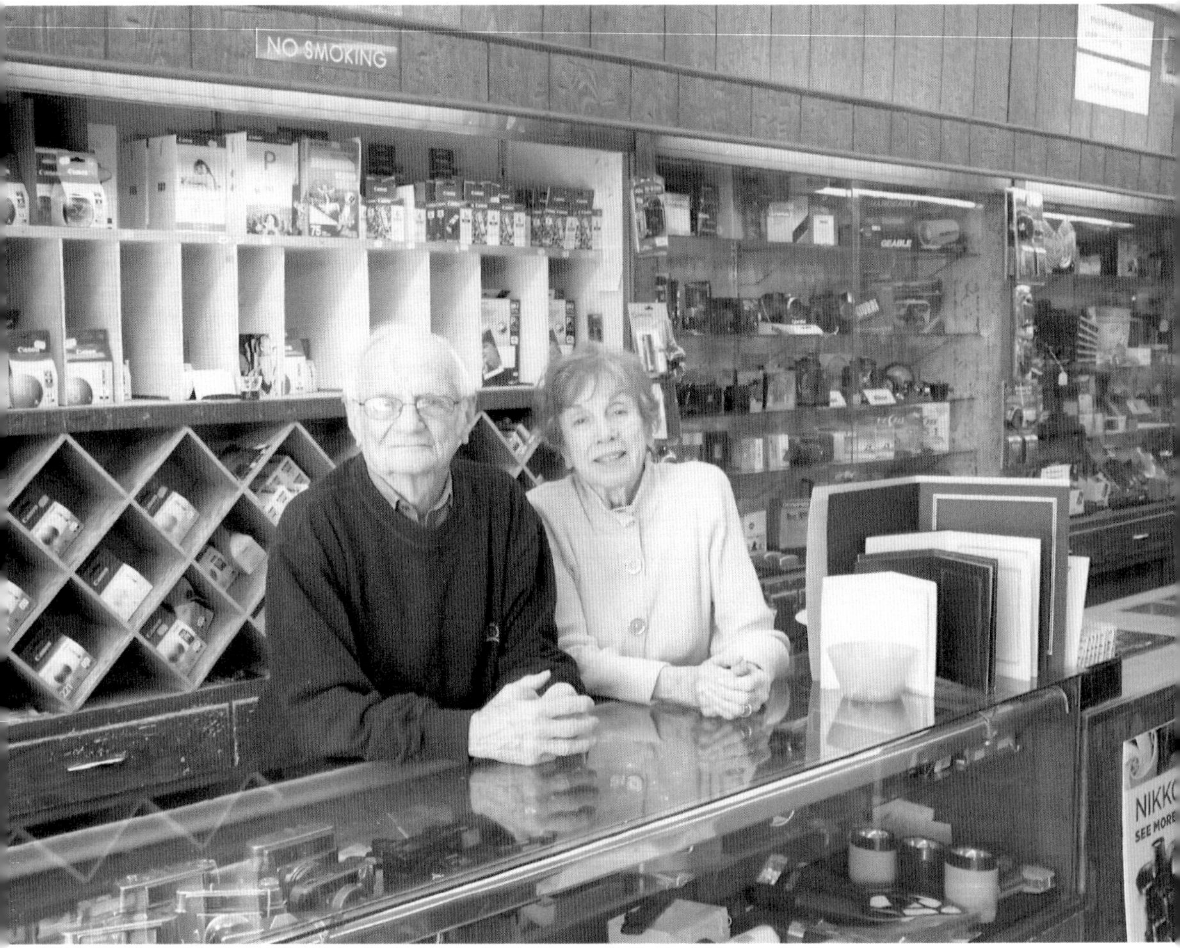

Joseph Herbert

To anyone living in the Chicago Lawn area within the last seven decades, the name Joe Herbert is familiar. To anyone with an interest in photography, Joe is the man to know. He and his Marquette Photo Supply have been the backbone of the Chicago Lawn Business District for over 70 years.

Joe, pictured here with his wife, Barbara, opened his business in 1945 when he was just 20 years old, turning one of his favorite pastimes into his life's work. The shop has been cited as the longest-running independent camera store.

Joe grew up right down the street. His father, Peter, was a barber and started his business at 6252 Spaulding Avenue, then moved to 3304 Sixty-Third Street and then 3312. Joe said when he was growing up he could see straight south to Marquette Road from the barbershop.

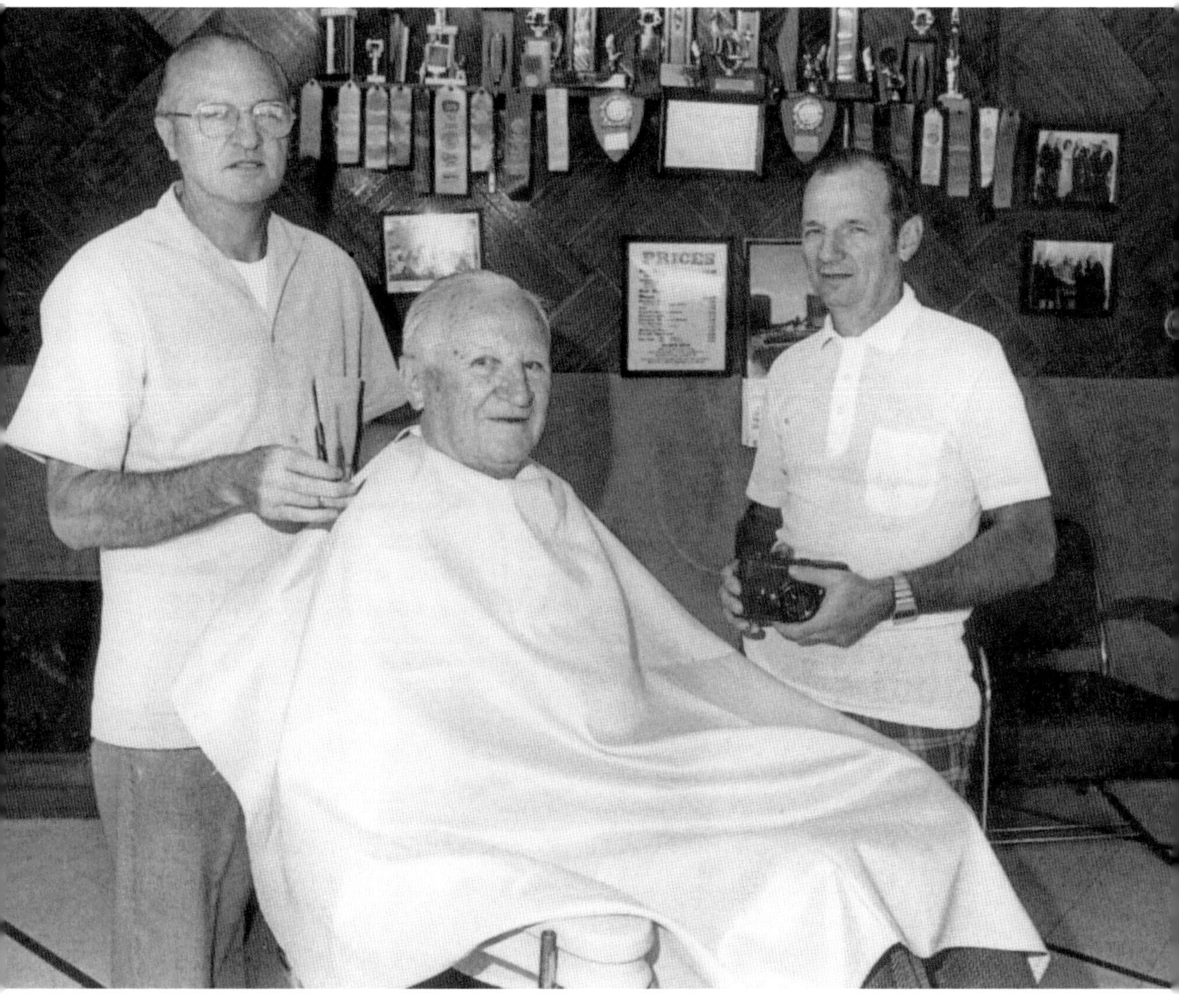

The Photography Expert

When Herbert first went into business, it was not easy to get camera equipment and photography supplies. He started with a small place at 3310 Sixty-Third street and three years later moved next to his dad's barbershop. As Herbert built up his customer base, he earned quite the reputation as the go-to guy for anything in photography. He has maintained quite a following and kept up with the times by using the Internet to his advantage, now selling to customers overseas as well.

Herbert's brother joined their father in the barber business next door, and they built a door so they could easily walk back and forth. His sister-in-law Marion also came on board, helping Herbert in the camera shop. When Herbert married his wife, Barbara, who had formerly owned the cleaners down the street, she joined the family in business as well. Throughout the years, Herbert has been active in the local business community, serving on the board of the chamber of commerce, several times as president. (Courtesy of Joe Herbert.)

Jack Klaus

Born and raised in Chicago Lawn, Jack Klaus was best known in his roles as an English teacher and senior guidance counselor at Hubbard High School and later as president of the Chicago Lawn Historical Society. And he seemed to love each phase of his life equally.

His students said he was the kind of teacher one could talk to about anything, and when they came back to visit, which they often did, he remembered each name.

He loved the historical society and spent countless hours organizing and preserving the collection. Klaus was not one for formality. He was also a big ice cream fan, so when he took over as president of the society, out went the silver tea service and china teacups used for refreshments at events and in came buckets of ice cream with three toppings—always chocolate fudge, strawberry, and butterscotch.

A confirmed bachelor, Klaus never strayed far from his childhood home, the one exception being his service in the Korean War.

Throughout his life, he gave a helping hand wherever and whenever he could to family, friends, students, and colleagues.

Klaus did not win the Nobel Prize, nor did he want to—he did better than that. He won the respect and admiration of all who knew him. (Courtesy of Donald Pointer.)

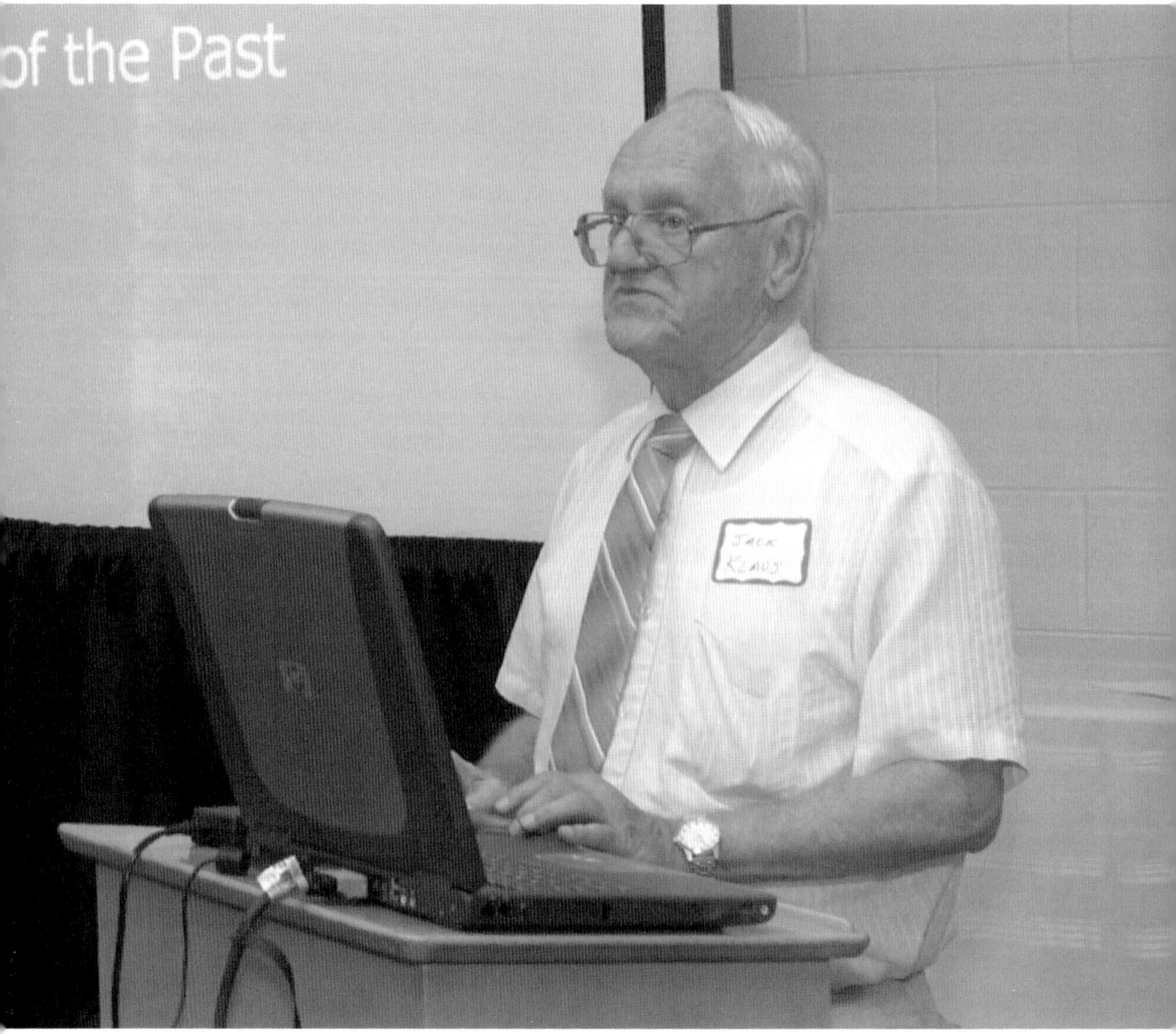

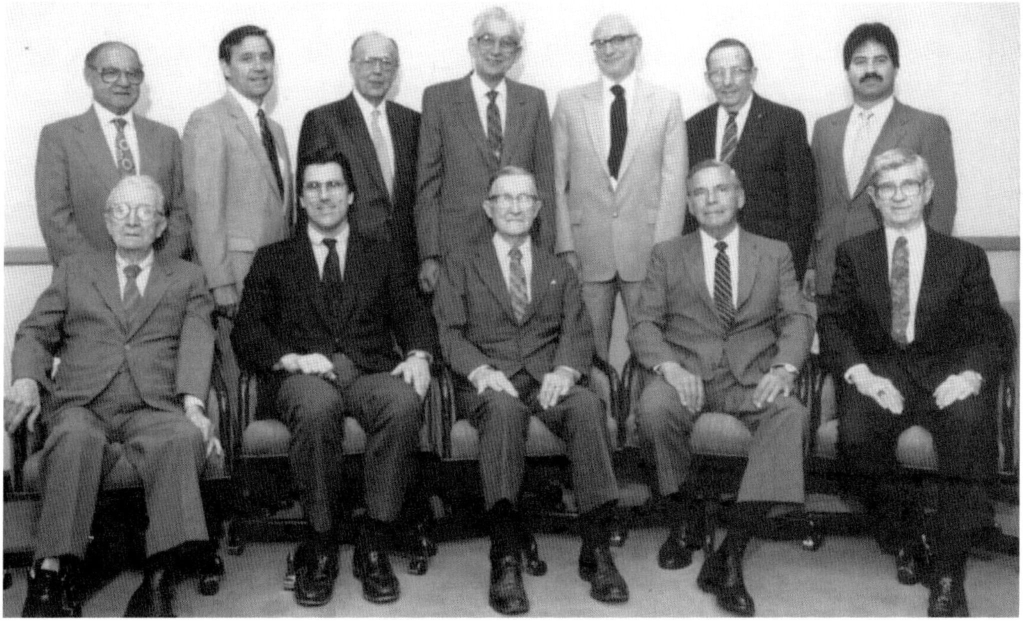

Paul McCarthy

Paul McCarthy succeeded his father, John McCarthy, as chairman of Marquette Bank. From the beginning, he held firmly to its South Side roots. While other businesses sought greener pastures, Paul made sure Marquette would grow and prosper in its flagship location while developing additional sites.

In 2007, Paul officially dedicated the newly renovated bank building and greatly enhanced grounds on Western Avenue.

"This renovation represents a $4 million investment in this community—and that is something that benefits all of us," said McCarthy at the dedication.

Marquette distinguishes itself from many other banking institutions by its commitment to community relations and community banking.

"As we have been since 1945, Marquette Bank is here to stay and here to serve the community. While this renovation took just 18 months to complete, the finished product will benefit our customers and the community for years to come," he affirmed. (Above, courtesy of Marquette Bank.)

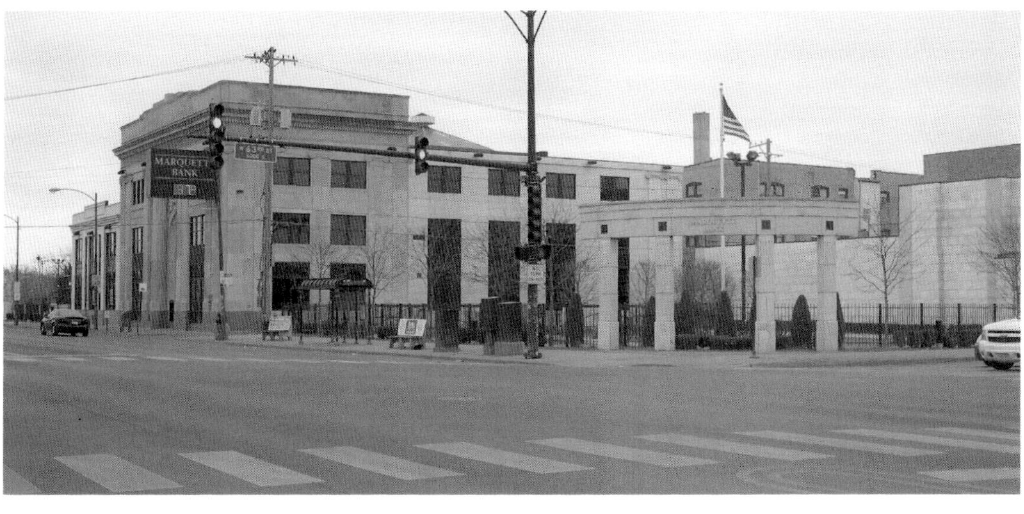

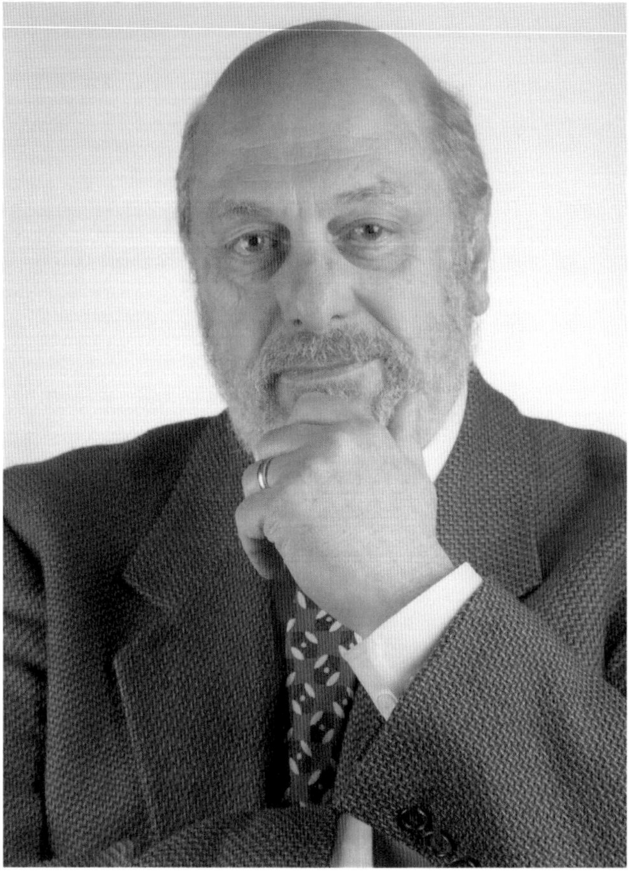

James "Jim" Capraro

Walk into any boardroom or community meeting on the Southwest Side. Mention the name Jim Capraro, and all heads look up, for the name Jim Capraro is synonymous with neighborhood vision and success. The son of Italian Catholic immigrants, Capraro grew up in Chicago Lawn in the 1950s and early 1960s. As a teenager, he witnessed a scene that profoundly changed his life—Martin Luther King Jr.'s march in Marquette Park. The demonstration, which met with people shouting obscenities, hurling beer bottles, and rioting, outraged the teenager.

As he was quoted in Mark Warren's *Fire in the Heart*, "How dare these people do this stuff? This is a democracy. People have a right to say things . . . and in fact be equal to everybody else."

This event sparked Capraro's life work in community development. In college, he got involved in organizing the antiwar movement and later took a job for the Southwest Community Congress working against block busting and redlining. As a community organizer he worked toward the passage of the Home Mortgage Disclosure Act and the Community Reinvestment Act.

Paul M. McCarthy, chairman of the board of Marquette Bank, recalled, "I remember some thirty years ago when my Dad (John F. McCarthy, a founding director of the bank and chairman of the board) said 'See if you can get Capraro on the board. He's a real go-getter.' He was exactly right. Many years later see what this go-getter has accomplished. It is because of Jim that the community has programs no one else has. Way back in 1978 Chicago Lawn had FHA Counseling. The real estate market was rampant. Jim got Chicago Lawn the only program in the country and avoided destruction of this neighborhood."

Jim Capraro was the founding executive director of Greater Southwest Development Corporation (GSDC). Under him, Greater Southwest achieved over $500 million in community development projects and created or retained over 6,000 jobs for his neighborhood. (Courtesy of Shawn Allee.)

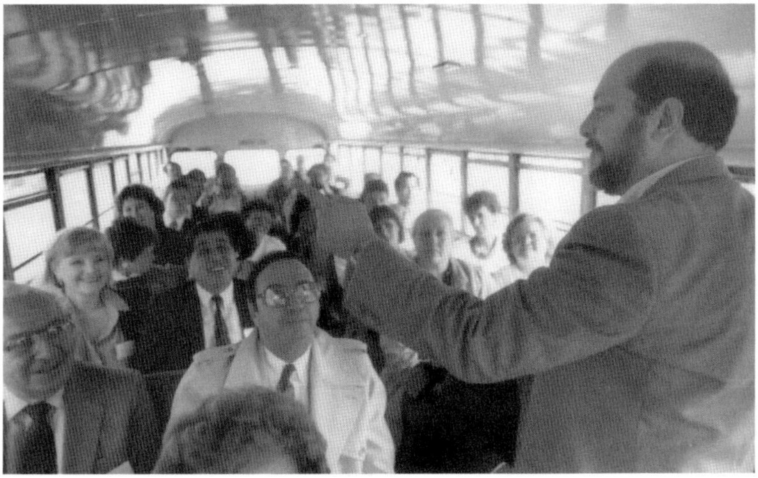

Jim Capraro

With Capraro's leadership, GSDC created Churchview Manor Apartments for seniors who no longer wanted the burden of home maintenance, then added Lawn Terrace down the street with 102 units of senior housing and a putting green in the back, and complemented the first project with Churchview Supportive Housing for seniors who need some help maintaining their independence.

His development projects included the $300-million expansion of Nabisco, the world's largest bakery under one roof.

Under Capraro, GSDC was designated by the National Neighborhood Reinvestment Corporation as a national model for commercial revitalization and selected as the recipient of the Outstanding Community Development Organization award.

Capraro himself has been honored with many awards, including the Chicago LISC Friend of the Neighborhoods Lifetime Achievement award, *Chicago* magazine's Chicagoan of the Year, and the Federal National Mortgage Association Foundation's James A. Johnson Fellow.

Capraro is pictured here leading a business tour, and in the next photograph he is giving his farewell speech.

The 1997 recipient of the Al Ruby Dream Catcher Award gave this advice to the community when he retired: "Be bold with no fear of failing."

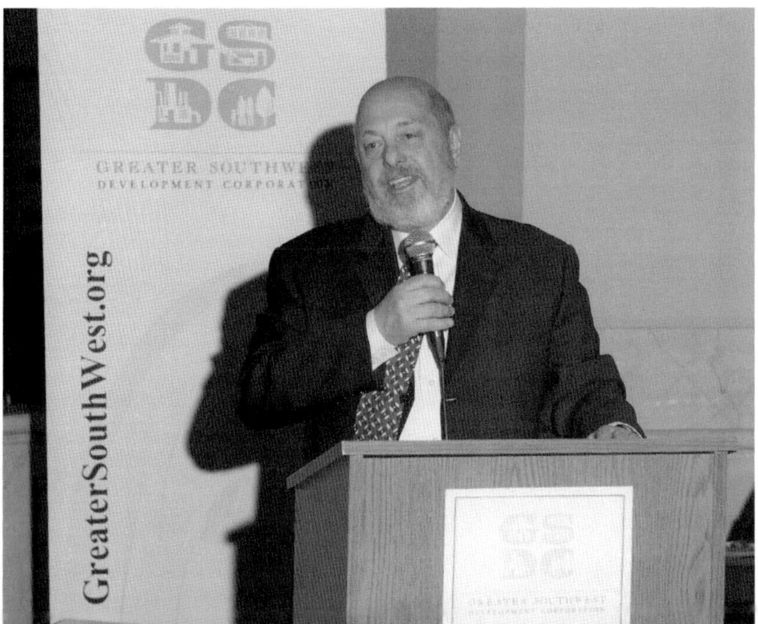

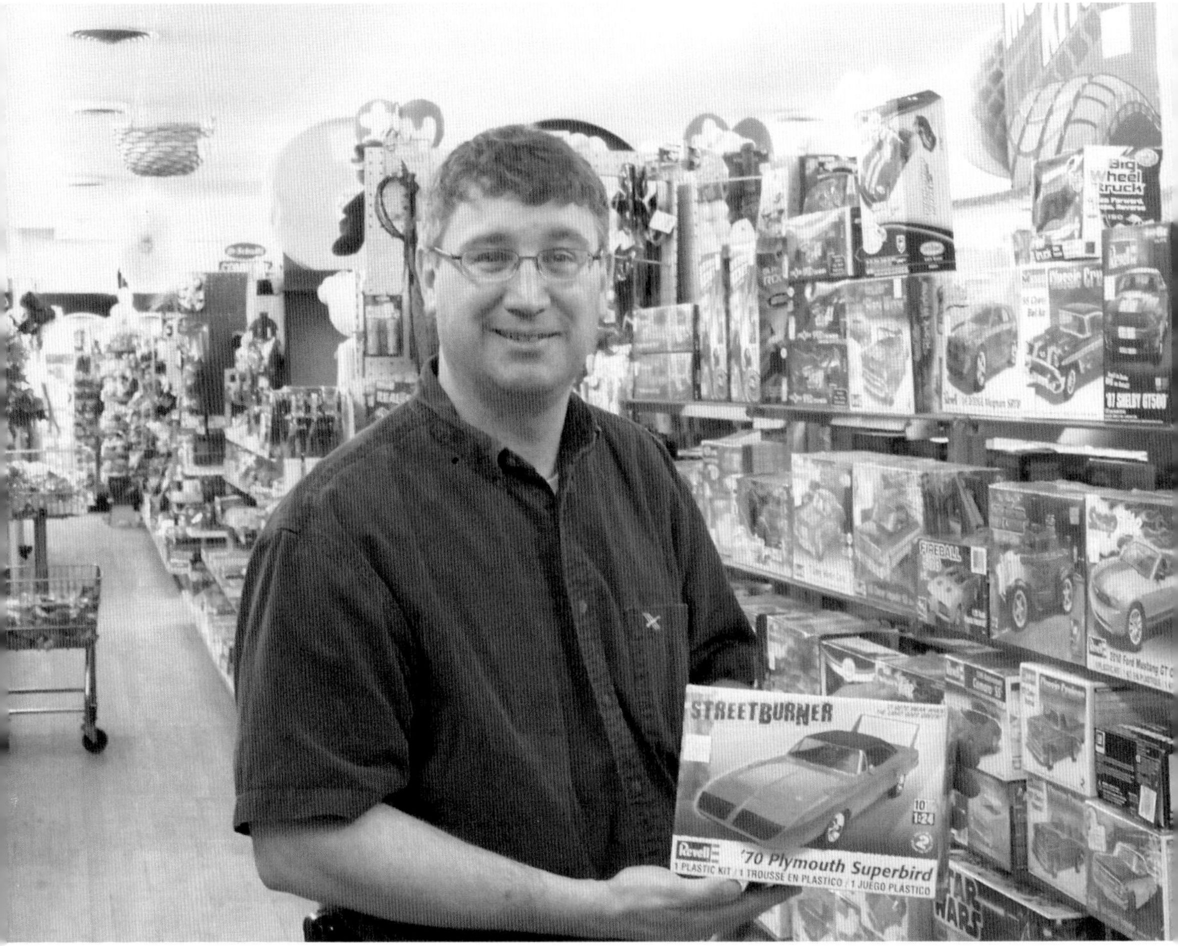

Michael Gehant

After World War I, the five-and-dime, originally selling merchandise exclusively for a nickel or dime, began to up the prices a bit. Over the next several decades, the stores were eventually referred to as variety stores. And thanks to Michael Gehant, West Lawn had the last remaining authentic variety store, one with wooden floors and old-school charm.

Gehant worked in the store since the first grade, initially by sweeping floors, then graduating to stocking shelves. He remembers doing his homework in the furnace room.

J & R had two stores at one time. In 1950, the store on the 7100 block of Western Avenue opened up. And in 1956, the Pulaski Road location was born. Both stores continued to operate until 1975 when the Western Avenue store closed.

Mike's father, Kenneth, was manager of the store and eventually the owner. Kenneth began in the variety store business at the age of 17 and at 21 became the youngest manager ever for the F.W. Woolworth chain. Kenneth purchased J & R in 1981 after having run the stores with his brother Stanley since the 1950s.

Mike worked steadily in the store beginning in 1985 and taking over completely when his dad passed away. Not counting his training years from first grade to 1985, Mike ran the store for 30 years, because, as he said, "It was in my blood."

J & R was a wonderful friendly store, and it will always hold a special place in the hearts of West Lawn and Chicago Lawn residents because of Mike Gehant.

CHAPTER SIX

Redirecting the Future

I know there is strength in the differences between us
and I know there is comfort where we overlap.

—Ani DiFranco

Throughout the years, neighborhoods take on different personalities. New people and ideas can bring new possibilities. Sometimes it just revolves around doing what one loves and holding onto dreams. It is how the old and new assimilate that determines the outcome.

Recognized time and again for his many efforts and accomplishments, Stanley Balzekas Jr. took his lifelong dream of opening a museum dedicated to preserving and promoting Lithuanian history and made it a reality.

Rhodel Castillo took his vision of showcasing his Garifuna roots while giving the Garifuna people somewhere to feel at home and turned it into a unique restaurant and cultural center.

While turning her passions into her first career, Anne Burke became one of the founders of the Special Olympics.

Turning his love of the sport into a livelihood, award-winning bowler Richard Supanich has kept Lawn Lanes as a West Lawn institution for over 50 years.

While nurturing his family's business, Frank Caldarone turned his parent's dream into an award-winning Italian restaurant.

Rami Nashashibi, the founder and executive director of the Inner City Muslim Action Network, has been named one of the 500 most influential Muslims in the world.

Nance Dulaj was named one of 100 Women Making a Difference by *Today's Chicago Woman* magazine and Woman of the Year by the American Biographical Institute for setting an example for her peers and entire community.

Lisa Madigan, recipient of the John F. Kennedy New Frontier Award, will go down in history as the first woman to become attorney general in the state of Illinois.

As proprietor at his Plaza Pub, Al Bartkus was dubbed the "Mayor of 69th Street."

Local leaders like Fr. Tony Pizzo, OSA, Rabbi Capers Funnye Jr., Betty Gutierrez, and Mary Ceil McManus have used their indomitable passion for neighborhood harmony to bring people together.

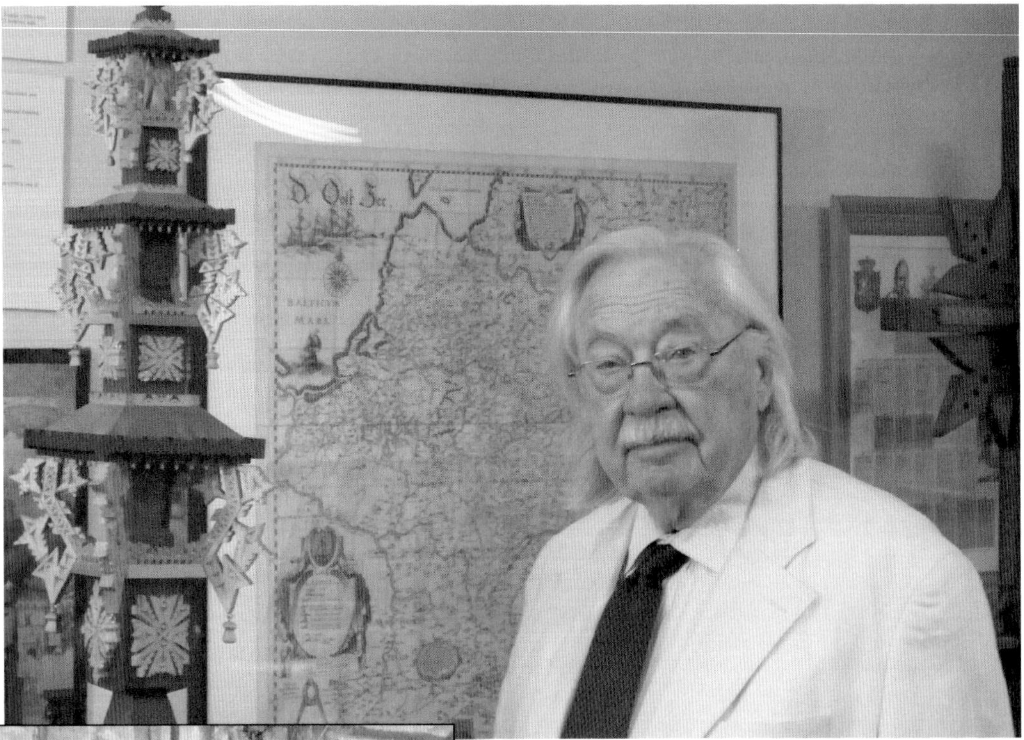

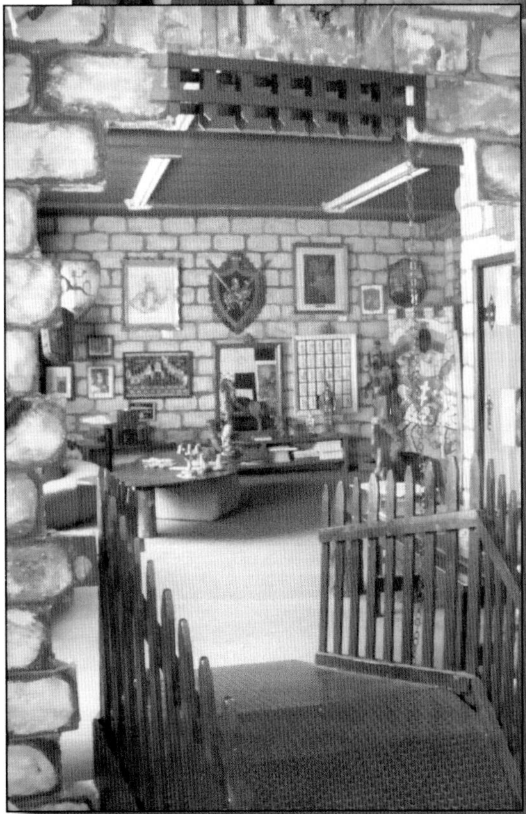

Stanley Balzekas Jr.

Stanley Balzekas Jr. started in what would be his future career during high school when he worked part-time in his father's automobile dealership. He served in the US Army during World War II and then studied business administration, earning his master's degree from De Paul University. Using his newly acquired business knowledge, he continued on at Balzekas Motor Sales, eventually becoming president.

Throughout his career in the automobile industry his lifelong goal was to preserve for posterity materials and artifacts of Lithuanian history. He realized his dream in June 1966 when he opened his first museum in a two-flat building next to the car dealership on Archer Avenue. He began displaying his personal collection of art, armor, and rare maps, with the oldest dating back to the 16th century.

The museum quickly outgrew its Brighton Park home, and in 1986 Stanley moved it to its current larger location on Pulaski Road. He added a children's area (pictured), a Lithuanian language library, amber, coins, stamps, ethnographic exhibits, a gift shop, and an extensive art collection as well as programs, classes, and events all promoting Lithuanian heritage.

Diplomat

This was his passion, and he has been recognized time and again for his efforts and accomplishments. In 2004, Rep. William Lipinski paid tribute to Stanley Balzekas with a declaration from the Illinois House in which he labeled Balzekas a remarkable gentleman and one of the foremost leaders amongst Chicago's communities.

"Mr. Balzekas has enriched the diverse fabric of our entire Chicago community by founding one of the largest ethnic museums and libraries in the United States. Through such measures, Mr. Balzekas has been a dedicated guardian of the heritage, history, and culture of this nation's Lithuanian ancestry."

He has worn many different hats over the years, serving as honorary consul general of the consulate for the Republic of Lithuania and vice chairman for the Lithuanian American Council, among others.

Pictured here in 2010, he was a speaker at the rededication of the Darius-Girenas plaque in Midway Airport.

In February 2014, Stanley Balzekas received the Lithuanian Diplomacy Star. Presenting the award was Lithuania's Foreign Minister Linas Linkevicius at a ceremony in Washington DC. The Lithuanian Diplomacy Star is the Lithuanian Foreign Ministry's award of honor.

Founder, president, businessman, promoter, diplomat—these are Stanley Balzekas Jr.

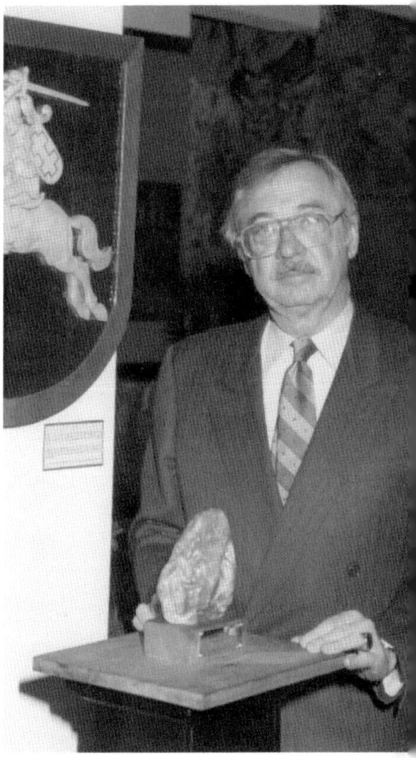

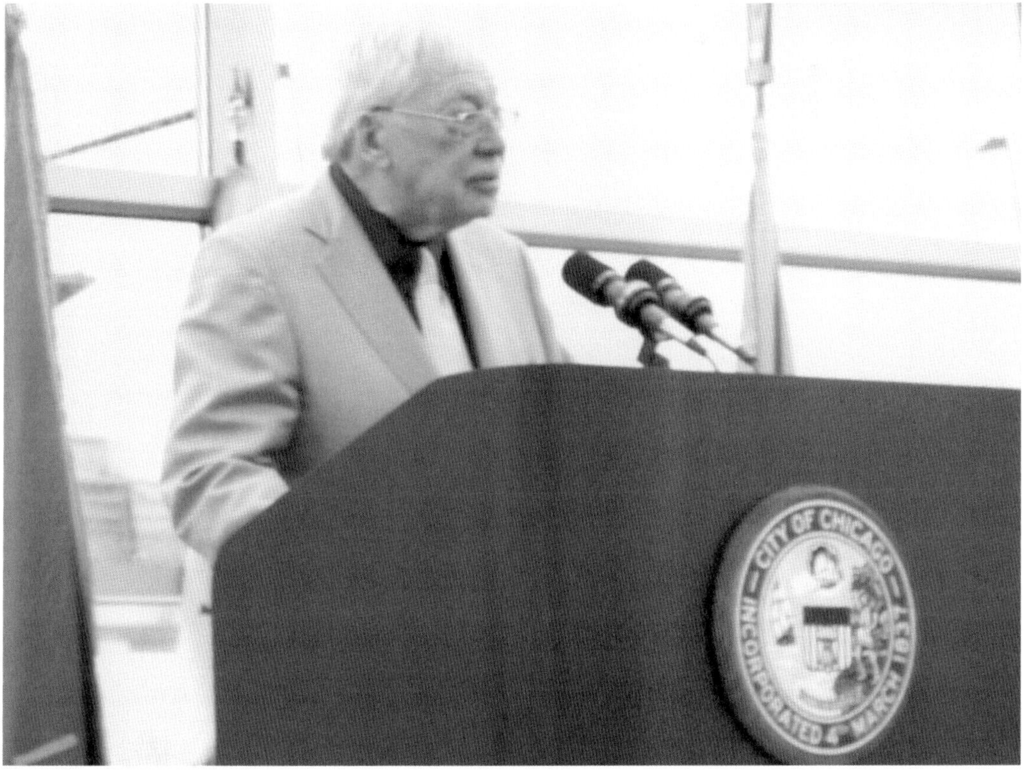

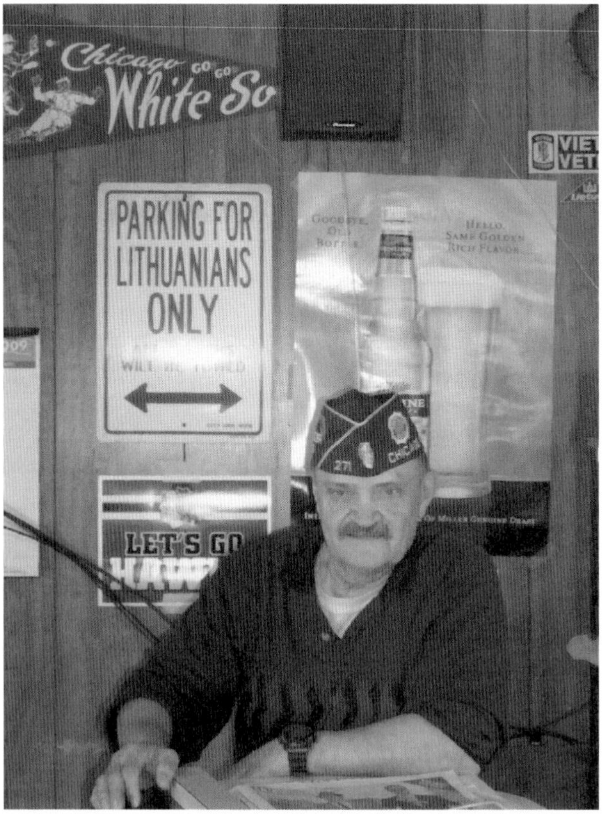

Algimantas Bartkus

In the heart of Marquette Manor, in a section that was known for its dense Lithuanian population and dubbed the Lithuanian Gold Coast in the 1970s, was a neighborhood meeting place called the Plaza Pub. But most people knew it as Al's Place.

For three decades, Al Bartkus, also dubbed the "Mayor of 69th Street," was the proprietor. Born in Lithuania, his family came to Chicago in 1949 and moved into a two-flat just a couple of blocks from the tap. After attending Nativity BVM Grammar School and St. Rita High School, he joined the Army, serving during the Vietnam years.

A generous and well-respected man, Bartkus was a longtime member of the Darius-Girenas American Legion Post 271, serving as its commander twice and offering Al's Place as the post home for several years.

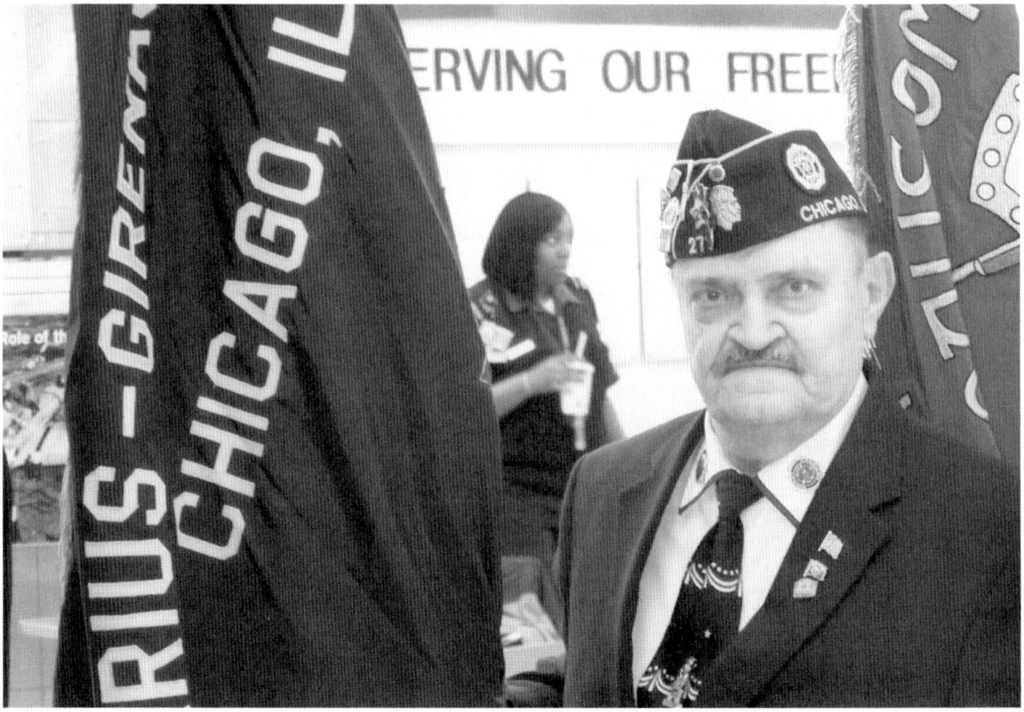

Nance L. Dulaj

Nance Lillian Irene Kopec Dulaj has worn many different hats during her lifetime. She has been a wife, mother, city worker, teacher, community activist, volunteer, and correspondent for the *Southwest News-Herald*, just to name a few.

She has danced and waved a flag during a parade scene in *Ferris Bueller's Day Off*. She sat in an airport waiting area while Catherine O'Hara argued with a flight attendant in *Home Alone*. She danced the polka in *Overexposed*. And those are just some of the roles her other career as an extra has taken her to on the silver screen.

In 1987, for her parts in *She's Having a Baby*, Dulaj won the Spark Award, which is a local honor presented annually to extras for versatility in film. In the movie she played a bag lady in one scene and a runaway model in another.

Today's Chicago Woman named Dulaj one of 100 Women Making A Difference in 2000. A definite jack-of-all-trades, at that time she was a state-certified teacher who substituted gratis at Queen of the Universe School, translated documents in both Polish and Spanish, worked as a docket clerk at the Commission of Human Relations, read for the blind on CRIS Radio, and was the president of the Queen's Guild, president of Chicago Legal Secretaries, and president of Phi Chi Theta Chicago Alumni Chapter.

In her spare time, she has volunteered as an usher at the Chicago Theatre, served on the nominating committee of the Coalition of Polish American Women, and volunteered with the United Cerebral Palsy Association, the Good Neighbor Food Drive, and the Grant Park Concert Society.

A West Lawn homeowner since her home was first built in the 1950s, she has also been a member of the Hurley Homeowners, the City Club of Chicago, the Queen's Seniors, and the Tarkington Seniors, volunteered with the Gallery 37 After School Matters program, and has been a commissioner on the Midway Noise Compatibility Commission.

Dulaj has been named Mrs. Ford City and recognized by many more organizations. Perhaps it was said best when the American Biographical Institute named her Woman of the Year in 1992, citing her for setting "a noble example for her peers and her entire community."

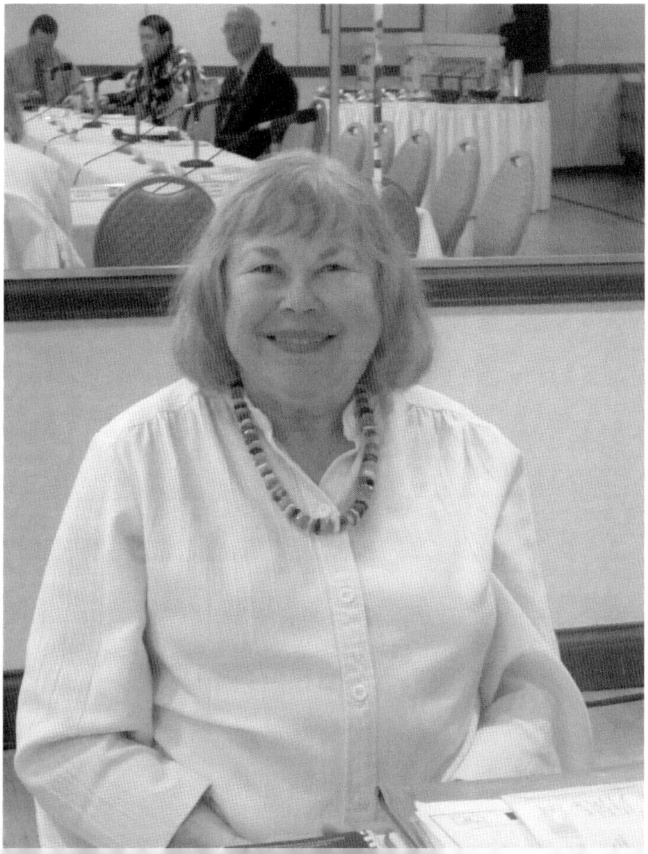

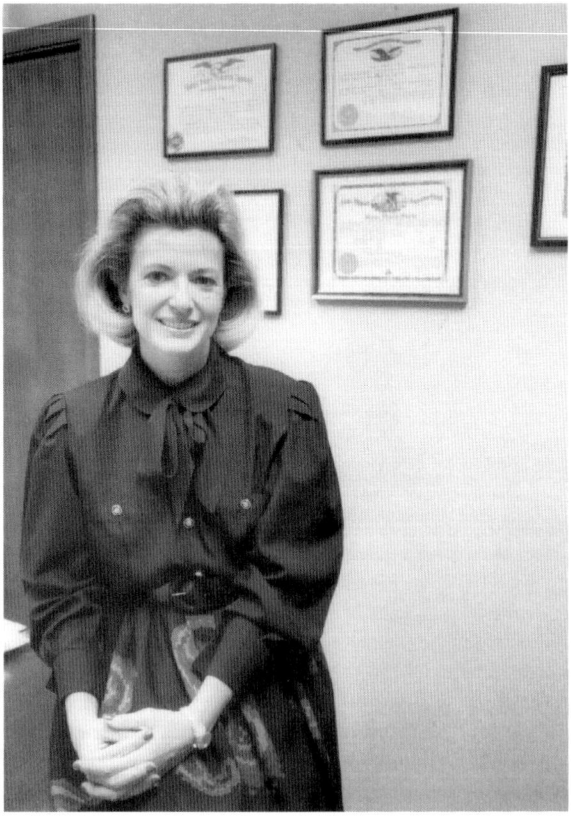

Anne M. Burke

In the world of politics, Anne Marie McGlone Burke has been known as a judge of the Illinois Appellate Court from 1995 to 2006 and then as a justice of the Illinois Supreme Court.

In the field of sports she is known as one of the founders of the Special Olympics, the world's largest sports organization for those with intellectual disabilities. In July 1968, Burke was instrumental in garnering the help of the Lt. Joseph P. Kennedy Foundation and the City of Chicago to host the first Special Olympics games at Soldier Field and in 2003 played a vital role in bringing the Special Olympics World Games to Dublin for the first time.

In the realm of the Sisters of St. Casimir, she is an esteemed alumna of one of their high schools who has honored them time and again as a benefactor that has found the time in her busy schedule to help.

The youngest of four children born to George and Helen McGlone, Anne grew up down the street from St. Rita Grammar School and attended Maria High School. Anne has noted on many occasions that she "grew up in Chicago Park District programs participating in everything from beanbags to track and field, basketball, swimming, baton, and tap."

Burke was a camp counselor and star athlete. Under the tutelage of her teacher at Maria she realized one of her passions could actually be a career. Loving athletics and working with children, she set her sights on becoming a gym teacher.

After freshman year, her college moved, and having no transportation, Burke had to drop out. However, she was able to pass the civil-service exam and become a physical education teacher, working with special-needs children.

Married to longtime alderman Edward Burke, and with four children under the age of 10, Anne Burke embarked on her next career and graduated from Chicago-Kent School of Law in 1983. Known as a staunch supporter of special-needs children and a stickler for professionalism, Justice Anne Burke has won numerous awards and been honored time and again for her accomplishments.

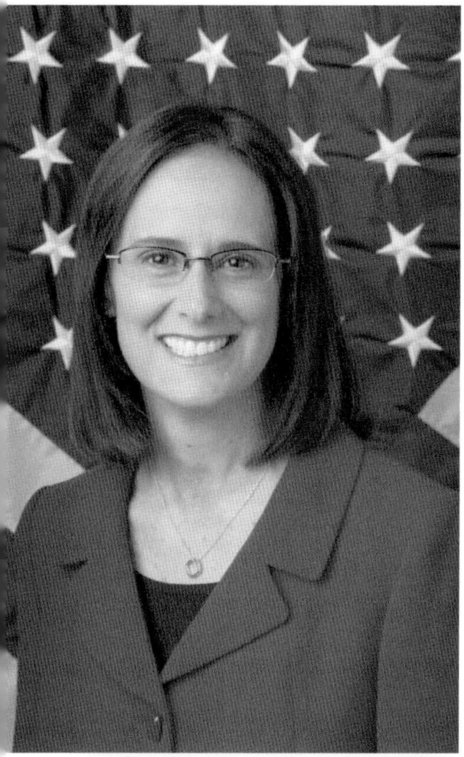

Lisa M. Madigan

Lisa M. Madigan will go down in history as the first woman to become attorney general in the state of Illinois. That was in 2003 and followed a four-year term in the Illinois Senate.

Of specific relevance to the people of Chicago Lawn and West Lawn has been her diligent fight against predatory lending practices and her willingness to stand with the community and hold major offenders accountable. They have showed their appreciation time and again with standing ovations.

Pictured below after taking a walking tour with the Southwest Organizing Project, Attorney General Madigan along with Ald. Marty Quinn and Sen. Jacqueline Collins, joined residents in listening to future plans for the neighborhood.

The stepdaughter of longtime Speaker of the Illinois House Michael J. Madigan, Lisa volunteered as a secondary school teacher in South Africa during apartheid in her early career. In 2005, she received the John F. Kennedy New Frontier Award, which is given annually to "exceptional young Americans under the age of 40 whose contributions in elective office, community service, or advocacy demonstrate the impact and value of public service in the spirit of John F. Kennedy." (Above, courtesy of Lisa Madigan; below, courtesy of the Southwest Organizing Project.)

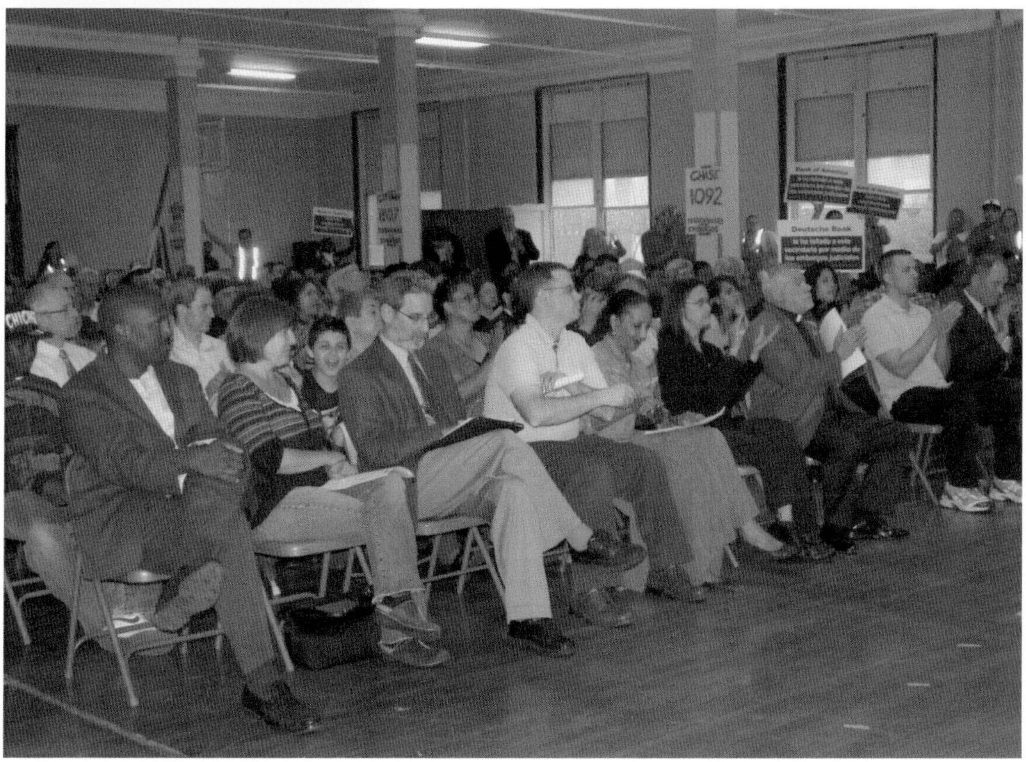

Rhodel and Hussein Castillo

Sitting on Sixty-Third Street between Campbell and Maplewood Avenues is what could be termed the Garifuna hub in the Midwest. Rhodel Castillo and his son Hussein are the owners of Garifuna Flava Restaurant. The uniqueness of this restaurant and cultural center are derived from Rhodel's passionate vision to showcase his Garifuna roots while giving the Garifuna people someplace to call their own. Yet the lively Caribbean music, yellow-checked tablecloths, and friendly hospitality beckon those from all ethnic backgrounds.

The Castillos serve Belizean cuisine, which is a unique blend of Caribbean, Latin, and Garifuna.

Immigrating to the United States in 1986, Rhodel received his bachelor's degree from Chicago State University and his masters from Roosevelt University in 1994. A musical artist, one of the things that struck Rhodel was the lack of anything the Garifuna people could really identify with in the area. He cofounded the Progressive Garifuna Alliance, an organization dedicated to preserving and advancing the Garifuna culture and worked on projects in conjunction with the Field Museum and the Museum of Science and Industry, but his focus was bigger.

Purchasing the building at 2518 West Sixty-Third Street in 2008, and along with his family, including his wife, Yolanda, and son Hussein, built a home away from home for Garifuna people while gaining a reputation as a go-to destination. Garifuna Flava has been featured on the WTTW Chicago's *Check Please*, ABC-TV's *Hungry Hound*, the Food Network's *Diners, Drive-Ins, and Dives*, and WGN-TV's *Chicago's Best*.

Impulcity has named Garifuna as one the nine essential South Side restaurants; Thrillist has included Garifuna as best of the South Side. In Newcity's November 2009 Best of Chicago, Garifuna was described as "a relaxing place to beat the winter blues."

Hussein said, "This is the cooking I have been eating all of my life, the kind my mother cooks. She is in the kitchen cooking now." Along with his dad, mom, sisters, and cousins, the family has hosted the prime minister of Belize at the restaurant and been invited to showcase their fare at the Taste of Chicago several years in a row.

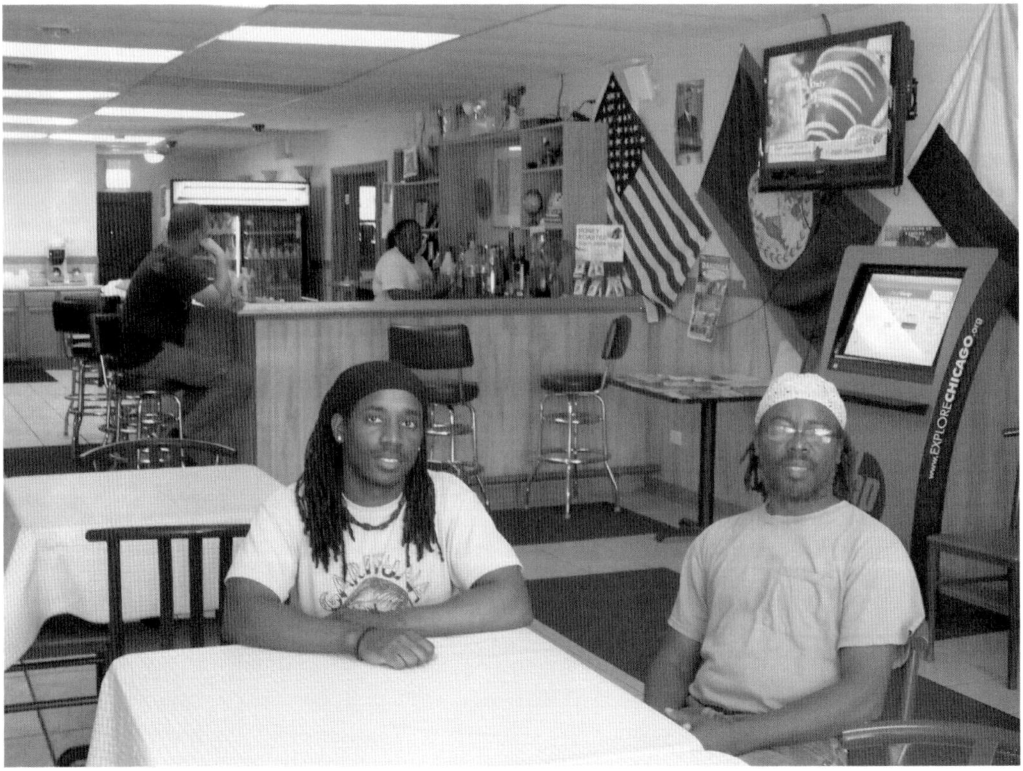

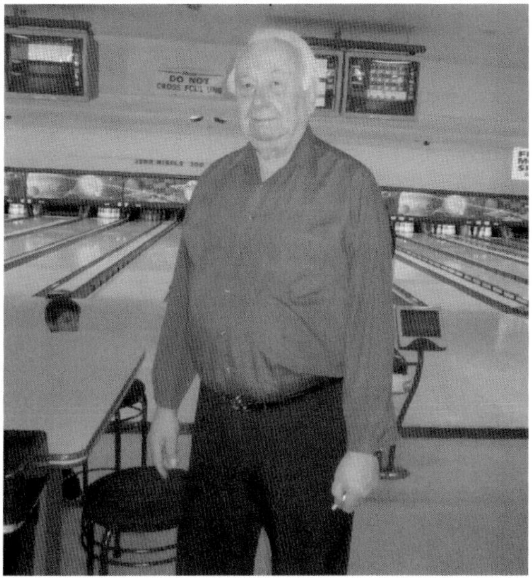

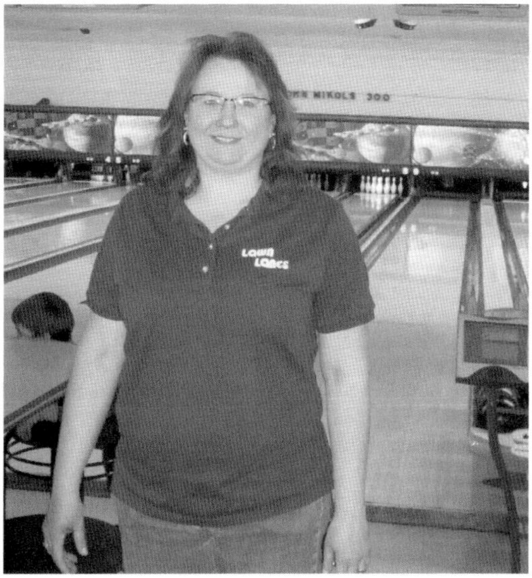

Richard Supanich

Lawn Lanes has been a West Lawn institution for over 50 years. It is owned by Richard Supanich and his family. Richard started working for Lawn Lanes as a mechanic while he was in college at Lewis University, and he stayed there for 18 years prior to purchasing the bowling alley in February 1977. His original partners were David Wright, Bob Bitunjac, and Dennis Misiak.

When asked why he chose a bowling alley, Supanich answered, "Because it is all I have ever done." He started bowling when he was 12. Even with a wall full of trophies and plaques, he is very humble about his accomplishments. Among his honors is a US Bowling Congress Hall of Fame award.

Richard's daughter Paula Supanich-Jarolim is the youth director and son David is the manager of the bowling alley. And his wife, Catherine, is the bookkeeper.

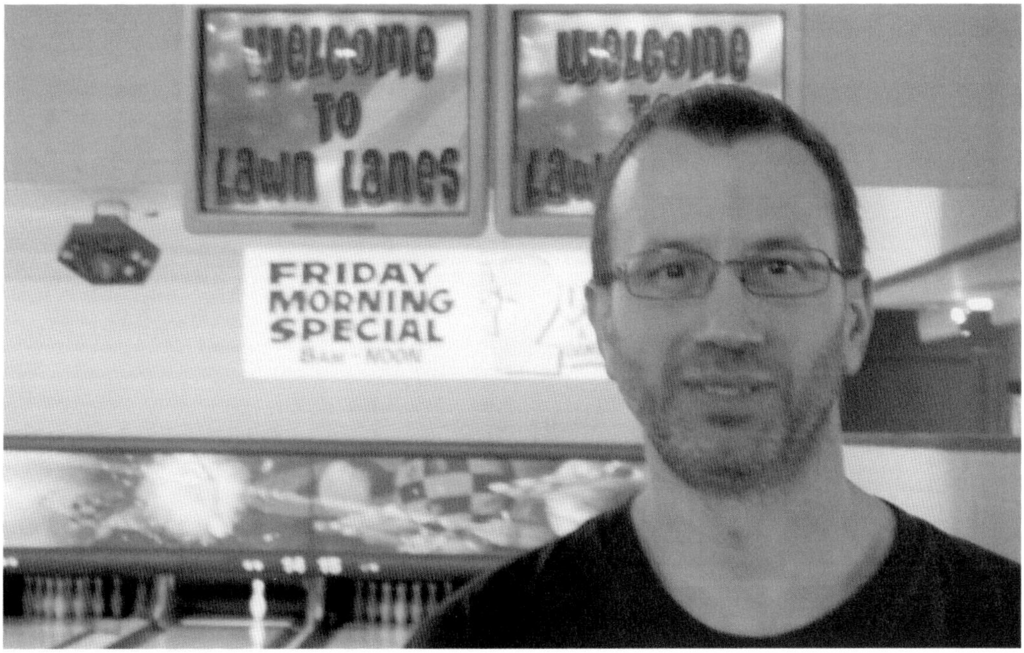

Rami Nashashibi

Named one of the 500 most influential Muslims in the world by the Royal Islamic Strategic Studies Centre and Georgetown University, Rami Nashashibi is the founder and executive director of the Inner City Muslim Action Network (IMAN). Dr. Nashashibi is the son of a diplomat, has a doctorate from the University of Chicago, and has been an adjunct professor at various colleges and universities across the Chicagoland area.

Though he was raised in Jordan, Spain, Italy, and Saudi Arabia, his mother, who was born in May 1948, grew up on the Southwest Side of Chicago as a part of one of the first Arab American families in the area.

It was a soccer scholarship that brought young Rami to America in 1990. By his own admission, he did not grow up in a very religious family, and it was not until he got involved in social-justice issues that he began delving into the Quran.

He founded the nonprofit IMAN in 1997 while still a student. He explained that IMAN stems from a core Muslim principle—the call for social justice.

One of his goals has been to inspire change through arts and culture. He said that IMAN brings musicians from all around the world to perform at its events, including opera singers and spoken-word artists. The annual Takin' It to the Streets festival draws thousands every year to Marquette Park and yet is one of the most peaceful events to be held in the park's history.

Since its inception, his organization has branched out to include a community health clinic, GED classes, and a computer lab as well as youth-development programming. Nashashibi and his organization have also become active members of the Southwest Organizing Project.

Nashashibi has been given the Courageous Voices Award by the Jewish Council on Urban Affairs and the Chicago Neighborhood Development Award. He has been featured on the BBC and PBS. In 2009, Chicago Public Radio selected Nashashibi as one of the city's Top Ten Chicago Global Visionaries.

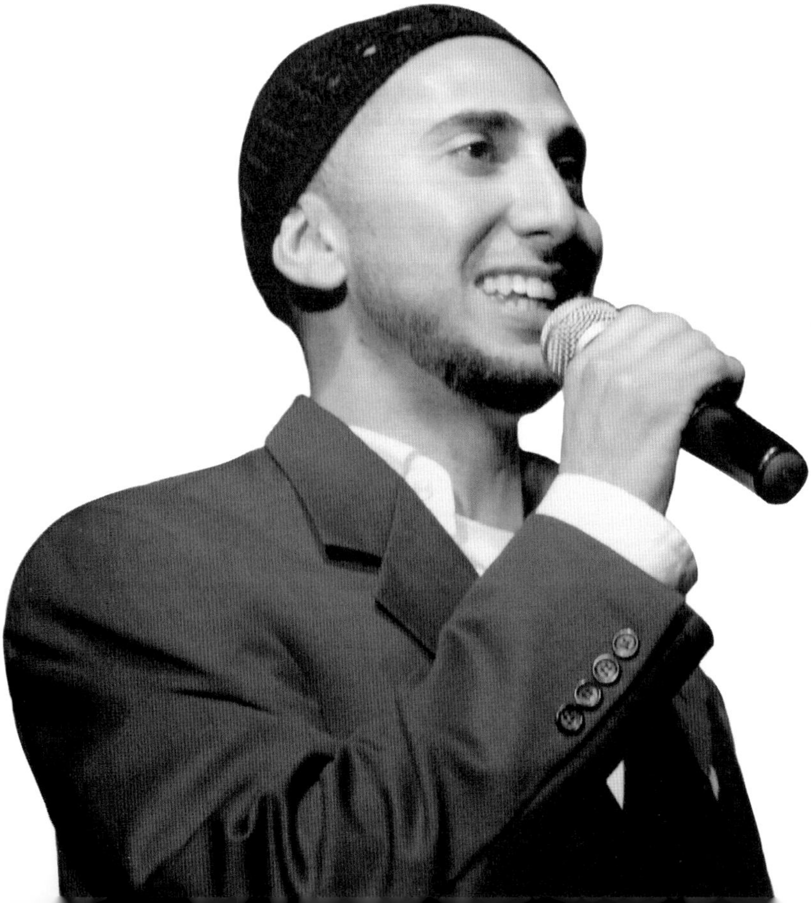

Rev. Anthony "Tony" Pizzo, OSA

Rev. Anthony Pizzo was named pastor of St. Rita of Cascia Parish in 2006. He is a native of the Southwest Side and in the recent past was also assigned to St. Clare of Montefalco, just down the street from St. Rita.

Prior to his arrival at St. Rita, the parish under the direction of Rev. William Lego, OSA, was a founding institution of the Southwest Catholic Cluster Project. Aspiring to include people of all faiths in the neighborhood, the Cluster Project grew to be the Southwest Organizing Project (SWOP).

Since his arrival, Father Tony has taken on a strong active leadership role with SWOP as well as many other groups on issues involving Chicago Lawn and West Lawn. He has taken seriously the Augustinian legacy begun by Fr. James Green back in 1905, that of concern and action on neighborhood issues, and it has been appreciated, as is evidenced by the honors bestowed on him. Recently he has received the Neighborhood Leadership Award from Neighborhood Housing Services of Chicago (2011), the Pope John XXIII Award from the Archdiocese of Chicago Office for Hispanic Ministry (2010), the Humanitarian Award from the Italian-American Executives in Transportation (2012), and a Community Heroes from the Keep Our Homes Campaign (2009).

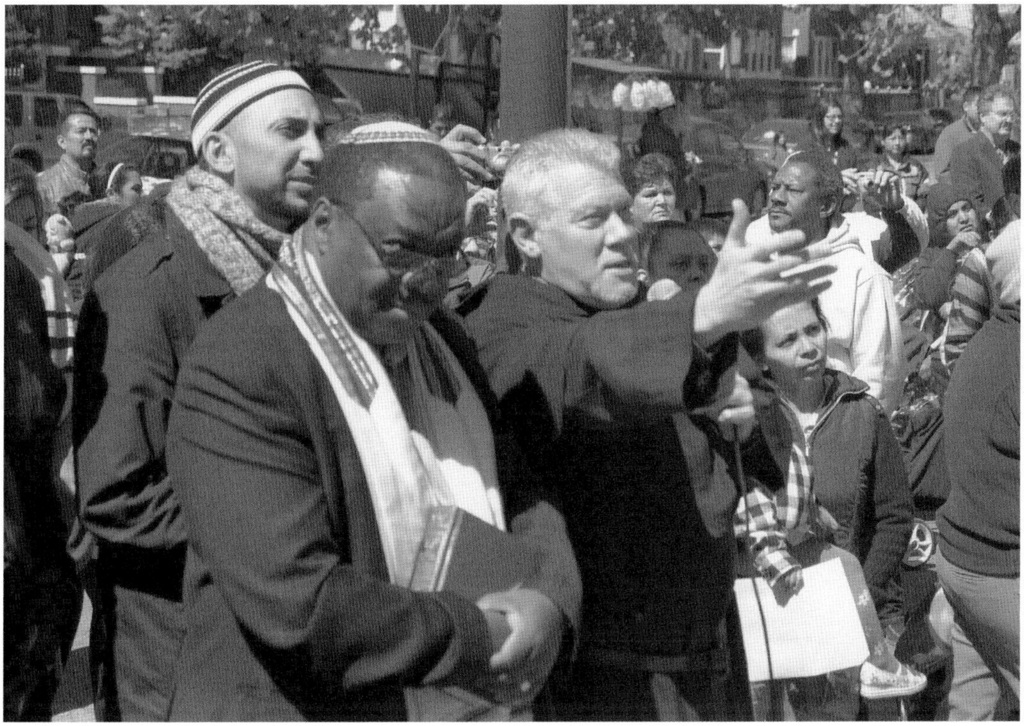

Rabbi Capers C. Funnye Jr

Rabbi Capers C. Funnye Jr. is the spiritual leader of the Beth Shalom B'Nai Zaken Ethiopian Hebrew Congregation in Chicago Lawn. It is currently one of the largest in the United States.

Although born in South Carolina, Rabbi Funnye grew up on the South Side of Chicago. He is a first cousin once removed of Michelle Obama. He has served as consultant to the Du Sable Museum, the Chicago Historical Society, and the Spertus Museum. Under his leadership, the congregation is an active member of SWOP.

Rabbi Funnye was the first African American member of the Chicago Board of Rabbis and is an interfaith activist. He was quoted in *Haaretz* as saying, "Why not take the richness of Protestantism, Islam, Catholicism, and be open to understanding and seeking ways to work together?"

Pictured here are three faiths working together for the betterment of the neighborhood. (Courtesy of the Southwest Organizing Project.)

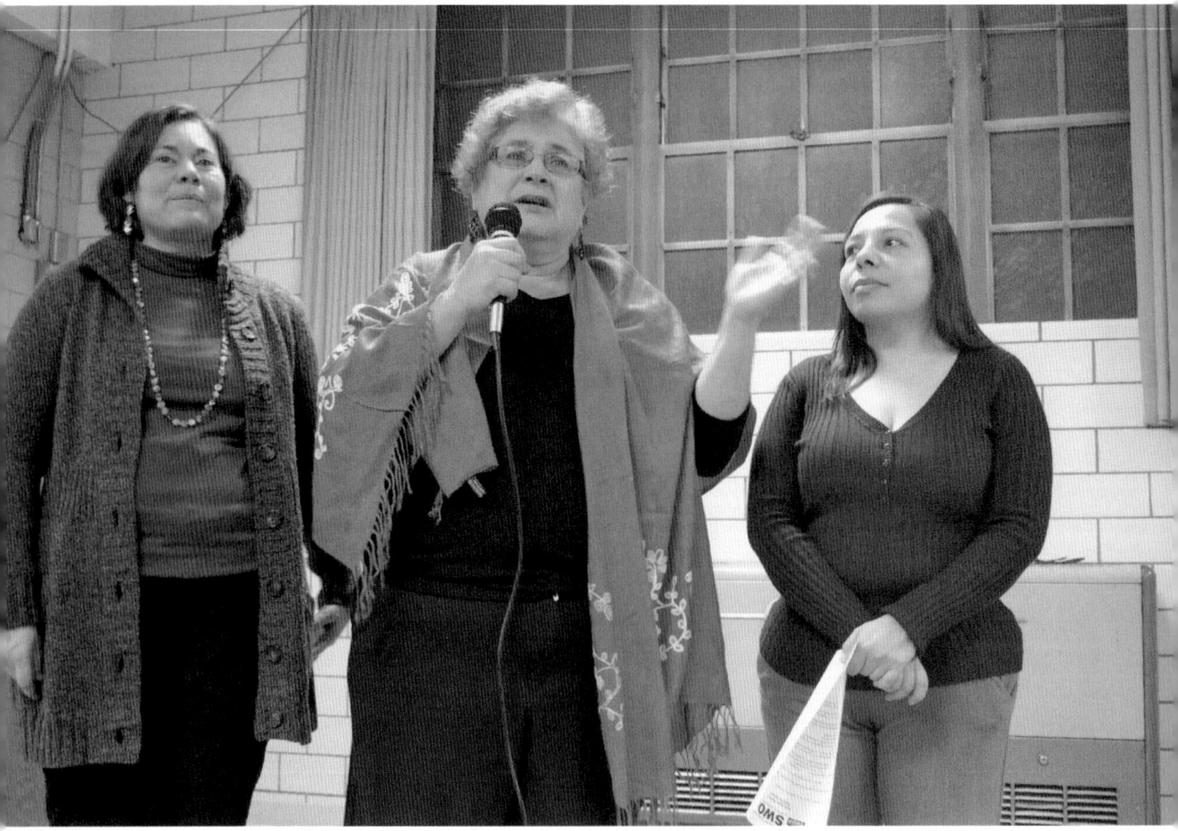

Betty Gutierrez

Since moving to her West Lawn bungalow with her husband, Francisco, and three daughters in 1984, Betty Gutierrez has never stopped working as a fervent advocate of her neighborhood.

At St. Mary Star of the Sea, she is on the parish council, has volunteered with other parents setting up bazaars, volunteered with the Girl Scouts, been a member of the Altar and Rosary Society, and served as president of the Our Lady of Guadalupe committee. On more than one occasion she has been asked if her bedroom was at the school because she is always there.

Gutierrez has been the team mom and helped out with the West Lawn Little League, been recognized by 8th District Commander Malloy for her involvement with CAPS, and was on the advisory board of the Southwest Youth Collaborative in its early years. She and her family have served meals to the homeless at the Pads shelter several times a year for the past 18 years.

During her tenure as director of housing at Greater Southwest Development Corp., Gutierrez coordinated three programs, which included the Housing Resource Center, the purchase and rehabilitation of foreclosed properties, and home repair, which included helping the disabled with accessibility options.

After her retirement from GSDC, Gutierrez has continued as a neighborhood advocate with the Southwest Organizing Project. She is pictured here with board members Esperanza Marrufo and Mayra Sarabia.

Organizers at SWOP have labeled her an inspiration, an outstanding example of leadership and building relationships. (Courtesy of Southwest Organizing Project.)

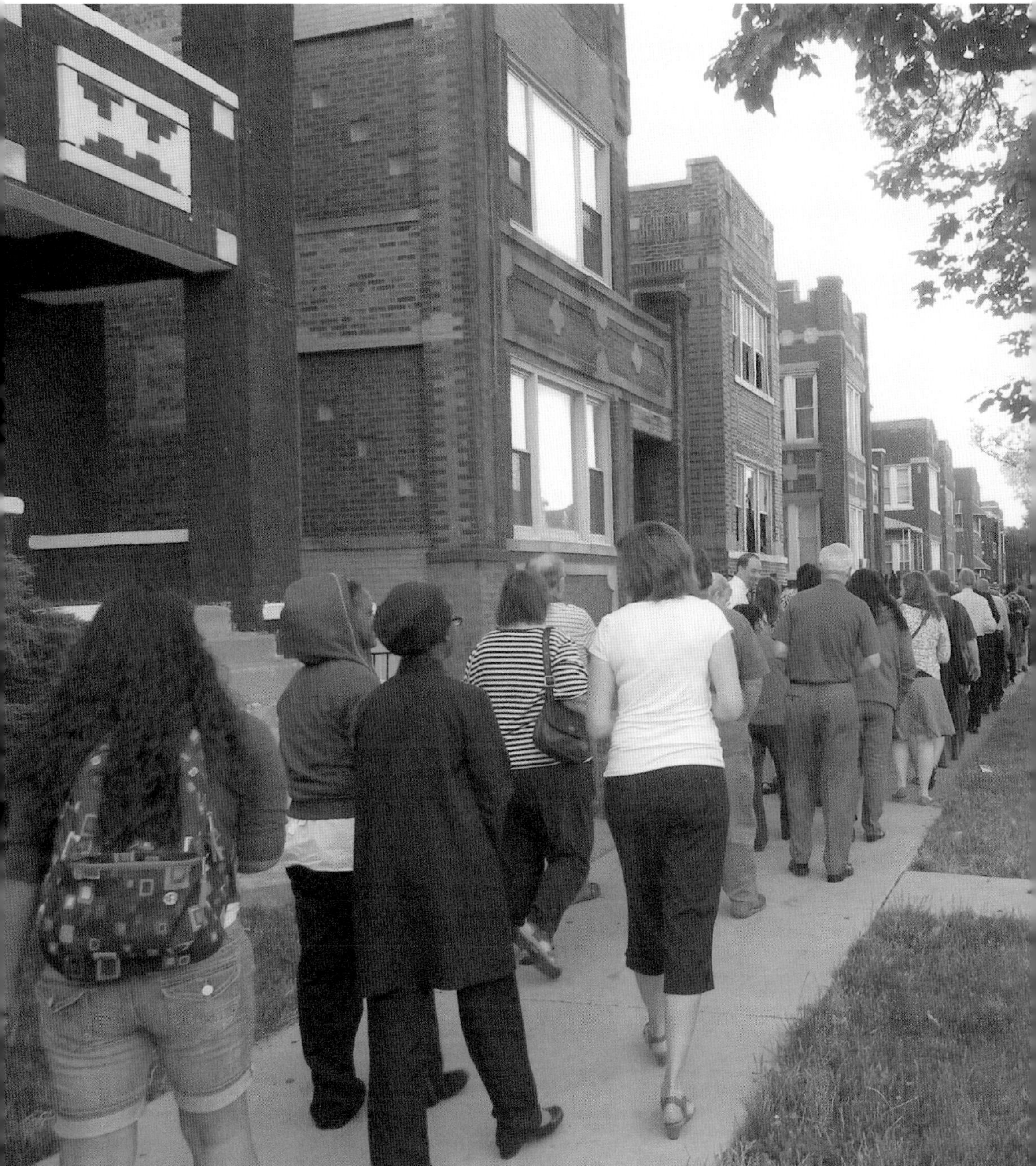

Southwest Organizing Project
In 2012, members of Southwest Organizing Project (SWOP), which encompasses all faiths and ethnic groups in Chicago Lawn and West Lawn, joined together to walk with Atty. Gen. Lisa Madigan on a tour of the eastern end of the neighborhood. Madigan visited the community at the invitation of SWOP to discuss housing. (Courtesy of the Southwest Organizing Project.)

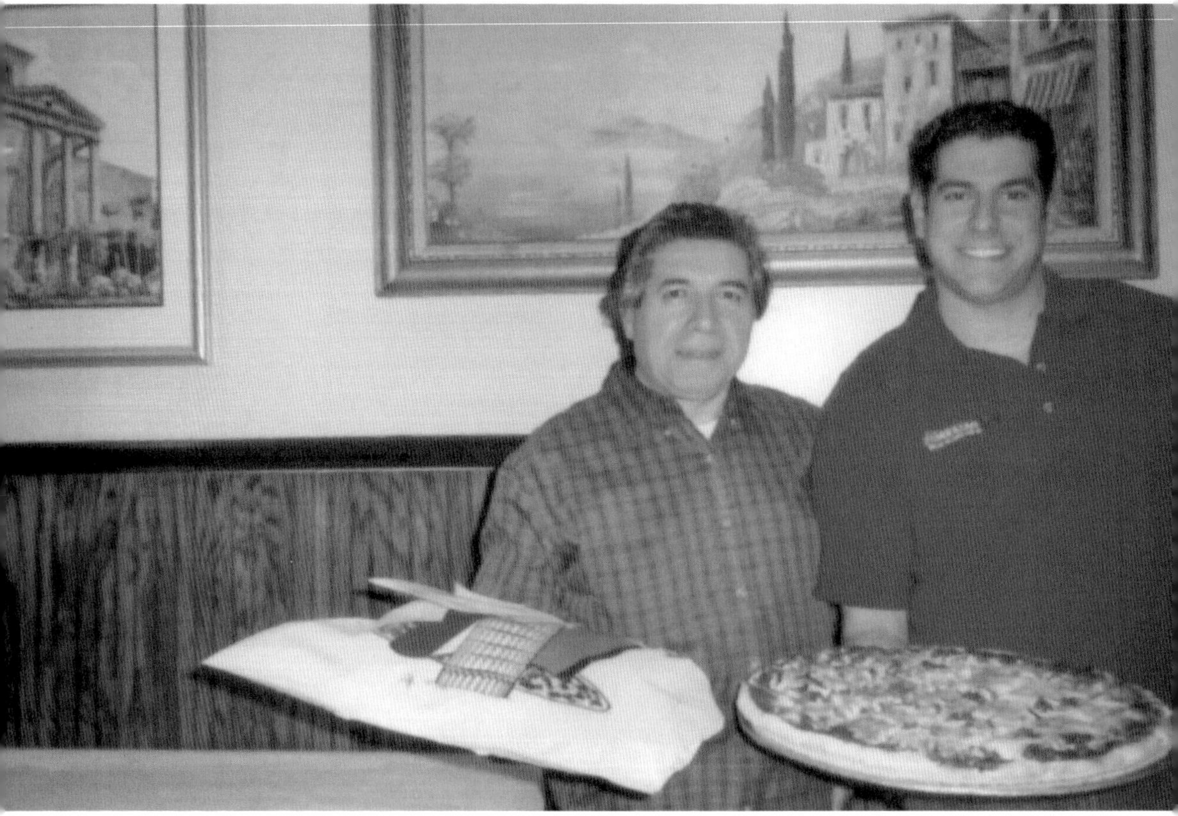

Frank Caldarone

For Frank Caldarone it is all about family and it always has been—family pride, family loyalty, and family camaraderie.

The proprietor of Palermo's of 63rd, Frank can boast among his ancestors the acclaimed 18th-century painter and playwright Padre Fedele Tirrito-Palermo. Frank's award-winning restaurant and his pizza have been referred to as the "Miracle on 63rd Street." He has a doctorate in Romance languages and has written *The Cycle*, a work based in Italian Verismo.

His story begins in Sicily, where his father, Antonino Caldarone, was active in the restaurant business. And his mother, Maria Carmela Tirrito Caldarone, was known in their town for her good cooking.

Frank was in a Capuchin seminary when Antonino and Carmela emigrated here with their children, Benedetto "Ben," Giuseppe "Joe," Ignazio "Frank," and Maria "Lia." Shortly after, in 1961 the Caldarones opened their first Palermo's, naming it after the town in Sicily where Antonino was born.

Using Old-World recipes passed down in the Tirrito family, they began with a modest pizzeria at Sixty-Third Street and Maplewood Avenue, take-out only. Frank attended St. Rita High School and also took some classes at Harper High School, dividing his time between the two until he had the credits he would need to graduate. It was also his job to open the pizzeria up after school and take care of things until the rest of the family arrived. Then he could go home to Sixty-First Street and Fairfield Avenue to do his homework.

Frank's dream was to become a teacher, but he could not leave the fledgling business, so he worked during the day and went to college at night, then student-taught Spanish at Hubbard twice a week.
In the meantime, business was growing. The restaurant's reputation escalated in 1970 when the *Chicago Daily News* named it one of the top five pizza establishments in the city, no small feat in a city the size of Chicago.

Dr. Caldarone

The next year, Antonino retired, leaving the business to his sons Frank and Joe. The brothers always hoped to open a larger place and in 1975 moved the restaurant to Sixty-Third Street and Hamlin Avenue. Before long they were enlarging that location as well.

Throughout the years, Frank and his restaurant have been acclaimed by newspapers and reviewers, and his pizza has ranked consistently high in reader polls. *Chicago Sun-Times* food critic Pat Bruno named it one of his Terrific Ten—the 10 best in the city.

Photographs of political, sports, and entertainment celebrities that have come to dine with Frank line the walls.

And while continuing on with his parents' dream, Frank has found the time to earn a bachelor's degree from Chicago State and a master of arts from the University of Chicago. He then went one step further and earned his doctorate.

The whole family is pictured here at his 1984 graduation: Lia (Caldarone) Baio, Joe, Carmella, Frank, Antonino, and Ben.

In 2005, Frank's nephew Paul Baio (Lia's son), joined him as a partner in the business. Paul was an engineer in car design. One of the first things he did was to redesign their logo.

And in April 2015, the Midwest Augustinians awarded Frank the highest honor a lay person may receive in the order, that of affiliation. The award is recognized by the Augustinian Curia in Rome.

Palermo's cuisine has been called the Miracle on 63rd Street, probably because it is all about family and has been since the beginning. Proprietor Frank Caldarone makes sure it continues that way. (Both, courtesy of Frank Caldarone.)

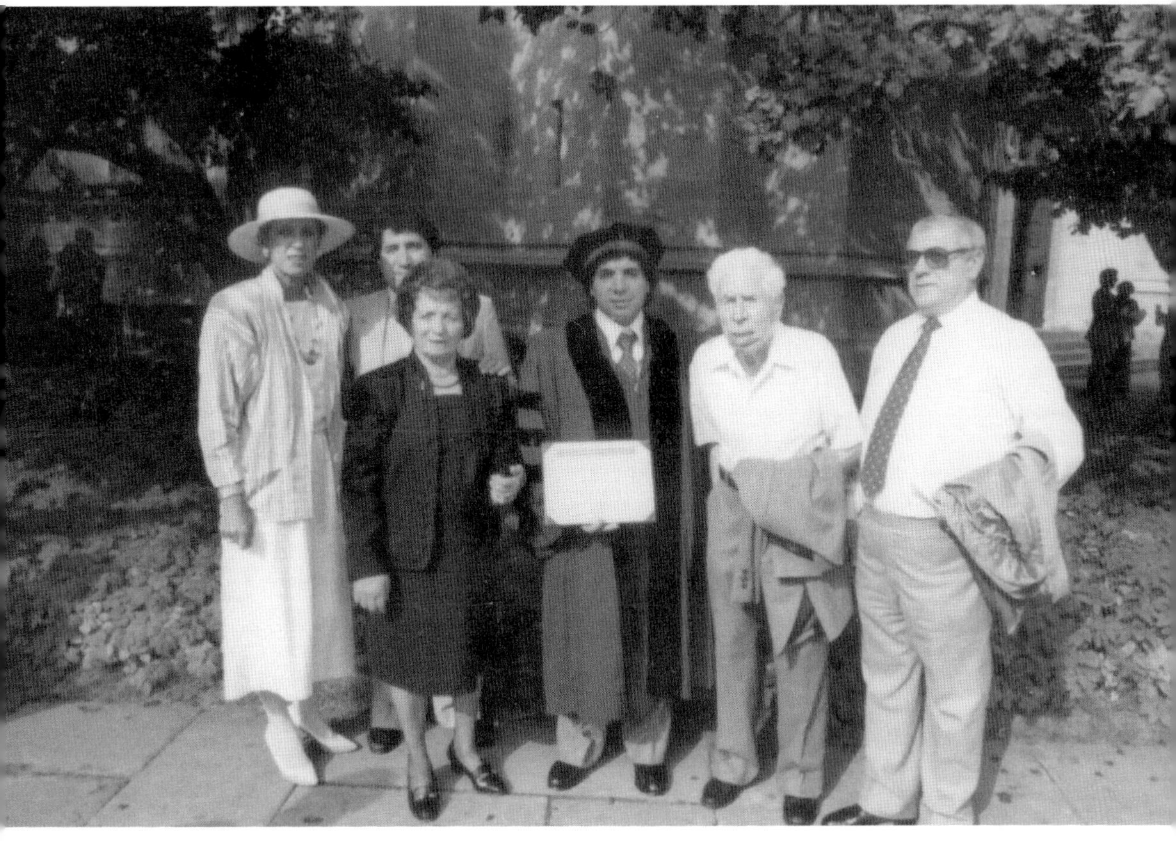

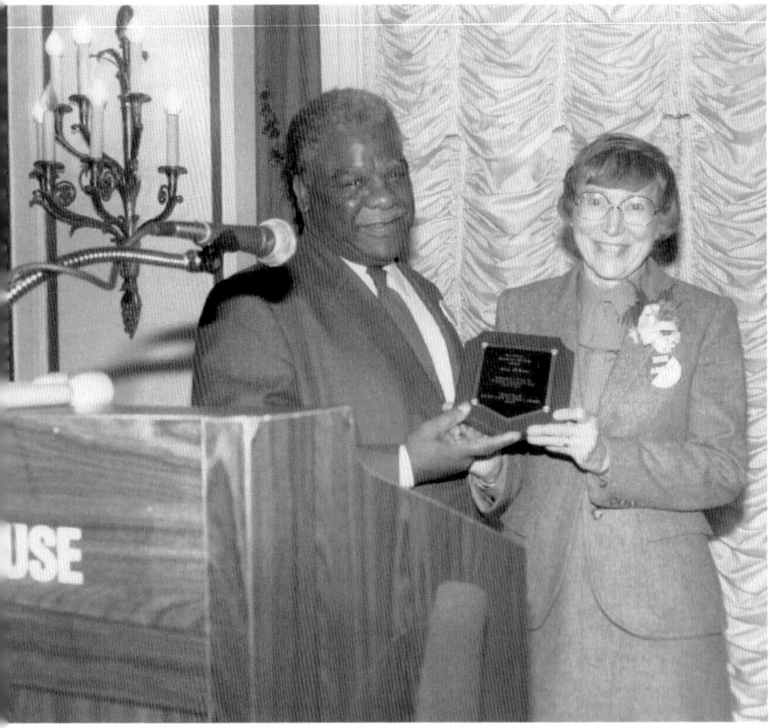

Mary Ceil McManus

Mary Ceil McManus worked toward neighborhood harmony for over 40 years, living in both Chicago Lawn and West Lawn. "Ethnic variety makes the community interesting," the librarian and longtime Southwest Community Congress leader once said.

As supervisor for the Senior Volunteer Program, she oversaw 140 volunteers for library, tutoring, and hospital work.

At a 2003 awards dinner, a story was told of seeing her sitting on the curb watching over a new neighbor's home during a time of particular neighborhood unrest. Beaming, she said, "It was the right thing to do." Mary Ceil McManus retreated to a standing ovation.

Marlene Mosqueda

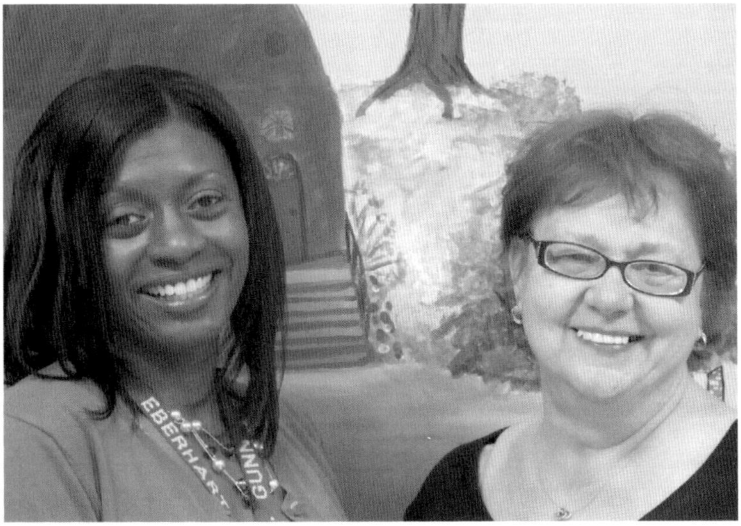

Marlene Mosqueda is the kind of person a teacher or principal really needs and appreciates. Even after her children graduated from Eberhart School, she continued to donate her time in innumerable ways.

Bringing together two book fairs each year is no small task. Add to that managing the Eagles School Store and coordinating the Birthday Books program. She serves on the Local School Council and has helped with Market Day, PTA, Gym Wear Sales, and more.

"Mrs. Mosqueda does everything!" said principal Nneka Gunn (left), pictured here with her. "She is a valuable member of our Eberhart School family."

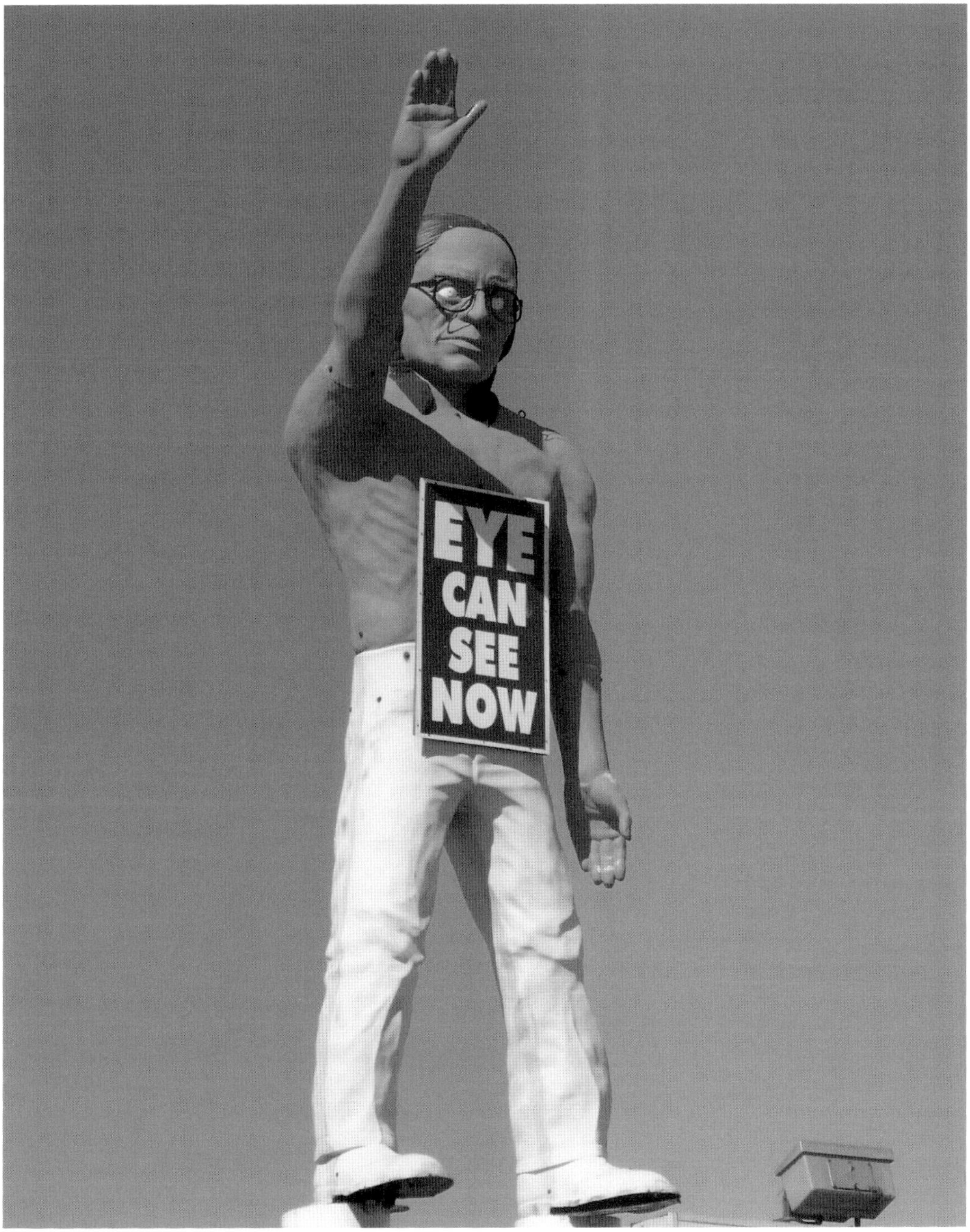

Our Indian

The most easily recognizable member of the community is the Indian standing atop the building on the northwest corner of Sixty-Third Street and Pulaski Road.

His first job was advertising White Owl Cigars for the Capitol Cigar Store. In this photograph over 50 years later, he is still in advertising, wearing eyeglasses promoting the vision store below.

In 1992, the Indian hit the silver screen when he was featured in Paramount Picture's *Wayne's World.* The Indian beckons to all who have called Chicago Lawn and West Lawn home, standing majestically with his hand raised in welcome.

INDEX

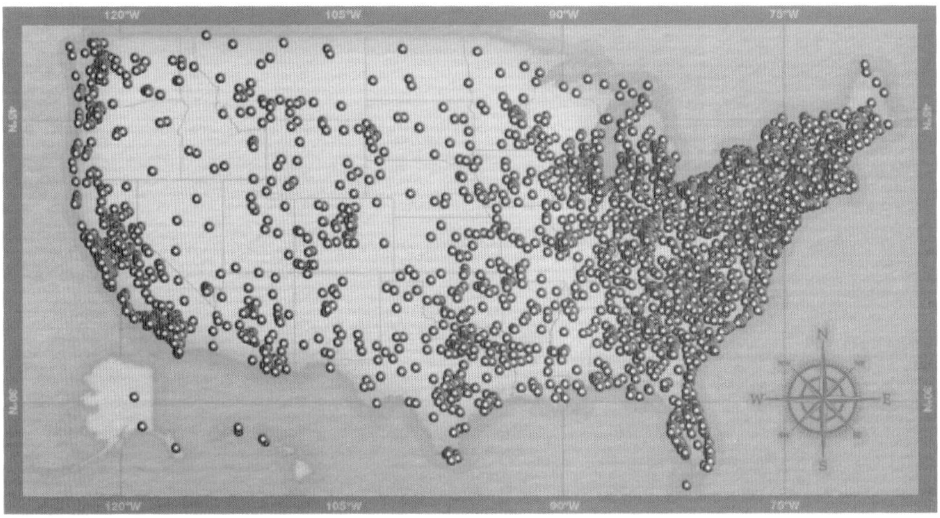